the art and science of
wine

the art and science of wine

wine

James Halliday and Hugh Johnson

MITCHELL BEAZLEY

The Art and Science of Wine

Edited and designed by
Mitchell Beazley International Ltd
Michelin House, 81 Fulham Road
London SW3 6RB

A CIP catalogue record for this book is available from
the British Library

ISBN 0 85533 946 2

The authors and publishers will be grateful for any
information which will assist them in keeping future
editions up to date. Although all reasonable care has
been taken in the preparation of this book, neither the
publishers nor the authors can accept responsibility for
any consequences arising from the use thereof or from
the information contained herein.

Executive Editor: Anne Ryland
Art Director: Tim Foster
Art Editors: Gaye Allen, Paul Drayson
Editors: Stephanie Horner, Susan Keevil
Indexer: Lyn Greenwood
Production: Sarah Schuman

Typeset in Sabon by
Servis Filmsetting Ltd
Manchester, England
Origination by Mandarin Offset, Singapore
Printer and bound by Cayfosa Industria
Grafica SA, Barcelona, Spain

This book is dedicated to

the genie in the bottle

Contents

A Propos 9
By Hugh Johnson

IN THE VINEYARD

The Vine 15
*From the historical perspective
to likely attitudes and practices of the
twenty-first century*

Terroir 19
*Does man matter more than
the natural environment?*

Climate 27
And, for that matter, weather

Which Variety of Vine? 36
The flavour starts with the grape

Sculpting the Vine 43
Too much vigour is as bad as too little

Quantity V. Quality? 50
Or can they be compatible?

Plague and Pestilence 57
Enemies of the vine

Irrigation 63
A necessary evil?

Mechanization 66
Simply a question of time?

IN THE WINERY

IN THE BOTTLE

Making the Wine   71
Winery equipment and how to use it

National Attitudes and
Regional Characters   76

Light-Bodied White Wines   86
Choices, consequences and techniques

Wooded and
Full-Bodied White Wines   100
Choices, consequences and techniques

Sparkling Wines   112
Choices, consequences and techniques

Sweet Table Wines   124
Choices, consequences and techniques

Light-Bodied Red Wines   137
Choices, consequences and techniques

Medium-Bodied Red Wines   149
Choices, consequences and techniques

Full-Bodied Red Wines   164
Choices, consequences and techniques

Fortified Wines   175
Choices, consequences and techniques

Oak and Wine   192
Choices, consequences and techniques

The Chemistry and Analysis of Wine   197

The Changes of Age   202

Wine Faults   212

The Manipulation of Wine   220

Glossary   227

Index   230

The vintage-scene as idyll, a familiar motif of artists from the ancient world to modern times. Penry Williams painted this idealized scene near Rome in the 1840s. Reality (and certainly the wine itself) was less idyllic. About 90 percent of the advances in winemaking have happened in the last 100 years, and perhaps 60 percent in the last 20.

A Propos

By Hugh Johnson

The rusty cannon gives the Moutardes' yard, divided from the village street by iron railings, its faint air of a comic opera set. It was last fired in 1964, when a cloud the colour of a decomposing aubergine and exactly the size of the vineyards of Muligny, hanging poised above the slopes of Chassard, the next-door commune, began to roll ominously towards the Clos du Marquis.

Père Moutarde had towed the weapon into the vineyards behind a borrowed tractor, loaded it with a canister of grape-shot of the vintage of 1815, levelled it at the heart of the threat, and plucked up his courage to apply the taper. The explosion was thunderous. Nobody in Chassard was sure whether what clattered down on several roofs was a flurry of hail or straying grape-shot. The cloud rolled on, menacing but still costive, over Muligny and three more communes before suddenly dumping its humbug-size hailstones on the scruffy oakwood on the hill above Beaune.

The oaks were shredded; not a leaf was left. But in Chassard relief for the spared vines was tempered by unneighbourly feelings towards Monsieur Moutarde – indeed towards Muligny as a whole. The two villages had never exchanged more than civilities; not in two thousand years. One must not put too much weight on the cannon incident; it was merely a symbol of the rivalry that had existed since the Romans.

Things were different then, in the early '60s, in several ways. For a start, nobody had any money – or if there was any cash in the mattress it meant a harvest mortgaged to a merchant in Beaune.

The way the Moutardes made wine had changed very little since the Middle Ages. The most evident progress lay in the vineyards, which since phylloxera had been far more uniform than before: orderly rows of grafted vines that got a good dusting of sulphur and a bright blue spray of *bouillie bordelaise* as often as the weather and Monsieur Moutarde's energy and resources determined.

The vats in the *cuvier* were Napoleonic, the barrels in the mossy cellar dark with indeterminate age. Only the basket press on its iron wheels definitely bore some relation to the Industrial Revolution.

Père Moutarde had a little cache of bottles in a corner of the cellar; no labels, but dates written in chalk which stood up very badly to any handling. In any case he knew the positions of all the bottles, whose vintages stepped back with irregular intervals to before phylloxera and his grandfather's death. To drink one of them was exceptional. The family's daily drinking came in litres from the *cave coopérative*.

In fact the Moutardes had little to do with their own wine at all. They were farmers, on a tiny scale, who picked their grapes, put them through a sort of grinder that tore off most of the stems, then piled them in a vat and waited for the heady stinging smell of fermentation to fill the barn. Then twice a day the younger male members of the family climbed the ladder to the open top of the *cuve*, wearing only shorts (and sometimes not even these), gripped the edge firmly and lowered themselves in. Their combined weight was sometimes barely enough, even with a fair bit of bouncing, to break the thick raft of skins and still-whole grapes buoyed up on the surface by the fizzing fermentation below. Once you got through into the warm half-wine the idea was to turn the fragments of raft upside down and tread them back in. This way none of the goodness, the colour and flavour of the grapes, would be lost.

Three weeks or so after harvest, with the weather distinctly chilly, the fermentation was finished; it was time to empty the contents of the vat into the barrels below, after washing them out energetically with a length of chain to scour the inside and endless cold water from the well.

That was almost the last the Moutardes saw of their wine. Before Christmas the négociant called, tasted each barrel, told them how bad business was, and named a price. In January a lorry came round, parked beside the cannon, and hoisted the barrels up to take them to Beaune.

Sometimes in good years (meteorologically and financially) Monsieur Moutarde would decide to keep a small barrel in the cellar, taste it from time to time with a neighbour, and at the end of three or four or even five years laboriously round up and wash enough bottles to hold all the dark fragrant liquid. Most of these he would distribute round the family, whose vineyard it was just as much as it was his. His own share would be chalked and squirrelled away.

Only he knew the almost celestial satisfaction that lay in the best and oldest bottles: a mingling of plums and earth and game, of heat and cool, of fungus and farmyard, of iron and leather, yet giving off, for all its strength and maleness, a scent as ringing-clear as violets.

This was Burgundy thirty years ago, the most prestigious and sought-after region in the world of wine, but in a world where even the rarest and finest of wines from the greatest vineyards went for a song.

Wine-growers dragged along at subsistence level, faintly hoping that some eccentric might come and offer to buy their burdensome inheritance, yet dreading the loss of their ancient bond with the land and its sweetest fruit. Monsieur Moutarde and his generation, like their forebears, were prisoners of their peasant suspicions and superstitions. By regarding even the next commune as a rival they spurned comparisons, they turned their backs on new ideas, they rejected progress. But they conserved and intensified the identity of their 'cru'. When they planted a new vine it came from their own cuttings. Every move they made at vintage time and in the cellar was ritualized. Muligny could only be made this way.

Frequently the results of such sleep-walking were catastrophic. It was often just as well the négociant took away barrels of faulty wine to treat them as far as possible, then blend them with Rhône or Algerian, to produce an approximation the world would accept as burgundy.

Occasionally ritual was blessed with luck, and the results were sublime. Certainly there was enough of this elusive sublimity to keep the legend of burgundy alive in waiting for the next generation – and to fire the imaginations of the very few wine lovers, mostly Americans, who aspired at least to collect, perhaps one day even to emulate, what they considered the loveliest of all wines.

Monsieur Moutarde's children live in a different world. They have been to technical colleges, even to universities with departments of viticulture and oenology. They exchange views, read trade journals – and openly compete with one another. They even see themselves as competing with other countries. Above all the peasant instinct for secrecy has evaporated.

The years between 1960 and today have seen the greatest change in the making, the quality and the distribution of wine in its 8,000-year history. This is not something to be surprised at. Which art, and which science, has not altered almost out of recognition in the era of technology?

Yet wine and our expectations of it are profoundly linked with age and time. Of all the food and drink we consume only wine can live (and indeed change wonderfully for the better) for decades – even, exceptionally, for a century or more. Yet its lifespan is never certain: its ageing process is unpredictable enough to seem to wear a mantle of mystery.

That cars should work better, or microchips have almost magical properties, are things we can accept without surprise, since they are the products of scientific inventiveness. But weren't we always told that the greatest wines are products of evolution, of tradition, of respect for the soil and patience in the cellar? How can technology improve on something that emerges from the womb of time?

Perhaps we need to ask how the standards were set in the first place. Who decided that one wine was 'better' than another – or indeed that there were qualities specific to wine that varied from place to place, season to season and time to time?

Wine was apparently discovered (or first exploited) in warm-temperate regions (the Caucasus and the warmer Middle East) before migrating, at first as merchandise, to such temperate ones as central Italy, then progressively to cooler areas in France and (coolest of all) Germany.

While wine-growing was limited to Mediterranean regions its quality was broadly measured in terms of strength and sweetness. As it left the Mediterranean and found niches along the trade routes of central, western and northern Europe these were presumably still the qualities that exacting drinkers looked for.

What they found, though, in regions where the vine was more and more of a marginal crop, was a drink of a different nature altogether. Sweetness could not be taken for granted. High strength was replaced by relatively high acidity.

This had been (and still occasionally is) the unimproved primitive style of Italian wine, made by growing vines up trees. The 'improved' state was achieved by pruning the vines low in what was known as the Greek style; even by drying the grapes to concentrate their sugar.

Using improved viticulture, that is low-pruned vines, in cooler regions gave rise to flavours more fruity, positive, juicy, aromatic and refreshing than either old or new Mediterranean methods.

How did France become the country where wine was brought to its fullest perfection? Not because she possesses any one physical characteristic which is unique. Nor is 'French genius' the answer – although no other country takes its nourishment so seriously. Simply in certain regions intensive cultivation led to the development of local strains and varieties of grape, which in turn led to a wine culture which was closely linked to local prosperity and local pride.

Not coincidentally these regions had either high local populations or strong trading links. Demand encouraged specialization; specialization led to experience, experience to accepted – even stereotyped – local methods, and the stability implied by these to distinctive local styles.

A French author wrote recently 'There are no predestined vineyards; there are only redoubts of stubborn civilization' – called Burgundy, Bordeaux, Champagne, the Moselle, the Rhône. . . .

This is the theory of natural selection of what were to become the world's model vineyards and their wines. Its most surprising aspect is that it all began nearly 2,000 years ago. Wine culture has had a very long time to develop its local traits; the characteristic style of each French region is the work of seventy or eighty generations.

In modern eyes (French eyes at least) what is most important about the great vineyards is their *terroir* – their combination of soil and climate. It is truer to say that this is what is most distinctive. The major factor in their foundation was not the precise characteristics of their soil. It was their strategic situation. But even where the two combine most luckily and effectively there remains a missing element to explain the ascendancy of France (and, for its white wines, Germany). Perfect *terroir* close to a rich and busy market could equally have been found in Italy or Spain.

The final building block is the pattern of climate; not just as it ripens the grapes, but as it dictates the moment of harvest and influences the progress of fermentation. The further north you go the narrower the band of choice of when to pick the grapes. Each vintage is a struggle to achieve full ripeness before cold or wet weather sets in. Perhaps even more important, once the grapes are picked, their fermentation has the benefit (in most years) of perfect natural temperature control: the northern autumn itself.

Without benefit of air-conditioning, of cooling coils or brine circulating in double-walled tanks, in the classic wine regions there is at least an even chance that the must will become wine at the ideal moderate, then gently falling, temperature. At higher temperatures the grape aromas boil off, yeasts become less efficient and bacteria flourish. If the vat gets too hot the fermentation 'sticks' altogether, leaving half-made wine which is fatally prone to becoming vinegar.

These were the problems that almost all winemakers in warmer climates had to contend with until electricity came on the scene. The one chance of avoiding them was a cool, deep-cut cellar. Modern wine-making dates from the introduction of artificial temperature control, first tried tentatively in Algeria a century ago using cold water, then more methodically in Australia, but not generally either available or accepted until the 1950s and '60s.

Until fermentation could be kept in check there was little purpose in planting the grapes that the north had developed for low-strength table wines. Once cool fermentation was mastered, even at the price of astronomical energy costs, the door was open to making balanced fruity light wines in a warm climate. From that moment on the production of sweet fortified wines, the mainstay of Mediterranean-climate vineyards round the world, went into accelerating decline. Technology had claimed its place as the indispensable ally of the winemaker. It was not long before what was seized on as essential in Australia and California had gained an interested following, to say the least, in Europe – even in parts of France. Today the range of controls open to a winemaker (with the money to pay for them) is so great as to be bewildering. European winemakers are at least limited by the conventions and traditions enshrined in their systems of appellations and denominations. Europe's governments want their wine industries, and now actively encourage them, to stay within conventional bounds, to exploit their regional traditions – above all to avoid simple varietal labelling. It is their best way of avoiding the head-to-head competition that increasingly threatens from the industries of the New World.

But New World winemakers still start with a clean slate. It is entirely up to them what grape varieties they plant (or buy), in what regions and soils, and how they turn them into wine. The United States is preparing the ground for what may one day become an effective appellation law. Yet its Viticultural Areas are a very long way from controlling or even influencing winemaking decisions.

South Africa has the most precise wine legislation of the New World. But it is still the farmer, not the government, who decides what he will plant and what kind of wine he will make.

Australia and New Zealand, meanwhile, flourish in a state of oenological anarchy. Anything goes, so long as the label 'tells the truth'. It is a cut-throat world, chronically short of cash, but it has proved more fertile in invention, more radical in technology, and overall more successful in pleasing its patrons than any other.

This book is about the range of choices open to a winemaker at the end of the 20th century. It is the fruit of collaboration between a most unscientific wine-lover and a passionate critic who is also a technocrat. I don't think James Halliday will object to my describing him in this way – so long as I also remind you that at Coldstream Hills in the Yarra Valley he makes some of Australia's most technically perfect wines, which just happen to be quite delicious.

It is no coincidence at all that James is Australian. Australia's winemakers and researchers have established themselves over the past decade as the world's most innovative, least reverent, most open-minded, most iconoclastic. And their ideas are taken very seriously indeed.

The vintage season in Europe falling in the least interesting part of an Australian winemaker's year, an increasing number of these iconoclasts are even migrating north in September to supervise the vintage at the invitation of proprietors and cooperative cellars in France.

I shall never forget the look on the face of a grower in south-west France when he tasted the first wine made by an Australian 'flying winemaker' from grapes he had delivered to the cooperative. All his life he had been accustomed to a rather hard, perfectly adequate but totally unexciting wine as the outcome of his labours. '*Mais mon dieu*', he spluttered, '*ça sent le fruit.*' That was just what it did smell of: grapes. And he was not at all sure that wine was supposed to do anything so obvious.

Australian wine-lovers are hard to restrain from playing a game they call Options. The rules are simple. An undisclosed wine is served to the company. Only the president of the game (Len Evans is the most infuriatingly skilful protagonist) knows what it is. He asks which three countries the wine comes from. Anyone who guesses right stays in the game; the rest drop out. Subsequent questions might name three grape varieties, districts, vintages or châteaux until the wine is identified.

'Options' might well have been the title of this book, because at each step in the making of any wine, from the choosing of the vineyard site to the opening of a mature bottle, there are choices to be made; options to be faced.

Many of the decisions are loaded by the economics of the business. Monsieur Moutarde of Muligny is an example of a wine-grower with very few options to give him sleepless nights. But many are not: as the choices and consequences charts show, such factors as timing and temperature can make as much difference to the quality of a wine as the most costly options: stainless steel tanks, air conditioning or all-new barrels.

The most costly option of all, perhaps, is one which is faced at every stage by a winemaker who aspires to quality. It is called selection. Only by constantly down-grading any wine which is not up to the standard you set yourself can you maintain a name and reputation.

Where, if anywhere, do you draw the line between art and science in producing or designing any product? It is a matter of judgment. Scientific decisions are made on the basis of measurements. Non-scientific decisions are made on the basis of habit or intuition; occasionally of inspiration. Might it be true to say that the first two amount to craftsmanship; only the third to art? Art is a grand word to use about the making of a drink. It is justified because exceptional wines can seem to transcend mere sensual enjoyment; to demand to be appreciated on a higher plane of awareness – for which art is the only appropriate word.

IN THE VINEYARD

The Vine

From the historical perspective to likely attitudes and practices of the twenty-first century

The grape vine in its wild state is a climber. Its natural home is the forest. Hence its botanical name of *Vitis vinifera silvestris* – the woodland wine-bearing vine.

Which woods did it originally inhabit? A vast stretch, in all probability, from western Europe to western Asia. Where was it first used to make wild wine? No-one knows. But archaeology can point out the place where it was first cultivated. The scientific evidence (like the Book of Genesis) points to the foothills of the Caucasus. Georgia has produced the earliest evidence of vine selection and hence the emergence of the cultivated variety: *Vitis vinifera sativa*. Carbon-dating puts this change to domestication at about 5,000 BC. Mankind was therefore still in his Stone Age when he first cultivated the vine – and presumably made wine.

To understand how the grapevine grows, and how it responds to cultivation, one has to remember that it is a climber, and that in its wild state it grows in a tight tangle with other plants and trees, competing with some, supported by others. Competition is for light, for soil moisture and nutrients. To reach the light the vine climbed higher. To survive in soils full of competing roots it built up a degree of tolerance to drought. The support came from the trees it climbed. These responses to the environment determine how the vine's performance can be manipulated in the vineyard.

European wine-growers have long known (and New World growers more recently) that vines react to sunlight, not only in spring but throughout the growing season – even in winter. Sunlight on the woody parts, especially the new shoots or canes, means a more fruitful vine. At the base of each leaf is a bud – the crop potential of the following year's vintage. The amount of sunlight on the vine when its new buds are forming acts as a signal, determining whether the buds become leafy shoots or embryo flowers for fruit. Thus the yield of each plant is initially dependent on the amount of light reaching the vine up to 15 months earlier – April

Wine from the woods

What the vine needs

Opposite: Vines in Mendocino County, California. The modern regimented style and scale of vineyard may seem unromantic but superb grapes can be produced.

to June in the northern hemisphere, October to December in the southern hemisphere. In this knowledge the grower will manipulate the vine to achieve an appropriate balance between the production of leaves and fruit, above all avoiding a dense canopy of leaves which shade the 'bud-wood'.

Pruning: 'vegetable editing'

Unquestionably the annual growth cycle of the vine stirs deep emotions in most wine-growers, and pruning has traditionally been regarded as an art-form of fundamental importance to grape and wine quality. Every possible means of vine training has been tried through the centuries. Close-planting and hard-pruning of vines, almost in the modern manner, to produce small hedge-like rows was introduced by the Egyptians between 4,000 and 5,000 years ago. When the focus of viticulture and winemaking changed from Egypt to Greece, the practice of pruning to increase the vine's fruitfulness and quality became standard.

The Romans, who learned their wine-growing from the Greeks and the Carthaginians, knew and practised most of the 'modern' pruning and training methods: the 'goblet'; cane-pruning, now credited to the 19th-century French researcher Professor Guyot; fan pruning; low bush training; high trellising, and so on. In the great vineyards of France this task is entrusted only to pruners who have been employed on the estate for decades, and who know every vine as an individual, every nuance of site and *terroir* as a fact of life.

The brutalist school

Is such attention lavished on each vine justifiable? In recent years Australian academics felt it was not. They proposed that a vineyard should be viewed as a modern commercial orchard: each row being treated as a hedge and trimmed with mechanical cutting-bars or even circular saws. Many grape-growers were only too delighted, since the crop itself was not harmed. And others have gone further, introducing 'minimal pruning', where the vines are not pruned at all in winter. There is an element of summer pruning but less than is practised on conventionally winter-pruned vines. It has proved an effective method. It works because of the vine's need for and response to sunlight. By not being pruned in winter, the vine's hormones are not stimulated to respond, and hence new growth is discouraged.

Above: *Egyptians, Greeks then Romans dominated winemaking in the ancient world. A few modern winemakers still prefer treading grapes to extract the maximum colour and flavour.*

Right: *Veneto, Italy. The undomesticated vine is a climbing plant, here growing through fruit trees. Any shaded bunches will produce less sweet grapes.*

What, though, of crop control? It is an axiom of European wine-growing that the grower must choose quality or quantity. Yet there is more to the equation than simply less is better : more inevitably means worse. If there is a single truth it is the concept of a vine in balance: one in which the ratio of roots, canes, leaves and grapes is correct. There is increasing awareness that this can be achieved in very different ways. The vines may be small, with either no trellis at all or with only the simplest support. For vines grown like this the density of planting will usually be very high – perhaps 8,000 to 10,000 vines per hectare. Or the vines may be very large, supported by an elaborate trellis, widely spaced at a density of 1,500 vines per hectare. In either system, high-quality grapes or poor ones can result, but that will depend on the skill of the wine-grower.

Planting at a density of 50,000 hectares, which was recommended in Roman times, precluded any form of mechanization. By mid-19th century densities of around 20,000 vines per hectare (with yields of 40 hectolitres per hectare or less) meant horse-drawn ploughs were in widespread use in all but steeply sloping vineyards. The reality of today is mechanization. In the future vine densities may be reduced as low as 1,500 per hectare (today they are certainly limited to 5,000 per hectare) to accommodate tractors and the increasingly sophisticated array of machinery capable of pruning, picking, summer hedging, lifting and dropping foliage wires, knitting the canopy, plucking leaves around the fruit to enhance exposure, even selectively thinning the crop itself halfway through the growing season. This all sounds distinctly unromantic, and so it is, but it is preferable to the do-nothing minimal pruning approach. Even with these vastly reduced planting densities, yields have increased and are continuing to do so. The question is whether the quality is dropping at the same rate.

The short history of plant-breeding and genetic engineering is a catalogue of successes and failures, benefits and disadvantages, opportunities and limitations, and while the French will have nothing of it, Germany and California, the two principal viticultural stud-farms, are forever playing with the genes of the vine.

The yield–quality equation

The vine in balance

The future

Mechanization

Grape harvesting still means working long back-breaking hours on many of the Bordeaux estates which do not accept mechanical pickers for their precious crop.

Healthier vines which consistently produce higher yields are the principal goals. Disease resistance and bigger harvests have both been achieved through the breeding of hybrids. Clonal selection is another route to the same goals. What has yet to appear in the commercial nurseries is a classic grape variety with enhanced disease resistance, or a classic variety with improved flavour, or a new variety which combines the attractions of the existing classics. Should such a vine make its appearance, it will almost certainly be due to genetic engineering.

Sprays and fertilizers

One of wine's great attributes is that it is among the most natural and stable of all food products. It is possible to make wine without any additions whatsoever, and in the vineyard and the winery there is a strong move to minimize human interference with nature. Many think we have been too clever and too profligate in our clonal selection and our use of herbicides, pesticides and fungicides – all in the interest of larger crops of 'healthier' grapes. European growers have less flexibility than their New World counterparts in warmer regions owing to the higher rainfall that threatens the crops in the northern hemisphere, but there is a tendency towards reducing the use of all but the 'natural' sprays such as lime and sulphur, elemental sulphur and copper oxychloride or copper sulphate – fungicides which are sanctioned by organic growers – especially in vineyards where quality rather than cost or convenience is at a premium. The same thinking applies to chemical fertilizers. The best vineyard practice is to apply even organic fertilizer very sparingly. A Médoc first-growth uses only cow-manure – once every 19 years.

The grower's key role

There is a remarkable consensus, as the 20th century closes, that the opening decades of the 21st century will belong to the viticulturist: to the grower in the field. The catch phrase of the New World winemaker is 'growing wine in the vineyard', echoing the old aphorism 'great wine is made in the vineyard'. How the consumers of the next century will define great wine will be the preoccupation of both grower and maker. The challenge will be to produce wines for a society which consumes over 95 percent of all the wine it buys within 48 hours of purchase, *and* ones that will be revered in the year 2100. The same wine will not serve both aims, nor will it be made in the same way.

The choice is not a new one. It is between convenience, using the short cuts offered by mechanization in the vineyard and chemical adjustments in the winery, and the time-consuming alternative of painstaking physical control.

Winemaking that aims for quality, let alone greatness, requires a high level of personal skill and commitment. It minimizes chemical intervention. It focuses on eradicating disease in the vineyard, and depends on hygiene and the control of temperature and oxidation by physical, not chemical, means in the winery. But it would be too simple to see a choice between art and science, between the old ways and the new. The proponents of each method can and should learn from each other: if they do, better wines at all levels will be the result.

Terroir

Does man matter more than the natural environment?

The French, who have cultivated and studied their vineyards with loving care for centuries, have a word with no precise equivalent in English or any other language. The word is *'terroir'*.

The proprietor of Château Cos d'Estournel in the Médoc, Bruno Prats, explains it thus:

> *'The very French notion of* terroir *looks at all the natural conditions which influence the biology of the vinestock and thus the composition of the grape itself. The* terroir *is the coming together of the climate, the soil and the landscape. It is the combination of an infinite number of factors: temperatures by night and by day, rainfall distribution, hours of sunlight, slope and drainage, to name but a few. All these factors react with each other to form, in each part of the vineyard, what French wine growers call a* terroir.'

Bruno Prats, proprietor of Château Cos d'Estournel, a 'super-second growth' in St Estèphe, is a spokesman for the whole Médoc – indeed for France – in his defence of the notion of terroir: *'. . . the combination of an infinite number of factors'.*

The identification and the delineation of different *terroirs* goes back to the monks of the Middle Ages, and perhaps beyond. First the Benedictines, then from the 11th century the Cistercians, worked and studied the soil, both in France (particularly in Burgundy) and in Germany, so closely that (according to one famous burgundy-grower) they 'even tasted it'. They were passionately concerned to make, not just the best possible wines, but wines that were as distinctive, as unlike each other, as possible. The patchwork quilt of named vineyards, the *crus* and *clos* of the Côte d'Or, the *Einzellagen* of the Mosel and the Rheingau, derives directly from this pious concentration.

Five hundred years later this approach was to be imitated in Bordeaux, though on an altogether larger and less precise scale, in keeping with a much broader, flatter and more consistent landscape. From this time (the 17th century) onwards, Champagne, Tokay, the port vineyards of the Douro, everywhere that proved capable of producing premium-price wines, saw the value of identifying the better and the best sites. Yet for some reason, which can hardly only be jealousy, the notion of *terroir* has stuck in the gorge of the New World.

To quote the American author Matt Kramer:

> *'. . . a surprising number of wine-growers and wine-drinkers – at least in the United States – flatly deny the existence of* terroir, *like weekend sailors who reject as preposterous that Polynesians could have crossed the Pacific navigating only by sun, stars, wind, smell and taste. Terroir is held to be little more than viticultural voodoo.'*

Viticultural voodoo?

Time will tell – and, one suspects, rather quickly. Already, in a mere 25 years, California and Australia have progressed from a fixation with grape varieties (in the 1960s and 1970s 'varietal character' was seen as the be-all and end-all), through the cult of the winemaker as romantic hero in the 1970s and 1980s, to the increasing emphasis on the vineyard we noted in the previous chapter.

It is now widely accepted that certain 'vineyard-designated' wines (Martha's Vineyard in the Napa Valley was the first famous example) are able to fetch premium prices. How long will it be before we hear of the *terroir* of the Rutherford

Bench? In South Australia, the bizarre strip of red limestone that defines the district of Coonawarra has exactly the distinctive qualities the Cistercians would have recognized.

Soil and *terroir*, however, are not the same. There is no specific chemical composition, no precise structure that guarantees that wherever a given soil occurs in the world it will produce wine of identical, or even vaguely similar, character and quality. There is, though, growing recognition that structure and drainage may be more important to grapes and wine than specific soil types. The two primary inputs which cause grapevines to grow and produce fruit are sunlight and water: in purely mechanical terms the function of soil is to provide anchorage (first), water (second) and nutrients (third). All scientific attempts to show a specific translocation of minerals or other substances from the soil, which then impact directly on the flavour of the grape (or the wine), have failed. The French expression '*goût de terroir*' is precisely that: the taste of *terroir*. So however hard it may be to disabuse yourself of the idea that in drinking, for example, a Grand Cru Chablis you are actually tasting the unique limey clay under the vines, it should always be remembered that soil is just one factor in the *terroir* equation.

'Goût de terroir'

Given a *terroir* that has proved its ability to make fine and distinctive wine, the degree of intervention by the winemaker determines how clearly the *terroir* will be expressed.

Terroir makes character: man makes quality

A close look at the 'character', 'quality' and 'personality' of a wine will reveal exactly how successful the winemaker's intervention has been. The assessment of these factors culminates in the philosophy developed by Peter Sichel, owner of Château d'Angludet and part-owner of Château Palmer (both in Margaux), who is also a leading Bordeaux *négociant* and one of the crispest commentators on the world of wine. Character, Sichel says, is determined by *terroir*; quality is largely determined by man. Incompetent winemaking can destroy the potential of a given site to produce wine of great character (first) and quality (second) and is precisely the reason why certain châteaux have fallen or risen in reputation; why the 1855 Médoc classification is perpetually under attack. Conversely, the most highly skilled winemaking cannot make a silk purse out of a sow's ear: above all else, the

Above: *The benefits of terroir take many forms, from the slope angle to the positive qualities of underlying rock and soil structure – seen here at Clos de Bèze, Gevrey-Chambertin, comprising a good proportion of light coloured stones in the soil which reflect the sun's heat.*

Gevrey-Chambertin

Burgundy is the best place to relate *terroir* to legal appellations. Gevrey-Chambertin in Côte d'Or (opposite) is a graphic example.

Immediately east of the 300-metre contour line, soil type and structure closely mirror AOC definitions: here, brown calcareous (chalky) soils overlie hard screes, and these, where located on south and east facing slopes, are the base for Gevrey-Chambertin's Grand Cru and Premier Cru vineyards.

The aspect and angle of the slope maximize climatic conditions – especially by providing good exposure to sunlight – and the subsoil provides the efficient drainage essential to a vine's development.

Further down the AOC spectrum, vineyards of the 'Villages' appellation, immediately south of Gevrey-Chambertin, are based on the same soil, this time overlying richer marls and alluvium. The difference this makes is that though fertile and well suited to most types of agriculture, these are too rich for the growth of top quality vines.

Further west on the flat river flood-plain, vineyards under 'Regional' AOC status predominate, reflecting the increase in rich river-deposited alluvium, more fertile still, and too poorly drained to grow vines that yield top quality fruit.

The cross-section (opposite) of Gevrey-Chambertin's underlying rock structure shows the slope

from the Côte in the east down to the river plain in the west. AOC status similarly declines from Grand Cru in the east to 'Regional' status in the west.

East of the fault line, Grand Cru and Premier Cru regions are situated on base rocks of calcareous mineral-rich marls, overlying clay. The better-quality vineyards are on the higher slopes, which provide better drainage and exposure to the sun. Marl conglomerates, alluvium and colluvial rock fragments occur as the slope declines: the base for vineyards of 'Villages' AOC status. As the harder layer of solifluction rock fragments at the foot of the Côte gives way to pure marls and clays on the flood-plain we are down to plain 'Bourgogne' status.

Gevrey-Chambertin – The Relationship Between AOC Classification, Soil Type, and Geological Structure

AOC Classification and soil types of the Gevrey Chambertin area

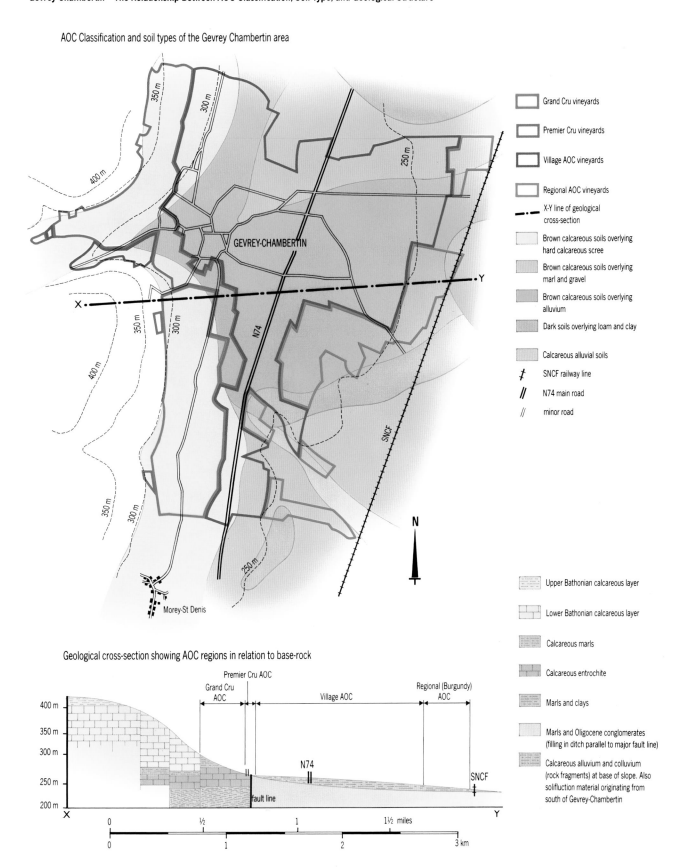

Grand Cru vineyards

Premier Cru vineyards

Village AOC vineyards

Regional AOC vineyards

X-Y line of geological cross-section

Brown calcareous soils overlying hard calcareous scree

Brown calcareous soils overlying marl and gravel

Brown calcareous soils overlying alluvium

Dark soils overlying loam and clay

Calcareous alluvial soils

SNCF railway line

N74 main road

minor road

Upper Bathonian calcareous layer

Lower Bathonian calcareous layer

Calcareous marls

Calcareous entrochite

Marls and clays

Marls and Oligocene conglomerates (filling in ditch parallel to major fault line)

Calcareous alluvium and colluvium (rock fragments) at base of slope. Also solifluction material originating from south of Gevrey-Chambertin

Geological cross-section showing AOC regions in relation to base-rock

winemaker cannot invest a wine with character not possessed by the grapes in the first place. He or she can make a good wine, one with commercial appeal, but never a great one.

. . . and weather makes personality

The third leg of the tripod in Sichel's analysis, 'personality', is largely determined by the weather. It is the difference between, for example, almost all the Bordeaux reds of 1982 – wines almost thick with ripeness – and the same wines in 1984, when the season produced barely ripe, often meagre wines. The 1984s can have the character of their site, the quality of well-made wines (though under difficult conditions) but their personality will never be extrovert or generous.

Character, then, can only come from a particular *terroir* or environment, a belief which substantiates a point of agreement between the New World and the Old – that the role of the winemaker, although critical, is nevertheless limited.

Illustrating this it is interesting to compare two winemakers' views. Australian Brian Croser of Petaluma, near Adelaide, has a rather more up-beat approach:

'I have a minimalist approach. It relies on an innate faith in the choice of an area; in the choice of a variety; and in the choice of a management technique in the vineyard to get the maximum expression of quality. That faith then carries through to the processing of the grapes. From my viewpoint if you put all the ingredients, all the building blocks, in place the resultant wine will share the quality parameters that all good wines of the world share. The personalities will be different, but they will share the fundamentals of quality, which are vitality, strength and intensity of flavour, length of flavour, subtlety, and reproducible uniqueness.'

Reproducible uniqueness

Great winemakers tend to be modest men. Jacques Seysses of the Domaine Dujac in Morey-St-Denis, Burgundy, casts himself as little more than a quality control officer:

'I believe we have been given the opportunity to have Pinot Noir vineyards at precisely the right place to make great wine. So it is my conviction that we should let nature do the work. I am happy to take advantage of modern oenology and to act if something goes wrong, but in fact I prefer to make wine the lazy way and let nature take its course wherever possible.'

The lazy way

And the New World?

If there is this measure of agreement on the importance of *terroir* between the New World and the Old, why has the New World not attempted to emulate the Old World more closely? There are two principal reasons. First, the scale of most New World viticulture makes precise delineation of *terroir* either difficult or of doubtful relevance. Secondly – and the two factors are inextricably linked – there is not enough evidence that it could pay.

The French classification system has ensured premium prices for the favoured vineyards. This in turn means that estates can afford to invest more in maximizing the potential of their grapes: for example, by buying new equipment, new barrels, and above all by the luxury of selection – downgrading second-best vats to a second or third label. The system is thus self-perpetuating, once given the accepted superiority of the site. How long will the lucky and successful among New World wineries be able to resist the attraction of some kind of classification?

Do the French waver?

The inevitable linking of *terroir* and classification in France has led to exalted land values and wine prices because it has created a finite resource in an ever-growing world market. A seller's market is comfortable in the short term, but in the longer term it creates real risks. It places the wines beyond the reach of those with more

taste than money, who in all probability would most appreciate them; it limits or eliminates the possibility of organic business growth from within; and it progressively opens up opportunities for competitors from without.

Nowhere is this more obvious than in Champagne. The Champenois have marketed their products brilliantly, and for the past 50 years have been vigilant in protecting their appellation and the use of the word 'champagne'. They argue this word should be used only for wine made within Champagne from the classic varieties and using the *méthode champenoise*; that, in a word, champagne is unique, and that all other sparkling wine – whatever and however made – is not only different but (by price implication) inferior.

But what is the public to think when the champagne houses themselves move to other countries and start making and marketing sparkling wines there? Moët & Chandon led the charge a surprisingly long time ago when it established a subsidiary in Argentina, and compounded the problem by using the word 'champagne' on its label (a practice believed to be required by Argentinian law, but recently discontinued).

More recently a dozen champagne houses have followed Moët's lead; some into the most improbable places. But there is no doubt many of the Champenois have found the decision difficult. Some have refused altogether to make the move, others have done so reluctantly, as, for better or worse, directly or indirectly, it carries with it the seeds of an attack on the special *terroir*-derived character of the wines made in Champagne itself. This is not to say the attack will succeed, or that the decision to begin production overseas was wrong. On the positive side it has not only increased their production and sales, it has allowed them to demonstrate that the word 'champagne' is not essential (as the world had supposed) to sell an expensive sparkling wine. So far, it appears they can have their cake and eat it.

It is clear, in other words, that even the French are attracted by the tremendous freedom from the restrictions of *terroir* the New World enjoys. The free-spirited Italians have followed suit without even leaving home. They have managed to turn their DOC system upside down in less than 30 years, generally engaging in good-humoured anarchy until 1992, when the entire wine law had to be revised.

Pinot Noir on northern slopes: the windmill at Verzenay on the 'mountain' of Reims in Champagne.

Champagne from Argentina?

Meanwhile, bogged down in an archaic set of laws (both too liberal and too rigid), the great German wine-growers contemplate revolution.

The New World contemplates its terroirs

In the New World (South Africa apart) full-scale classification is still many years away. In some countries, though, primitive appellation systems are beginning to take shape. America leads with its AVAs (Approved Viticultural Areas): regions which are supposed to have special viticultural and oenological characteristics. However, this demarcation does not carry with it the constraints of Appellations Contrôlées – most importantly, there is no stipulation as to which varieties may be planted. Nor are pruning methods prescribed, or yields proscribed.

Australia is tentatively headed down the same path. In both the United States and Australia there is a plethora of laws, some specifically directed to the food and beverage industry, some of wider application, which (theoretically at least) guarantee truth in labelling. In Australia the major gap is any effective and comprehensive system of defining regional names. Certainly, one cannot name the Hunter Valley as the region of origin of a wine coming from Coonawarra, or vice versa: the regions are over 745 miles apart. But in late 1990 a heated debate was taking place among vignerons in or near to Coonawarra about the boundaries of the district. It focused on the cigar-shaped strip of red soil (9 miles long and varying in width from a few hundred metres to less than two miles) which is generally agreed to be of critical importance in making Coonawarra Australia's greatest red wine – or at least Cabernet Sauvignon – region.

Red earth in Coonawarra

Not only is the soil unique to Coonawarra, with a few isolated pockets elsewhere in southeastern Australia, but so is its uniformity. In the Barossa Valley there are 27 different soil types found in vineyards, and a small (15 hectare) vineyard may have half a dozen different soil types. When one adds the impact of ubiquitous irrigation it is not hard to see why Australia downplays the importance of soil. But it is moving to a limited form of appellation precisely for the reason Bordeaux did in 1855: to assist in the marketing of the wine.

Barossa: 27 soils

In doing so it will hopefully learn from the experiences of Germany and Italy. The system must not be too complicated: while the infinitely precise and detailed subdivision of Burgundy, and the Bordeaux château system, have become accepted and known over the centuries, these are exceptions unlikely ever to be emulated. No-one in London or New York is the least bit interested in the parish-pump politics of differentiation between Seville, Gruyere, Coldstream, Lilydale, Yering, Yarra Glen, Woori Yallock or Dixon's Creek, which happen to be different subdistricts within the Yarra Valley. It is more than enough to establish the Yarra as a point on the map 25 miles east-northeast of Melbourne, and Melbourne as the capital city of Victoria on the bottom right-hand corner of that vast and far-away continent, Australia. The fact that it has different soil types, including two radically different groups, or that microclimate variation can see Pinot Noir from one vineyard in one subdistrict ripen a full four weeks earlier than that from another, will remain, for many years if not forever, strictly its own business.

Yarra: microclimates

On the other hand the star system does have obvious attractions. If one Yarra estate could emulate Heitz's Martha's Vineyard and attract the following that leads to a hefty premium, who knows how interested the world might become in Yarra Valley geography? All New Zealand felt the benefit when one winery called 'Cloudy Bay' established its delicious Sauvignon Blanc on the world stage.

The message on the bottle

Certainly the success of Martha's Vineyard has led a number of winemakers in California, and rather fewer in Australia, to identify precise vineyard sources on their labels. This has met with varying degrees of success; so far it seems to be significant only to domestic markets. Perhaps a more intelligent – and successful – approach is that adopted by such lateral thinkers (and great winemakers) as

Miguel Torres in Catalonia and – most conspicuously – Piero Antinori in Tuscany. These winemakers have simultaneously established new styles of wine, by employing new varieties and new winemaking techniques, and strong brand identity. The varietal and vineyard sources of Torres' Black Label Gran Coronas (now Mas la Plana), of Antinori's Tignanello, Sassicaia and Solaia are no secret, but the bold front labels make no mention of them. This approach allows for flexibility in shaping each wine according to the needs of the vintage, but more importantly, it builds up goodwill in a proprietary name.

The red soil of Coonawarra in South Australia is a geological freak – which produces Australia's best Cabernet Sauvignon. Only one small area, nine miles by less than one, remote in the outback, is blessed with this eccentric pedology: half a metre of mineral-rich perfect drainage, then a metre and a half of pure limestone: then the water table. Could there be a more perfect argument for appellation laws?

Australia's one acknowledged first-growth, Penfolds' Grange Hermitage, comes from an unidentified swag of small vineyards spread across much of South Australia and which change (albeit not dramatically) from one vintage to the next. The criterion for production is simply highly coloured, rich, concentrated fruit, from old, low-yielding Shiraz vines.

The varietal honeymoon

Most New World winemakers have fallen into the trap of using simple varietal names for their wines, focusing attention on Chardonnay, Cabernet Sauvignon, Sauvignon Blanc or Pinot Noir. Yet there is no proprietary goodwill attached to those varieties. There is a delirious honeymoon as they make their début in markets previously unused to them, but the risk is boredom. Not *another* Chardonnay?

To quote Peter Sichel of Bordeaux again:

> *'The wine culture based on appellations and soils has been phenomenally successful and one simply must not put it in danger. If you can produce wines with character you should not emphasize their varietal composition. Sooner or later varieties will cease to mean very much because of the infinite variety of wines which can be made from (say) Chardonnay or Cabernet Sauvignon, depending on soil, weather, viticultural practices, yields, winery techniques and so on. If you simply call your wine Cabernet Sauvignon the consumer is going to have difficulty in relating it to other wines: if you are producing a wine which really has to be upmarket, people say "why should we pay four times as much for this Cabernet Sauvignon when there are Cabernets which are so much cheaper?"'*

Not only is the proportion of the different grapes of Latour or Lafite nowhere mentioned on the label of the wine, but it is considered largely irrelevant. Until Edmund Penning-Rowsell wrote his *Wines of Bordeaux* in 1969 there was little or no published information on the subject, and few people realized just how widely the relative proportions of Cabernet Sauvignon, Merlot, Cabernet Franc and Petit Verdot varied from château to château. Not until even more recently has the extent of the annual variation in proportion (largely owing to flowering conditions) been understood: an abundant year for Cabernet Sauvignon may well be a poor one for Merlot, and vice versa. How far a château succeeds in stamping its character on a wine made from an abnormal mix of grapes is one of the measures of its quality.

. . . and the fruit of experience

Burgundy's great vineyards grow only a single white variety (Chardonnay) and a single red (Pinot Noir). But just as in Bordeaux, the variety is subsumed into the vineyard: we make Latour, not a Cabernet Sauvignon-dominant blend; we make Vosne-Romanée Les Malconsorts, not Pinot Noir; Puligny-Montrachet Les Pucelles, not Chardonnay. What is unique is the vineyard, the *terroir*, not the grape variety which happens to grow there so perfectly. You can make Cabernet Sauvignon almost anywhere in the wine world; you can make Latour only at Latour.

Climate

And, for that matter, weather

Grape vines will grow in any temperate climate. Whether they will produce healthy grapes, or make good wine, is another matter altogether. Europe has been living with this question for so long that its vineyards have become fully adapted to local climatic conditions. Its preoccupation now is not with climate, but with weather – and of course *terroir*, and the way the two interact.

The New World sees things from the opposite perspective. While weather can be a considerable irritant, and *terroir* is something for long-term observation and definition, climate is the determining factor in deciding where to plant vineyards, and which grapes to plant in them.

One should be clear, first, about the difference between climate and weather. Climate is measured or described in long-term averages; weather is the day-to-day variation of those averages. Weather may make or break a vintage, and may explain the particular characteristics of a given wine, but it is climate that determines which grapes (if any) will grow and ripen well in any given locality.

The Japanese have been making wine for over a century in a climate where almost everything militates against the vine. Their answer to hot and humid summers and the diseases they bring is a high canopy allowing air to circulate. Traditionally most of the grapes were for the table: perfect bunches were the priority.

Climate and microclimate: a question of scale

If you look at the Médoc, you have an area of gently undulating land, six miles wide and 30 miles long, with a marked maritime influence. In a given season, the weather may vary significantly from one commune to the next, but the climate will be roughly the same. The same applies to Burgundy, although that critical – and ever so narrow – gently rising slope to the west of the N74 does cause significant variations in what is commonly referred to as the 'microclimate' (the climatic conditions peculiar to individual subsections of the vineyard).

If, however, you turn to Tuscany, Piedmont, Alto Adige, the Penedès, the Rhine and Mosel Valleys, the Barossa Valley (and attendant ranges) or the Napa Valley (and its adjacent hillsides), to name but a few well-known regions, you are dealing with areas which are far greater in size and with infinitely more variable topography. The 'climate' will almost certainly vary significantly according to altitude, aspect and degree of slope. Spring frosts, for example, are such a common problem on the floor of the Napa Valley it is hard to say they are merely a manifestation of weather; they are a climatic factor, but one absent a few kilometres away on the first slopes and on the hillsides, because the cold air drains down the hillsides and collects on the valley floor. Most critical, in California, is the climatic effect of the coastal hills in either excluding or admitting the famous clammy coastal fogs.

So, as many aspiring growers have discovered to their cost, in the real world it is often necessary to differentiate climate site by site. A practical illustration: in the 1990 vintage in the Yarra Valley, Australia, the first and last grape harvests, crushed in one winery some six weeks apart, were of Pinot Noir grapes. In between it crushed Chardonnay, Sémillon, Sauvignon Blanc, Shiraz (Syrah), Merlot, Cabernet Franc and Cabernet Sauvignon. The first Pinot Noir came from a warm site in the valley, the last from one of the coldest sites. This is a pattern which will continue from year to year, reflecting climatic variation, not weather. It is, incidentally, an illustration of one reason why in California, Australasia, South Africa and South America, one producer is likely to grow four or five different grape varieties. He or she has approximations to the climates of Bordeaux, Burgundy and the Rhine in the backyard.

Perfect growing weather

Given an adequate supply of nutrients and moisture, the optimum temperature for photosynthesis and vine growth is between 23 and 25°C. At this temperature the growth mechanism should be in perfect balance, with canopy and leaf development using the full sugar production. Whether these are the perfect conditions for ripening grapes is another question. For one thing a too-leafy canopy deprives the grapes of sunlight and therefore sugar.

If the temperature rises much above this level, the vine does not gain additional nutrition through increased photosynthesis, but instead begins to use sugar for increased respiration, leaving progressively less available for the grapes, and leading to the characteristic light colour and soft, flabby flavour of wines from excessively warm areas.

If the temperature falls below it (as far below as 15°C) photosynthesis continues perfectly happily. Other factors, though, slow the growth of the vine.

In winter a mantle of snow and temperatures as low as 18°C will not damage a dormant vine.

The consequence is that a mean average temperature of around 21°C is ideal for the ripening of red grapes, and around 19°C for the ripening of white grapes. At these temperatures the vine will produce the maximum amount of sugar surplus to its requirements for growth. This surplus is then used up by the grapes – at first it is accumulated, then it is used for ripening as enzymes come into play to produce colouring and flavouring substances.

The slower the better?

There is a myth that slow ripening produces the greatest flavour in all types of fruits and vegetables, and hence that the slower the ripening, the better. In reality, given certain basic temperature limitations, the faster the rate of ripening of grapes between the moment they turn colour (or '*véraison*') and harvest, the better will be

colour, flavour, sugar and acidity. It is one of the reasons why, in cool climates, the warm years are the best.

Growers have sharply differing ideas about the significance of seasonal temperature variation, about the effects of short periods of heat, and about day-to-day and day-to-night temperature swings. Those who grow grapes in warm climates often argue that cold night-time temperatures are very beneficial for keeping the acid levels in the grapes relatively (and desirably) high. This may well be true, for virtually all metabolic changes will come to a halt at temperatures below 9°C, and cold nights will delay all aspects of ripening. If this means that

In the vast vineyards of central Spain the most basic of pruning methods, the bush, gives the vine the best chance of surviving constant intense sunshine and desiccating winds.

Riesling wines, the glory of Piesport on the Mosel, have the unique property of achieving intense flavours in cool ripening conditions and at very modest levels of alcohol.

harvest is delayed until the onset of cooler late summer or autumn weather, so much the better. An equally valid point of view is that the more even the month-by-month growing season temperatures are, and the less the daily temperature range, the more certain and predictable will be the quality. How high this quality will be then finally depends on the average temperatures (and whether it is Riesling or port you are trying to produce).

The benefits of even ripening temperatures are most frequently met with in strongly maritime climates (such as that of Bordeaux) or in warmer continental climates (as in the Rhône Valley). Less reliable conditions occur in Germany, where the climate is cool and continental, marked by cool to cold springs and rapidly falling autumn temperatures which mean that a hot, sunny summer is essential for a good vintage. Germany, however, has the perfect grape for such conditions. The Riesling can attain full physiological ripeness, and hence intense flavour, at very low sugar levels, or in other words when it is (in chemical terms) barely ripe at all.

It can certainly be shown that a marked and consistent change between winter and spring temperatures is beneficial. The grower wants his buds to burst in unison, and not too early. Vacillating spring temperatures (all too common in maritime northern Europe) mean ragged budburst, longer periods of risk from spring frost, and probably uneven flowering, too. The continental temperature pattern is clearly a benefit here. At the other extreme, in strongly maritime areas (such as the Margaret River in Western Australia) the vine can scarcely differentiate between winter and spring. Its winter dormancy is disrupted, leading to the bizarre sight of Chardonnay enjoying (if that is the right word) budburst in mid-winter, then barely changing for the next two to three months. In summary, it seems that the more even the growing and ripening temperatures (both in terms of month-to-month ranges and daily fluctuation), the greater will be the progressive accumulation of colour, aroma and flavour at any given sugar level.

Less fluctuation: more flavour

The reasons are both negative and positive. Negative because sporadic very low temperatures at the start or finish of the season can cause severe frost damage, while extreme heat can cause leaf burn, defoliation and berry scorching. Positive because research indicates that at night-time temperatures of between 15 and 20°C, photosynthetic ripening continues, and with it accumulation of colouring and flavouring substances.

This phenomenon occurs across a range of temperatures. In the coolest quality regions, full flavour ripeness can be achieved at relatively low average temperatures. In warm but not hot climates, maximum flavour is achieved before acidity drops and sugar and pH levels rise too far.

Sunshine hours

Temperature and hours of sunshine are by no means the same thing, however interrelated they may be. The paradox is that in warmer climates the vine needs more sunshine hours than it does in cooler climates; conversely, it is temperature, rather than sunshine hours, that determines growth rates in those cooler climates. The further one moves from the equator, the longer are the summer days, and the greater the potential sunshine hours. It is a complex equation, made more so by cloud and rain (which are generally both more frequent and more sporadic in the cooler regions).

Rainfall: when and how much?

How much the vine drinks depends on how much it transpires – and, of course, how much water is available. In most of the northern European wine regions nature supplies adequate (at times more than adequate) rainfall throughout the year, while in the southern regions a Mediterranean climate provides a strong winter-spring rainfall (the most critical) and a dry, sunny summer. In much of the New World the patterns of rainfall and humidity are very different, and so-called water stress (the old word is drought) is much more common. The question of rainfall, stress and irrigation are discussed in later chapters.

It is probably the Germans, whose vineyards need all the heat they can get, who have studied the effects of wind most closely. They conclude that less is better, and align their vine-rows at right-angles to the prevailing wind accordingly. But, as growers in districts such as Carneros in California or Marlborough in New Zealand will attest, wind has a three-fold effect. Blowing hard, it will interrupt flowering and reduce the crop. Gales break the tender parts of the vine, removing growing tips, breaking canes and bruising leaves. Even stiff breezes can be damaging: the 'wind-chill factor' to the vine means leaf-pores close and photosynthesis is reduced; so the plant is working below its full efficiency. At the other extreme air stagnation can just as easily inhibit the vine's growth – a slight breeze, however, will refresh the microclimate around the vine and allow healthy respiration.

Wind: less is better

Serious vineyards in England were thought an infeasibility only 15 years ago. Spring is late; flowering is delayed until July, therefore ripening time is at risk from cold autumn weather. Nonetheless good light aromatic wines are now consistently produced.

The climate of the French Alps, with a short but sunny summer and low temperatures at night, stamps its personality on the low-key, all-refreshment wines of grapes traditionally grown in Savoie: the Altesse and the Roussette. Here the variety and the terroir *produce wines which precisely express the uniqueness of their origin.*

Chardonnay is the most forgiving and the most flexible of all varieties. It will make satisfying wine in any climate from cool to very warm – but the personalities of these wines will be vastly different. Its specialized use in sparkling wine apart, its most restrained manifestation is arguably that of Chablis. Chablis is traditionally described in terms of gun-flint and sucking river pebbles – images for the totally-dry, only just ripe aspect of cool-grown Chardonnay. Primitive production methods and uninhibited use of sulphur dioxide in the past may have contributed to this image. But Chablis of a fine vintage today (the vintages of 1985, 1986, 1988, 1989, 1990 for example), made in the traditional way without new oak, is Chardonnay at its purest and most refined – coloured only by the elusive, elemental *goût de terroir* of its pale clay.

As Chardonnay moves from cool to warmer regions, its flavour develops from suggestions of apple, fig and melon, to grapefruit, peach and finally to honey. Overlaid on these flavours is (in most cases) a greater or lesser influence of oak (toast, butter, tar), but the increasingly ripe, round and dense personality of the same grape grown in a warmer climate is clear. It is true that these changes are in part structural, associated with increasing natural levels of alcohol, although chaptalisation can be a wild card which upsets this neat pattern. Very ripe, warm-grown Chardonnay has precocious appeal, but quickly cloys: one glass is enough. That was the California Chardonnay of the early 1970s.

Cabernet Sauvignon grown in excessively cool conditions has a weedy, thin, herbaceous flavour, and a bitter, 'green' finish. Under perfect ripening conditions it develops its central aroma and flavour of blackcurrant, given tension by echoes of the green pepper character lent by less ripe (or more heavily shaded) fruit, and by the variety's typically astringent tannins. In warmer regions it acquires a more lush aspect, sometimes showing eucalypt or mint flavours, sometimes a distinctive taste of dark chocolate. Hot-grown Cabernet Sauvignon has a jammy, stewed mulberry and prunes character, and is usually flabby on the finish. If the acidity is as low (or pH is as high) as one might expect, the hue will have an unhealthy, dull blackish edge right from the outset, which will rapidly degenerate into a dispirited brown.

Pinot Noir is the opposite to Chardonnay. It ever so reluctantly reveals the glorious perfume, the sappy-silky taste and texture of great burgundy – a reluctance which starts at home, and intensifies away from it. Chardonnay takes the vicissitudes of the Burgundian climate in its stride: one has to go back to 1975 to find a really bad year for white burgundy. How different the position of red burgundy. In the 1970s one can approach only three vintages (1971, 1972 and 1978) with confidence that the bottle may well be great; in the 1980s, only 1985, 1988 and 1989. Why? Because with a little too much heat, or a touch too little, with rot at harvest-time or (as in 1976) drought that produced unbudgeable tannin, that elusive fruit disappears, and dull, soapy and bitter unripe wines or burnt, flabby, smelly overripe ones result.

Pinot Noir flavours in ideal conditions range from slightly simple red cherry or raspberry fruit (as in Volnay) to more textured and voluptuous plum (as in Vosne Romanée). Dotted around the world are a few areas where Pinot Noir gives glimpses of its inherent greatness: the Central Coast of California (Santa Barbara in particular), the Willamette Valley of Oregon; Carneros, California; the Yarra Valley and other regions grouped around Melbourne, Australia; Martinborough, New Zealand; and perhaps the high Penedès, in Catalonia. Pinot Noir will simply not tolerate excessive warmth: it ripens well enough, and the bunches look perfect, but it produces an utterly nondescript red wine (briefly red before it turns brown) which is devoid of any varietal character. If the climate is too cool, as in Germany, one ends with the anaemic character of Spätburgunder or with wine as thin, herbal and weedy as the most unripe Cabernet Sauvignon.

Climate: how varieties react

Chardonnay

Cabernet Sauvignon

Pinot Noir

Riesling

Riesling is a conundrum. On the basis of its distribution in Europe, one would say it needs the coolest of climates, yet if one looks at dry Riesling, its performance in other countries points in another direction. Australia (with 3,600 hectares) has some of the largest plantings outside Germany, and until the dramatic rise of Chardonnay recently, Riesling was by far the most important premium white wine in that country. There Riesling reaches its stylistic peak in the uncompromisingly warm climate of the Clare Valley and the marginally cooler Eden Valley, both in South Australia. With between 11 and 12 degrees natural alcohol, the wines are very reserved in their youth with overtones of passion fruit (Eden Valley examples always smell a little more floral, with a definite suggestion of lime juice). But over ten to 20 years in the bottle they develop a fine tannin between their lime-like acidity and a broader flavour often likened to gently browned toast. At least to Australian palates, the somewhat harder, faintly spicy Rieslings from cooler areas such as Coonawarra and southern Victoria are much less successful.

One characteristic, however, sets all warm-climate Rieslings apart from the German model. A singular scent, usually referred to as kerosene or petrol, gradually creeps into German Rieslings in maturity (which can be after 15 or 20 years). In the great majority of Australian or California Rieslings, the same aroma arrives after a mere year or two in bottle.

The evidence from North America, South Africa and New Zealand is similar. Clonal selection, yield and the winemaker's intentions all play a part; so far, though, areas outside Germany with similarly cool climates have failed to produce Rieslings to compete with those grown on warmer sites. The exceptions are sweet wines. The noble rot botrytis is evidently less pernickety than its host-grape. Once it has taken hold it can be hard to tell whether the wine was made in the northern hemisphere or the southern, the east or the west.

Syrah

Syrah – or as it is known in Australia and South Africa, Shiraz – is another grape which responds positively and enthusiastically to a range of climatic conditions, taking warmth in its stride. France (the Rhône and the south) and Australia are its two strongholds. Paradoxically, Australia provides some of the coolest areas in which it is grown (as well as the hottest – at Alice Springs in the centre of the country). These cool regions – Macedon, just north of Melbourne; the Mornington Peninsula; and cooler sites at Great Western, also in Victoria – produce wines redolent of fresh ground pepper and sundry spices. These wines have caused much excitement and attracted much praise in Australia, yet masters of the grape such as Gérard Jaboulet of the Rhône take the view that pepper and spice are seasonings which should be held at threshold level, and that in excess the flavour simply indicates unripe grape character from a poor or mediocre vintage.

As the climate warms, pepperiness diminishes and (while the wine is young) sweet, warm berry-fruit flavours take over, but with a range of secondary aromas and flavours more akin to the ephemeral Pinot Noir than to the imperious Cabernet Sauvignon. The greatest Syrah wines are Jaboulet's Hermitage La Chapelle, the very rare Côte Rôties of Marcel Guigal, and Penfolds' Grange Hermitage – wines made in roughly similar climates, albeit from very different *terroirs*, the last showing none of the pepper and spice flavours of the Rhône wines. Then there are the Syrahs of the very hot Hunter Valley in Australia (traditionally, if cheekily, called Hermitage) in which secondary characteristics of tar, leather and a certain smokiness are immediately apparent, and pepper and spice are notably absent.

Sauvignon Blanc

Whether one regards Sauvignon Blanc as flexible or limited in its climatic range depends on whether one is an aficionado of Sancerre and Pouilly Fumé – and indeed whether one accepts it as one of the great grape varieties in the first place (other than in its role in contributing to the great Sauternes). The American palate, consciously or unconsciously, seems to reject its pristine varietal character as expressed in the Loire Valley: tart, crisp, gooseberry with a vegetal-tobacco bite, less charitably described as canned peas or cat's pee. Californian winemakers go to considerable lengths to mute these characteristics, making sure the grape is very ripe before it is harvested, blending in a percentage of Sémillon, and surrounding it with a coating of oak. In most parts of Australia no such effort is needed: the variety easily detunes itself, and it takes skilled viticulture, favourable vintage conditions and special site selection to produce a wine which (in its unwooded state) combines recognizable varietal character with reasonable ripeness and body.

On the other hand, New Zealand (with an ease tantamount to promiscuity) and South Africa (surprisingly) produce Sauvignon Blanc wines with pungent and precise varietal character. New Zealand does it best of all in Marlborough, with a climate which must be very similar to that of the upper Loire Valley and with the type of meagre, stony soil which would bring a smile to the face of the most chauvinistic and hard-to-please French grape grower. Quite why South Africa does so well is not easy to understand: its climate is much warmer – warmer than that of the Barossa Valley around Stellenbosch, and warmer still at Paarl (though cooler on the Simonsberg hills) – but even Sauvignon Blanc made in the modest cooperatives towards Paarl retains distinctive character.

Sémillon

Sémillon, like Syrah, finds its greatest expression in France and Australia, producing, when made dry, wines of almost unrecognizably different style in climates which, viticulturally speaking, are as far apart as the Sahara desert and the South Pole. Given that it is a ubiquitous variety, found in almost all the wine-growing regions of the world, it is strange that it should manifest its greatest character at these extremes – Bordeaux on the one hand, and the Hunter Valley on the other. All the two areas have in common is humidity. Paradoxically, Bordeaux is still only in the process of investigating Sémillon. While it is the foundation-stone of Sauternes, its role in dry wines in the past has been merely to round out the edginess of Sauvignon Blanc. Its affinity with new oak, with Sauvignon as the junior partner, is a discovery with an exciting future.

Overall, it must be seen as a flexible variety. Although in the relatively warm, strongly maritime climate of Margaret River in Western Australia and all of New Zealand it produces wine which is hard to distinguish from a slightly thin Sauvignon Blanc, with pronounced herbal and tobacco overtones, there are a few good examples from South Africa (where the grape is widely planted) and there is potential to produce good wines in South America (there are vast plantings in Chile) with the rapid improvement in fermentation technology and oak handling in that country. Washington State also grows it very well. But to date it is the voluptuous, nutty, honeyed 20-year-old Australian Hunter Valley Sémillons – tasting for all the world as if they were fermented in new oak or at least matured in it, which they were not – which show the Sémillon grape to its greatest advantage.

Chenin Blanc

Chenin Blanc has not yet had a fair trial. Even in its home in the Loire Valley it demands exceptional conditions to produce great wine. Yet no one who has tasted a 30- or even 50-year-old sweet Vouvray or Coteaux du Layon can forget its potential. For acidity braced against richness it is France's only answer to the masterpieces of the Mosel.

This aptitude to maintain its high acidity stands it in good stead in much warmer climates than the Loire – where it is understood. South Africa has long relied on it for everyday wine that stays lively and fruity even in primitive conditions. One or two Californian winemakers regularly make an excellently structured dry wine from it. New Zealand is just starting to discover its potential affinity with the Loire. This is a grape (rather than a fashion) to follow.

Which Variety of Vine?

The flavour starts with the grape

Varietalism

Each long-established wine region has a story to tell about its own grape varieties. Perhaps the Greeks introduced them, perhaps the Romans, perhaps the Cistercians; perhaps they evolved by selection and mutation from some such introduction – or even from wild woodland vines.

In most cases they are so important to the identity of the local product that, ever since there have been appellation laws or their equivalents, the grape variety or varieties have been specified as clearly and definitively as the region itself.

What is perhaps surprising is that very little of this history is particularly old. With the unique exception of Pinot Noir, which was made mandatory (with only mixed success) for the region of Beaune in the 14th century, the designation of varieties comes very late in wine's long history. Not until the late 18th century was Riesling heavily planted along the Rhine and Mosel, or Cabernet Sauvignon recognized as the best of all grapes for the Médoc. Only a hundred years later growers in the Napa Valley came to the same conclusion.

We should not think, then, of two totally separate developments, one Old World and one New World. In terms of modern winemaking, in many ways both worlds have been working out most of their grape preferences over the same short period of time.

Grape preferences: a new concern

The great difference between the two is that the vineyards of Europe – whatever was planted in them – were a long-established going concern. Changes in old

Cabernet Sauvignon, the classic 'claret grape', has shown itself to be surprisingly adaptable in climates quite different to that of Bordeaux: in California's Napa Valley, in Australia, Chile, the Penedès region of Spain, and in Italy. It is proving in every sense to be an international variety.

practice (and old planting) were made reluctantly, circumspectly, and probably only by those who could afford to make mistakes without risking starvation. Besides, who would pull up an old vineyard and lose several years' harvests? Better to patch a plot where vines had died and see a gradual transformation.

Old practices, old plantings

The case of New World growers has always been totally different. The land is bare; there are decisions to be made. Do I want red wine or white? What vines are available from the nurseries? What do the neighbours say, think and do? What do the boffins advise?

True, in the first century of Californian and Australian winemaking most of the wines went to market as 'Burgundy', 'Chablis', 'Claret', 'Rhine' or 'Sauternes' – or, more strictly speaking, most as 'Port' or 'Sherry': table wines were very much in the minority. But the growers had planted their vineyards with Cabernet, Riesling, Shiraz (Syrah) or Zinfandel. It was inevitable that they saw them as blocks of certain grapes, rather than peculiar parcels of land with an immemorial, usually only vaguely identified, vine population.

Peculiar parcels

'Varietalism', to coin a word, was therefore built into the structure of New World viticulture from the start. Then, from the 1930s, the journalist Frank Schoonmaker, advising Almadén Vineyards (California), hit on the idea of making the grape variety the sales pitch. It was harmless, it looked like truth in labelling, and Europe had reason to be pleased that its geographic designations were no longer to be plundered wholesale.

The idea that half a century later a French wine might sell not because it was burgundy, but because it was Chardonnay, would have seemed absurd. No longer, though. Varietalism has come to Europe, and given legitimacy to regions with little or no history. A few classic regions apart, it has already all but destroyed the fragile 'traditions' of Italy, while even in France growers in regions without strong traditions now effectively get their vine-manipulating and vineyard-managing ideas, their marketing strategies and even their winemaking techniques straight from Australia or California.

'White burgundy' or 'Chardonnay'?

Above: *Riesling, Chardonnay's rival for the title of the world's greatest white grape.*

Left: *Chenin Blanc, cultivated in the Loire since the 9th century, has happily travelled the wine world producing a variety of wines: luscious sweet, off-dry, sparkling – even appearing in fortified wines.*

Blending

Parallel to varietalism, and by no means at odds with it, lies the tradition and practice of blending. In most old wine regions blending (of varieties in the vineyard) was taken for granted. The 'purity' of Pinot Noir was very much an exception – and very probably a chimera, too: Pinots Blanc, Gris and Meunier, some Chardonnay, a certain amount of the outlawed Gamay, and a little Aligoté might all have been found in a red-wine Côte d'Or vineyard. At Château Margaux in the 18th century it was the practice to make the white wine (Sauvignon) separately from the red and blend them together to make the *grand vin* – according to the owner's taste. At Lafite it was more likely to be Hermitage from the Rhône that was blended into the château wine, to give it the weight it often lacked.

Dom Pérignon: kid-glove care

Dom Pérignon was celebrated in his day not, as the legend goes, for inventing sparkling champagne, but as a blender of genius who conjured luxurious white wine almost exclusively from Pinot Noir by using grapes from different *terroirs* and handling them with kid-glove care. He was no fan of Chardonnay: he found it too prone to refermentation, producing the bubbles he tried so hard to avoid.

Chardonnay and Riesling, it is true, are grapes that have nothing to gain and much to lose from blending, but port has always been a blend of grapes, and Châteauneuf-du-Pape has 13 permitted varieties in its appellation; similarly the formulas for Rioja and Chianti both call for a balancing of darker and lighter, more aromatic and more weighty wines.

The New World, though, has generally been hesitant about sullying the purity of its 'varietals'. The assumption has been that if Cabernet Sauvignon is good, 100 percent Cabernet Sauvignon must be best. For better or worse 'varietal character' has been and still is pursued as a goal in itself.

It is true that well-selected New World sites should not need the insurance-policy element of a mixed planting. For them the reason for blending (apart from stretching the supply of an expensive grape as Australia has been known to do by adding Sémillon to Chardonnay) must be found in the flavour.

Of all the 'classic' varieties Cabernet Sauvignon is the only one that regularly benefits from a partner in the vat. Memorable as its flavour is, with a structure that demands long ageing, anything less than ideal ripening conditions can lead to a

The 'doughnut' effect

'doughnut' effect on the palate: the wine starts and finishes powerfully in the mouth, its finish in particular boosted by astringent tannins, with the result that the 'mid-palate' seems to lack something.

Bordeaux has its answer, arrived at by centuries of trial and error. It blends in the rounder, fleshier Merlot and more aromatic Cabernet Franc – but still in proportions very much dependent on the vintage. Australia has attempted an answer of its own, whose logic appears impeccable. Shiraz (Syrah) rises in flavour in the mouth just where Cabernet seems to fall. Structurally the two are ideally matched. For all that, though, Cabernet-Shiraz blends are going out of fashion.

A feeling for orthodoxy?

Whether due to a feeling for orthodoxy (which does not sound very Australian) or due to disillusionment with the local formula, winemakers are switching over to the classic 'Bordeaux blend'. The current argument against Shiraz as a companion for Cabernet Sauvignon is that, while structurally compatible, rather than producing a whole greater than the sum of its parts each 'blurs' the varietal flavour of the other. A plausible explanation may be that Merlot and Cabernet Franc are genetically part of the Cabernet 'family': Shiraz is not.

Talk of 'varietal character', in other words, is simply an acknowledgment that a few outstanding grapes have flavours we appreciate for themselves. Others need a supporting cast.

Clones

A clone is a population of plants all members of which are the descendants by vegetative propagation of a single individual and are therefore, in theory at least, genetically identical.

Left: *Pinot Noir at 'véraison', when the grapes turn from green to purple. Uneven flowering caused by bad weather (below) can lead to the berries ripening unevenly – a serious problem when it comes to harvest.*

The Stone Age selection

The selection of clones has been carried out for just as long as the selection of varieties; indeed, in a sense it preceded it. It has also had a single purpose for almost all of the thousands of years for which it has been practised: to increase or to ensure a healthy yield. The first selections were made in Neolithic times. Wild vines are predominantly female, depending on a lesser population of male vines for fertilization. If properly fertilized, the female vines would bear good crops, but the process was far from certain. The male vines bore no crops at all. There were then a few vines which had a percentage of hermaphrodite flowers; flowers which could self-pollinate. It seems reasonable to assume that the early viticulturists would have been anxious to rid their vineyards of any barren male vines, but the result of rooting out the males would have been to leave the females barren. The hermaphrodite vines, therefore, were seen as the most reliable. Attempts to propagate them by seed would have been both slow and risky. But propagation by transferring cuttings enabled quick and reliable selection resulting in vineyards of the modern day composition of totally hermaphrodite vines.

Health and consistency

Today clonal selection has two overt aims: to achieve a defined and consistent level of quality and to eliminate viruses and other diseases. Its effect, whether or not recognized as an aim, has almost invariably been to increase the size of the crop. For its first aim it depends on genetic mutation – however slight. In any given field of vines some will stand out as having all or most of the desired qualities: above all a good, healthy crop of grapes in bunches which are not too tightly packed together, or too loosely spaced on the stem.

Some varieties offer far more mutants than others. Pinot Noir is famously genetically unstable. All the other Pinots (Meunier, Gris and Blanc) are apparently mutations of this promiscuous parent, while there are said to be some 1,000 clones of Pinot Noir in Burgundy, ranging from the ubiquitous easy-to-prune and heavy-cropping 'Pinot Droit' (easily recognizable by the peculiar upright and straight growth of its canes) to the tiny population of the shy-bearing 'Pinot Fin' which the Domaine de la Romanée-Conti claims as its own.

The German model

If the French have been backward in using hybrids, the Germans have more than compensated, with Müller-Thurgau their flagship. A century after its discovery the parentage claimed (or supposed) by Dr Müller is in doubt. Rather than being of Riesling × Silvaner it may in reality be a cross between two clones of Riesling.

Müller-Thurgau did not in reality combine only the advantages of each parent: its soft wood makes it particularly susceptible to winter frosts, it is more prone to a range of diseases than either parent, and it is not particularly easy to grow. If this were not enough, no-one disagrees that the wine it produces is exceedingly ordinary.

Hybrids and crosses

A distinction should be drawn between a hybrid (the union between a Vitis vinifera *vine and another species of* Vitis – Vitis amurensis, *for example) and a cross, involving two varieties of* Vitis vinifera *(such as the crossing of Riesling and Sylvaner to produce Müller-Thurgau).*

To breed grape vine hybrids is no less painstaking and costly than are the mechanics of clonal selection, although plant geneticists argue it is more certain and focused in aim: it does not rely on chance mutations for its source. Its purpose is quite different: rather than seek improved versions of existing varieties, it creates new varieties. The process may take place in stages, and be repeated many times. Step one involves the selection of two parents. Since the female might self-pollinate, it must be emasculated by removal of the stamens from the flowers. Pollen is then taken from the flower of the male, applied to the female, and a bag placed over the pollinated flower to keep out strange pollen from other flowers. Step two involves removal of the ripened berries from the vines and planting the seeds. Not all will germinate, but those that do will all be different from each other. Several years later step three involves the selection of the most promising vines, and step four, propagation of multiples of these by cuttings (not seeds). Most will be discarded, perhaps all. If one is selected, it may be both propagated commercially in its own right and/or used for yet further crossings (step five).

Genetic engineering

Intractable French opposition to hybrids and crosses – and some would say the conservatism of wine producers and wine consumers everywhere – has played some role in slowing the development of the next phase: genetic manipulation. Biotechnology was one of the buzz words of the 1980s, but its application to woody plants has been slow compared to cereal crops and vegetables. Nonetheless, there is great potential in taking the best features of both plant breeding and of clonal selection, and in particular in making directed and deliberate improvements in existing grape varieties. The method used is the 'in vitro' growth of grapevine cells, which are manipulated and subsequently nurtured into an entire plant. The advantages of this approach are numerous and its perfection will undoubtedly preoccupy viticultural research scientists over the next few decades.

As the German experience graphically demonstrates, technique (and technology) must never be allowed to become an end in itself. Clonal selection and vine breeding have to be seen as tools to be used sensitively and with discretion. In the early decades of experimentation, the viticulturists made all the running. The winemaker was scarcely consulted; nor the consumer. The indices of success were vine health, yield, and ability to ripen the crop within a stipulated time.

The next phase of experimentation was marked by more thorough chemical analysis designed to give a better idea of quality; research was often substantiated by the making of small quantities of wine from trial plots. The problems with these winemaking trials were, first, their very small scale. They seldom provided any close correlation with the results of commercial winemaking. Secondly the calibre, experience and expectations of the judges called upon to judge the wines.

Quis custodiet?

Plant health and yields, however, continued to improve. In some instances quality improved. But the problem in many areas was (and is) the divergence in interest between the grape-grower who sells the grapes and the winemaker who makes and sells the wine. In areas such as Bordeaux, where estates are the rule, this conflict scarcely arises, but in most of the grape-growing regions of the world much of the production comes from small contract growers.

To compound the problem, the years since World War II have bred generations of winemakers who have focused their attention on the winery, believing that modern machinery and techniques could (as it were) make silk purses out of sour grapes. Behind them stand the bankers and the company accountants, ever anxious to reduce costs and entirely insensitive to – indeed oblivious of – the special nature and requirements of fine wine.

Silk purses out of sour grapes?

The result has been the proliferation of clones which satisfy the economic tests easily, and scrape through the lowest common denominator of not impairing quality. Or do they? The following are descriptions of some new Pinot Noir clones given in an appendix to a paper delivered by Monsieur Raymond Bernard, a world-respected authority on clonal selection, to the Australian Society of Viticulture and Oenology on 20 November 1986:

> **Clone No 111, Pinot Fin:** approved 1971
> Colour: good. Nose: undeveloped, undistinguished. Palate: lacks body, roundness and finesse.
> **Clone No 291, Pinot Fructifère:** approved 1973
> Colour: average. Nose: not very representative. Palate: acid – unbalanced.
> *(To be fair, both clones were damned in their overall assessments.)*
> **Clone No 291,** summarized thus:
> Very productive clone with a long cycle. Low alcohol, quality inadequate for Bourgogne-Franche-Comté. To be rejected for the refinement of red wines.

Nonetheless, these clones were originally approved, and remain available to those interested in high yields. Whether growers are prepared to reject such 'advancements' ultimately depends on what their customers are prepared to pay.

Since phylloxera attacked the world's vineyards in the 19th century prudent growers have grafted their chosen variety onto a rootstock of American parentage. Phylloxera originally came from North America and had coexisted with the native vine species over the millennia which gradually became largely resistant to it. It soon became apparent, though, that the balance between the American rootstock, the scion (chosen vine variety) and the soil was almost infinitely variable. Some rootstocks are so vigorous that uncontrolled vegetative growth (and hence sharply reduced crop levels) result. Others are too weak. Some, such as hybrid rootstocks ARGI, AXR and 1202 used in California, are not sufficiently resistant to

American roots

Above: *A bunch of newly grafted vines: the pale wood at the top is the 'scion' – the chosen variety – with one bud, dove-tailed onto the darker wood of the selected root stock.*

Right: *The grafts are planted out in dense rows in a nursery bed with a plastic mulch covering to form roots before going into the vineyard.*

phylloxera. Vulnerability to nematodes is another problem: tiny worm-like creatures which are not as devastating as phylloxera but which also attack the roots and debilitate the plant, compel growers in several phylloxera-free New World regions to use grafted vines.

In the outcome, much the same pattern has emerged as with clones: those rootstocks which (however insidiously) gave increased yield came to be preferred. Worse, much of the evaluation work was carried out in France, on infertile 'low-potential', soils: to this day there has been insufficient work done on sufficiently devigorating rootstocks for the fertile 'high potential' sites of the New World.

Selection and breeding v. the flat-earther

Only a flat-earther could deny the potential benefits of clonal selection, hybrid crossings, genetics and rootstock selection. Many parts of the world have indifferent clones which are neither high quality nor high yielding. They need to be able to start again with 'clean', well-adapted vines. As we shall see in later chapters, phylloxera has had devastating affects on plant health and the spread of viruses, and no-one would argue that low yields from sick vines are desirable. Genetic engineering offers all sorts of possibilities for the natural control of diseases, a subject of increasing significance in a world increasingly wary of the use of chemicals of any kind. And the use of rootstocks, quite apart from saving the European wine industry from oblivion, offers real scope for improvement in wine quality at all levels. In other words these are tools: if used skilfully and intelligently, they will help make better wine; used clumsily and without sufficient thought, they will make rubbish.

Sculpting the Vine

Too much vigour is as bad as too little

The vine is the most adaptable of plants, accepting with equanimity the transition from its forest origins to the ground-hugging, stumpy little bushes of Beaujolais or the Rhône Valley, or Rioja, the form it also traditionally took in the Barossa Valley of Australia, the Napa Valley and in many other New World vineyards. This severe 'bush-pruning', taking the vine back to only a few buds on each branch, seems orderly and natural, while the ancient Italian (and Portuguese) method of growing the vine up poplars, across high latticed pergolas, interplanted with every type of crop or fruit tree imaginable, seems chaotic and unnatural. In truth, the Italian approach far more closely resembles the vine's natural habit, even though today it is a fast disappearing anachronism.

All the great wine regions of Europe have one thing in common: very moderate soil fertility, leading to low natural vigour in their vines. French wine-lore is full of aphorisms about vines growing where nothing else is worth planting, and conversely, that where corn will grow well, the wine will not be worth drinking.

In the bizarre jargon of today the term for such ideal vineyards is 'low potential sites'. Over the centuries a priceless bank of experience has been built up and passed down from generation to generation: the formulas for growing vines in perfect balance on such low potential sites, to make the highest quality of wine.

In Europe, whatever the traditional, regional or local system of vineyard management (pruning, training and trellising), its common features are very close vine-spacing, low yield per vine, small individual bunches, and shoots and grapes well exposed to light; these achieved by repeated and meticulous hedging or trimming of the vines through the growing season. In European vineyards the low vigour means that by mid-summer the vine's growth has slowed, and it reacts mildly to trimming. This is where the fertile, 'high potential' vineyards of the New World have a peculiar problem: trimming provokes a burst of lateral growth (laterals are shoots springing from the base of the leaves on the current year's canes). It exacerbates the very problem of shading which it is intended to cure.

The unflappable vine

Trim in Europe

These Egyptian vines of 3000 BC were planted in richly manured beds and trimmed high on pergolas. The quality of their wines is unknown.

A Year in the Vineyard

Every vineyard has the same essential annual routine, but there are scores of options open to the wine-grower as to how and when each job is carried out. This chart indicates some of the more important tasks.

The decisions of the growers will be dictated by climate, tradition, economics and the pursuit of quality. Over the past decade or so there have been enormous advances in the science of growing grapes. The results of academic research are now shared world-wide, so that progressive growers have an uncomfortable amount of often conflicting advice to ponder. The majority settle for the certainty of tradition, while staying alert to the new products and techniques that promise a less gruelling workload.

1 WINTER

Pruning
There are four basic choices:
(a) *Cane-pruning*
(the most skilled)
(b) *Spur-pruning*
(easier and quicker)
(c) *Machine pruning*
(effectively spur-pruning)
(d) *Minimal pruning*
(effectively no pruning at all during winter)
Mechanical pruning is often followed by a certain amount of hand pruning or 'cleaning up'.

2 SPRING

Planting
The optimum time for planting is in early spring as the ground is starting to warm up yet still retains good moisture. If the rootlings are planted too early the roots may rot; in the New World vines are sometimes kept in cool stores and planted in early summer.

3 SUMMER

Irrigation
This period of flowering and fruit-set is a critical time in which the vine needs warm, calm weather and in which the intervention of the grower is limited. Irrigation will begin at this time in dry regions in the New World.

4 AUTUMN

Harvest
The choice lies between the speed and economy of machine harvesting (where the vineyard permits it) and the gentler, slower and more controllable hand-picking.

In all cases late pruning will delay the development of the buds and result in a more even bud-break.

In Champagne (far left) and Alsace (left) it is an accepted part of vineyard hygiene to burn the prunings from the vines in winter. Some growers leave them lying between the rows to decompose slowly and add to the structure of the soil – or the risk, say others, of harbouring fungal diseases.

Foliage sprays

The first of the lime-sulphur sprays are applied at woolly-bud stage (as the buds swell and soften) to guard against fungal disease. Organic growers or those wishing to minimize spraying will still accept the use of these sprays and of Bordeaux mixture.

Working the soil

There is an increasing recognition of the choice between the traditional agricultural practice of ploughing the soil, and of leaving it untilled – relying in the latter case on the use of herbicides to control unwanted weed or excessive grass growth.

In frost-prone areas a billiard-table smooth, bare surface between the vines allows air circulation and hence protection against frost. Organic growers, however, encourage a variety of plants to grow there, thus providing a natural food chain (protecting the grapes) and adding nitrogen to the soil.

Canopy trimming and training

Directing and, later in the season, limiting the exuberant new growth is of critical importance in establishing the balance of the vine and achieving appropriate exposure of the grape bunches to sunlight. Traditionally a skilled hand job, it can now be done by machines which can lift wires and shoots or weave support strings through the canopy.

Vine maintenance

(a) *Foliage sprays*
In cool, humid regions the vines must be sprayed to prevent botrytis attacking during flowering. Such attack destroys the grapes before they can begin to form.

The vines also need to be sprayed regularly against oidium and other mildews: Bordeaux Mixture (a solution of copper sulphate, lime and water) or systemic fungicides are frequently used. These latter chemical sprays are absorbed into the sap-stream of the plant. Unfortunately, fungal diseases rapidly develop resistance to specific chemicals, making it necessary to vary the formula.

(b) *Trimming the vine*
Throughout the growing season the canes must be trimmed and the remaining foliage raised and attached to the trellis wires to allow the maximum sunlight to reach the leaves and grapes.

Working the soil

While the area under the vines will not be disturbed, traditional growers still lightly plough the soil between the rows of vines in order to prevent run-off and thus conserve moisture.

Pest control

Caterpillars, moths and, towards ripening, birds have to be controlled. Other pests to which vines and grapes are lost include: rabbits, foxes, snails and, in Australia, kangaroos.

Post-harvest sprays

At approximately 50% leaf fall, a spray is applied to kill mildew spores which would otherwise establish themselves on the vine over winter.

Working the soil and applications of fertilizers

Traditional growers will work manure and fertilizers into the soil and bank the soil up under the vines – thereby also protecting them from frost. The choice lies with the type and amount of fertilizer. On steep sites, to counter any run-off, the soil may be brought back up the hillside.

Vineyard maintenance

Between the end of harvest and the commencement of pruning, much vineyard maintenance is carried out: prunings are removed – and either burnt, or chopped up and incorporated into the soil – and trellising is checked.

So different are the problems of balancing the metabolism of a typical New World vine on a high potential site that academics and growers have gone back to basics, analysing the influences at work so that they can study them one by one. Mechanization appears to be the first step towards a solution.

Australia: brutally radical

In the early 1960s Coonawarra in South Australia was the testbed for a completely radical experiment, lasting until 1979. The sequence of events was: first, the abandonment of all soil working and the use of herbicides to create a billiard-table smooth and completely bare vineyard surface between the vines; then the introduction of mechanical harvesting (by no means a world-first, although a relatively early one). Next mechanical harvesters were adapted to perform the function of a mechanical pruning machine; finally came the implementation of what is euphemistically called 'minimal pruning', which in reality means no winter pruning at all.

. . . but wonderfully cheap

The cumulative effect of putting these techniques and practices to use was to reduce the cost of producing each tonne of grapes (including picking), in an area renowned for making some of Australia's finest wine, to a quarter of the cost of producing the same quantity using traditional methods – hand-pruning, summer training, some cultivation or grass mowing, and hand-picking.

From an economic viewpoint, therefore, these techniques have everything to commend them. As one might expect, however, the implications for quality are very much less clear, and analysis of the rationale and effect of each viticultural step explains why.

Old hat to till?

Working the soil is a time-hallowed practice with strong emotional overtones. It starts in the home garden; there is something intensely satisfying in the sight of a freshly turned plot, the moist, dark brown earth proclaiming its fertility, worms burrowing indignantly downwards from the unwelcome light, weeds vanquished

Mechanical harvesters have many virtues: not least the fact that they can be converted to hedging-machines in winter and 'prune' a whole vineyard in no longer than it takes to remove its grapes.

and lying in limp heaps beside the beds. Similarly, the sight of a freshly worked vineyard, weeds and grass removed, the vines in soldierly rows, and bright green canopies in stark contrast to the brown soil, brings a feeling of deep satisfaction.

And yet, working the soil with modern tractor-drawn equipment can be and often is very destructive. For a start, every time a conventional tractor is driven along a row of vines it compacts the subsoil, and the tractor tyres necessarily run over the prime root zones. Working the top 30 centimetres of the soil does no more than hide the problem underneath. Of course, tractors cannot be eliminated from vineyards, although the lightweight over-the-vine tractor common in France has advantages: its tyres run down the middle of the row, and the compaction is less. Equally undesirable, conventional cultivators destroy the all-important structure of the top soil in which the fine feeder roots of the vine are so active during the growing season. In its undisturbed state, the soil builds up an active ecosystem with bacteria, worms and other organisms all helping create nutrients and nitrogen for the vine to use. Paradoxically, undisturbed soil can also be much more effective in capturing water falling on its surface, be it from rainfall or irrigation. It establishes a capillary action which sucks the water downwards, and surface evaporation is also less than that from worked soil.

If the decision is taken not to work the soil in any way, the question then arises what to do with the weed and grass growth. Weeds vary from a mere visual nuisance to serious competitors for moisture and nutrients. Apart from specialized applications with organic farming, they need to be eliminated. The almost universal solution is to establish a weed- and grass-free band directly under the vine canopy, and these days herbicides are widely used to do this. After several years' application the top few centimetres of the surface soil become sterile, and occasional weed growth easy to control.

Soil satisfaction

A Napa Valley grower favours an eco-friendly solution: sowing mustard between his vines and ploughing it in as 'green manure'.

Machine pruning

Mechanical pruning is now so widely practised that it has almost ceased to be controversial. The basic technique calls for the vine to be hedged by horizontal and vertical cutter bars, so that the pruned vines look like endless rows of hedgehogs. This process only works, though, where the vines are trellised at a constant height which is within the working range of the pruning machine. It also necessarily involves the vines being spur-pruned rather than cane-pruned. Traditionalists predicted at first that the vines would strangle themselves and die. They do not, although experience does show that a certain amount of cleaning up by hand pays handsome dividends.

The initial reaction of the vine to machine pruning is to produce much higher yields; these eventually settle back and production then tends towards smaller berry and bunch weights, which help counterbalance loss of quality.

Minimal pruning

Minimal pruning remains the most controversial technique. All formal pruning and training systems have one aim: to ensure that this year's crop and next year's fruiting wood get enough sunlight to ripen. The great attribute of the minimally pruned vine is that this occurs naturally; without pruning it has no stimulus to grow a heavy, shading canopy, and the bunches naturally position themselves on the outside of the canopy. Another attribute is the formation of more numerous, smaller-than-usual bunches. The drawbacks, though, are the risk of mildew and other diseases growing unchecked in the cluttered, untidy interior of the vine, a

No vineyards are lovelier than the pergola'd alleyways that surround the fields of the Minho in northern Portugal. Their vinho verde *does not call for very ripe grapes: freshness and an acidic bite are guaranteed by growing them in the shade of their own canopies in a picturesque polyculture with vegetables and maize.*

tendency to over-crop, and irregular ripening of shoots of varying lengths.

Given the conditions of a fertile, 'high-potential' site it works well within its limitations. Few would argue, though, that minimal pruning has any place in high-quality vineyards.

Vines on fertile soil, supplied with everything they need to grow lustily, can become like spoilt children. They will establish a massive root system loaded with carbohydrate reserves, grow excessively, and smother their own grapes (and next season's latent buds) in dense shade. Such vines will produce a relatively low yield of grapes (as little as the 'magic' number of 45 hectolitres per hectare) but their wine will have low colour intensity, a high pH, high malic acid content, low flavour and only moderate alcohol content.

'California sprawl'

Some call this phenomenon California Sprawl; when a vine dedicates most of its superabundant energy to growing leaves and canes, and only a small part to growing and ripening grapes. It is a no-win situation because however the vine is pruned the result will be more or less the same.

How, then, does one satisfactorily control vigour in a high-yielding New World site and how does one measure (or quantify) the success of such control? One of the answers has been to increase the planting density from the traditional 1,500–2,250 vines per hectare to around 3,300 vines per hectare. But in practice this has a negligible effect on vine vigour. It may well result in a more efficient land-use and, coupled with an appropriately complex trellis, may result in an increased yield of higher quality grapes, but it is not an answer in itself.

Vigour control

On the contrary, very close planting on fertile sites can lead to a vicious circle of furious growth, leading to an impenetrable canopy of shade where few buds receive any worthwhile light. The few that grow just add to the mass of sappy vegetation.

Leaves properly exposed to sunlight have a much higher photosynthetic capacity than those which are shaded, leading to higher levels of sugar (carbohydrate) in the vine's system. Conversely, shaded shoots borrow sugars from elsewhere in the vine (including the grapes) to acquire energy for their growth. Buds which have been shaded in the previous growing season are less likely to break (or shoot) the following spring, and if they do break, are likely to be significantly less fruitful. Flowering and fruit set are also impaired. It is thus not hard to understand why a shaded canopy will be less productive than one which is well exposed.

Too much shade

And as we have seen shade also plays a major role in reducing grape quality. Shaded leaves and shaded bunches produce thin, soapy wine which has aberrant flavours, excessively herbaceous in the case of Sémillon, Sauvignon Blanc and Cabernet Sauvignon, overly peppery in the case of Syrah, and so on. The incidence of botrytis, powdery mildew and downy mildew also increases sharply.

One answer to the problem is to go in the opposite direction, and plant the vines as widely apart as three metres by three metres (1,110 vines per hectare). This allows the grape-grower to control vine vigour naturally by exposing to the light a sufficient number of buds upon an appropriately designed trellis. If one measures all of the features of the resultant canopy one arrives at similar characteristics to those of classic French vineyards.

Australian viticulturalist Dr Richard Smart says that the ideas that a struggling vine makes the best wine and low yields give highest quality are widely held in Europe:

A struggling vine

> 'A common feature of both struggling vines and low-yielding vineyards is that, associated with lower vigour, the canopies have a good microclimate, ie most leaves and bunches are exposed to the sun. It is my belief that many of the quality attributes of low yielding, struggling vineyards can be explained by this fact.'

Quantity V. Quality?

Or can they be compatible?

No wine-grower will seriously attempt to deny that there is a relationship between quantity and quality. Every era of wine-growing has acknowledged the fact; the assumption is built into almost all systems of wine law, and obvious extreme examples of what the French call *'faire pisser la vigne'* are known to all wine-lovers.

Wine-lovers also believe, even if they have no scientific proof, that the sensation of intensity and depth in certain very old wines that still live on from the early years of the 20th century, or even before, derives at least in part from the tiny 'yield' (by modern standards) of their vineyards. Whether for good reasons or bad most of the established vineyards throughout the world used to yield only a quarter of what they produce today.

Yet the relationship is not a simple one. In the words of Bruno Prats, owner of Château Cos d'Estournel and President of the Syndicat des Crus Classés of Bordeaux:

Bordeaux in the '80s

> *'If a mathematician were to study the relationship between the quality of the last ten vintages of Bordeaux'* . . . he said this in 1989 . . . *'and the volume of the harvests, he would inevitably conclude that the bigger the harvest, the better the wine.'*

Within reasonable limits, in other words, when all goes well in a healthy vineyard both quantity and quality increases.

When it comes to longevity, though, these words from Etienne Grivot, a respected and conservative grower in Vosne-Romanée, give a rather different perspective:

Bordeaux in the '20s

> *'In 1980 I tasted many of the wines in our cellars. The wines of the early 1970s were then very nice, but are no more. But the 1929 was incredible; it is and always was very young and fresh, with big fruit, perfect colour, good acid and great elegance. We also have some* villages appellation *wine from 1952 which tastes younger than our 1980, with more body. So for me my first objective is to make wine from good fruit. And with the fruit of 50 years ago even if there was a lot of rot it would be impossible to make bad wine because production was so small, and the potential was so big. Even if you extracted only 40 to 50 percent of the potential of the fruit it was enough to make a good wine. Today you are working with a much smaller potential but much better technique. In the old days, with all their difficulties and mistakes, they still made great wine.'*

Lip service to limits

There is – and one suspects there always will be – a certain lack of reality in the discussion about yield, and about the relationship between quantity and quality. Producers of wine which aspires to anything above the status of *vin ordinaire* all pay lip service to the necessity of limiting production. An increasing number in both the Old World and the New go further and talk of the need to reduce it. Yet there is a gap between the theory and the reality; all over the world yields are inexorably increasing.

In the simple world of jug wine, *vin ordinaire*, or what Australians call 'Château Cardboard', yield is of little account. So long as the grapes are able to reach satisfactory sugar levels, the more the merrier. But then comes a distinction which is much less clear, and where yield is intensely debated: that between wine which is merely good, and wine which deserves to be called great.

Those who produce great wine, those who buy and consume it, those who write about it, and most of those who read about it, need no persuasion that it is a world apart from good wine, even very good wine. Many of those who make good or very good wine seek to deny that the gulf really exists. They ascribe it to clever marketing, or Gallic romancing. Those who cannot afford to buy great wine tend to be equally dismissive; particularly if they have never tasted it.

The wine professional who over the years tastes several thousands of good, very good and great wines (many in blind tastings) knows that there is indeed a difference, and that it cannot be explained by marketing alone. Certainly, labels (and reputations) have a powerful influence: confronted with a bottle of Château Latour or Romanée-Conti you have to be brave and very experienced (or naïve and exceedingly foolish) to criticize it. What is more, one can (and should) draw upon the knowledge of bloodlines in assessing such wines in their youth.

So, the perception engendered by the label *is* important in establishing the difference. But there is more to it: the makers of great wines almost invariably invest more time and money in the process, if only because the price at which it sells means they can afford to. Certainly, there have been periods when great estates have fallen temporarily into decline, but these have been the exceptions which have proved the rule.

The French rule of thumb is that you cannot make great red wine if the yield exceeds 50 hectolitres per hectare. It brings forth vociferous protests from New World growers and also from more than a few who make what ought to be great wine in the Old. This chapter is concerned with justifying the proposition.

The quality ladder

Gallic romancing?

Even the hand-made wines of the great Bordeaux châteaux vary widely in yield from vintage to vintage. In the '80s top growths often found themselves with far more grapes than they wanted, and had to resort to thinning the bunches in mid-summer.

The measurement of yield

Yield is usually measured either in tonnes of grapes or hectolitres of wine. The conversion factor between the two is not entirely simple. One tonne of grapes at normal maturity will yield between 550 and 750 litres of juice. The range depends on two things: the size of the berries (and hence of the bunches), what type of press is used and how heavily the must is pressed. In a low yielding vineyard, the berries will usually be smaller, with a higher ratio of stalks, skins and pips to pulp – in other words, there will be less juice available in each kilogram of grapes. As the berry and bunch size goes up, so does the relative proportion of juice.

However yield is measured, there is no question of relating it directly to quality. As any student of elementary logic will tell you, the mere fact that great wine is made from a yield not greater than 50 hectolitres per hectare does not mean that all 50 hectolitres per hectare yields will produce great wine.

An almost inane example is a 100 hectolitres-per-hectare crop reduced by hail and rot to 50 hectolitres per hectare. Another rather more realistic example is a 50 hectolitres-per-hectare crop produced from virus-infected vines in an ailing condition; another is a crop produced from an old vineyard in which one-third of the vines are dead (or missing altogether), a fifth are barren, and less than half are producing; another is a crop produced by vines suffering severely from drought.

Less can be worse, too

Nor is the yield–quality relationship (if it exists) a simple linear one. As one dips below 50 hectolitres per hectare it by no means follows that there will be any increase in quality. It may be maintained, but more probably it will decrease, reflecting vines which are either diseased or excessively stressed. Very old vineyards also complicate the question: the chances are that many of their vines will be either decrepit or even missing. A helicopter flight over long-established vineyards is very revealing. Some have so many gaps that the yield-per-vine of what is left must be alarmingly high to maintain even the 50 hectolitre standard.

As the yield exceeds 50 hectolitres per hectare, the implications are very different. There is a strong and respected school of thought which says that once the yield exceeds this amount, quality immediately reaches a level which can – with appropriate viticulture and canopy management – be increased to 100 hectolitres

Tight, narrow-row planting in Alsace (left) is typical European philosophy of letting vines compete with, yet shelter, one another. In total contrast the Madonna vineyard in California's 'high-potential' Carneros region (right) has rows up to three metres apart. In spring the vineyard looks strangely empty. By vintage-time the wine canopies will almost touch across the rows.

per hectare without any further significant drop in quality. Like the primary benchmark of 50 hectolitres per hectare, this secondary plateau will prompt a spirited response from some quarters, though it too has to be qualified and expanded. There are many variables which have to be taken into account, of course, including grape variety, clonal selection, rootstock selection, vine age, soil status and site potential, vine health (nematodes, viruses and phylloxera), and use of fertilizers, fungicides and herbicides.

Quality plateaux

Of these, the most significant is grape variety, and most particularly – as we shall see later in the chapter – whether it is white or red. It seems to be generally accepted that the quality of white wine is much less susceptible to deterioration through yield increase; certainly most winemakers aspiring to make great wine would support this view, suggesting that yields 10 to 20 percent higher than for red varieties will give wines of equivalent quality. The challenge to this proposition comes from vineyards such as Le Montrachet, whose average yield is half that of most of the other white burgundy appellations, and whose wine has a wonderfully distinctive power and flavour in the mouth.

Even when one comes to red grapes and wines, there are significant and commonly agreed variations. Pinot Noir is the most sensitive of all varieties to increased yields, readily losing colour and flavour. Syrah reaches a certain point and then abruptly collapses. The most resilient is Cabernet Sauvignon, with its naturally small berries and thick skins, which provide stout resistance to excessive water from any source.

Relative sensitivity

Bordeaux yields up

Not even the first-growths of Bordeaux have escaped the net of significant increases in production (only a small part of which may be explained by increases in vineyard area). The period 1945–1949 was one of unusually low yields. The most obvious reasons are that the vines had been starved of fertilizers during and immediately after the war; that all replanting came to an end with the onset of the war; and that the timing of the massive replanting after phylloxera meant that the majority of the vineyards were not at this stage fully mature. Add it all up, and the results were low-yielding vines, sub-economic by the standards of today, but capable of producing great wine even at artisan level, let alone first-growth.

On the other side of the ledger there have been a number of 'advances' since 1945. The well-run modern vineyard should have 100 percent of its vines either actually or potentially bearing a roughly equal crop per vine, in total contrast to the situation 50 or 100 years ago. Before questioning whether this is indeed a perfect situation, how has it occurred? Briefly, through clonal selection of vines which are certain to crop well and regularly; through rootstock selection, which can according to some views though not others, support higher than desirable yields; through a successful war on viruses; through use of fertilizers; through better canopy manipulation; through the use of highly effective fungicides and insecticides; and finally through the economic imperative which says the producer cannot afford the luxury of a dead, diseased or infertile vine on hallowed ground.

A warning note If all this seems positive, let Peter Sichel sound a warning note:

'*Clonal selection is a major concern. Clonal selections have been primarily for health, and some attention has been paid to colour, sugar, acidity, balance and that kind of thing. But there has been very little work done on clones that more or less transcribe the character of the soil. That worries me, because if we are not careful it seems to me – although remember I am not a technician on this kind of thing – it will be easy to develop clones which have a lot of colour, a lot of personality, but which will completely dominate the soil-character aspect of our wines; and that, quite apart from the problem of excessive yields, people seem frighteningly unconscious of this danger of the clone dominating the soil.*'

The German débâcle Yield changes in Germany have exceeded all others. Since the last century yields have risen from 17 hectolitres per hectare (the average for 1870–1879) to 104 hectolitres per hectare (the average for 1970–1979). Prodigious yields, even up to 400 hectolitres per hectare have been obtained; 200 is routine in some areas. In the 19th century (and earlier) German Riesling from the Rhine Valley was regarded as the longest-lived of all table wines and was frequently sold when 50 or more years old, with 100-year-old bottles not uncommon. In 1830 at Hochheim, 1775, 1776 and 1748 were the 'fine old vintages' commonly offered. Price lists published in the latter part of the 19th century show that the top Rhine wines cost more than Bordeaux first-growths or the finest champagne.

The all-encompassing malaise which overcame German wines in the 1970s and 1980s, notwithstanding some great vintages, can be ascribed to many things: the deliberate lowering of quality thresholds by the new national wine laws in 1971 is fundamental, but excessively complicated labelling, unpredictable shifts of fashion between sweeter and drier wines, and (paradoxically) the success of 'reliable' brands such as Blue Nun have all played a part. But to most observers the root cause lies in the dilution and attenuation of flavour intensity and structure, brought about by the prodigious increases in yield.

More wine, less taste

Happily the great estates have become aware of this just in time. Today a top wine from the Rüdesheimer Berg or Johannisberg will have a similar yield to a Bordeaux *cru classé*. It will, however, take decades to undo the damage caused by past over-production.

Yields have risen in the New World just as they have in the Old. The figures for Australia show the same dramatic escalation since 1945, from less than 20 hectolitres per hectare, to more than 88 hectolitres per hectare in 1989. And many of the same factors are at work. But the debate becomes more complicated: what is an acceptable yield and how do you limit it when your 'high potential' vineyard is so fertile that the sky is the limit?

Australia: up 440%

Dr Richard Smart goes straight to the heart of the problem:

'*Most New World vignerons select vineyard sites which are too high in potential to give them top quality wine, yet they all want it.*'

We saw some of the means used to limit yields (and the reasoning behind them) in the previous chapter. Here it is sufficient to accept that, in the New World, just as in the Old, yields in most vineyards have over-reached their potential to make outstanding wine. (There are exceptions though: the great California Cabernet Sauvignons from the dry-land vineyards on the Rutherford Bench, and Penfolds' Grange Hermitage from South Australia, are good examples.)

If out of all of this you sense a feeling of crisis and confusion, you are not far wrong. What, in broad terms, has happened is this: since the start of the 20th century growers have gained access to a large number of scientifically derived techniques and tools previously undreamt of. As these became available, growers enthusiastically adopted them with minimal consultation with winemakers, and even less consideration for the style or taste of the wine. This trend extended well beyond grapes: the story of the breeding in California of the perfect tomato, a perfect sphere which was of a constant size, which would withstand packaging and transport without bruising or marking, which would ripen perfectly when gassed in a cool store, and which had absolutely no taste, is but one example.

Back from the abyss?

Somewhat grudgingly, the growers were forced to agree that the winemakers should have some say. Trial batches of wine were made, and full chemical analyses undertaken. The growers were still interested primarily in increased yield, but they began to accept that the chemical composition should not suffer unduly. The next step forward was the admission that perhaps the wine should be tasted. The problems here were (and are) that the tastings tended to be of one experimental wine against another, and of very young wines at that, conducted by technocrats or winemakers with limited vision. There was little or no attempt to place the wines in a broader context, either in terms of history or in terms of absolute

Grudging agreement

quality. Now, the final phase has been reached: winemakers of all ages in all parts of the world are tasting wines and assessing grapes in an appropriately broad context.

Yield and white wines
If one does taste wines in the appropriately broad context, how does one draw conclusions about yield and its influence on quality? First, as previously noted, white wines are less obviously affected by increased yield, and most varieties can produce at least slightly higher yields than red grapes without appreciable loss of quality. The basic reason is simple enough: the skin of the grape, which plays a central role in red winemaking, plays almost no part in white winemaking. The white grapes are either pressed immediately after they have been crushed, or are pressed as whole bunches. The latter technique reduces the extraction of colour and flavour from the skins to an absolute minimum. Only in parts of the New World do we find any deliberate attempt to extract flavour from the skins of white grapes, and then on a limited basis. Since it is the ratio of the pulp to skin which changes (by increasing) with higher yield, the proportionate loss of skin content is understandably less important.

Less important does not mean unimportant, however. One only has to look at the German experience with Riesling. As we have seen, as yield goes up the tendency is for bunch and berry weight to increase. This in turn leads to higher pH, lower acidity and lower total flavour content at a given sugar level. In terms of taste this means lower flavour intensity, less total flavour, and softer wine which will not age so well. A young wine made of grapes from high-yielding vines will lack entirely the length of flavour of its low-yield counterpart; it will be less profoundly fruity and have less of the character of its variety. As it rapidly ages, the light, crisp, fresh fruit of its youth (if it was particularly well made) will fade, leaving a wine which is flabby, soft and rather empty on the palate. Such varietal character it may have once had will have all but disappeared.

Yield and red wines
Red wine derives all of its colour and a great deal of its flavour from its skins. It is perfectly possible, though it takes care, to make white wine from red grapes by pressing them before fermentation has had a chance to start (the use of Pinot Noir for champagne is the best-known example). Assuming normal red winemaking, the most obvious diminutions with increased berry-size (the usual result of higher yield) are in colour, in stability of colour, and in 'structure', derived from tannins and acids. Quite obviously, too, flavour intensity will be less.

But much depends on the winemaker's response. Doubtless he or she will seek to extract more from the grapes of high-yielding vines; if he or she is very skilful, that additional level of extraction may partially compensate for the inherent weakness. What is technically called 'over-extraction' results from less skilful winemaking. The result is a tough, hard, tannic wine in which the fruit will never have the aroma or flavour to balance the tannins: by the time the latter soften, the fruit will have gone. It must be said, though, that it is easier still to 'over-extract' concentrated, low-yield grapes.

The point of balance
The searching questions are: how much is too much, and how does one tie in sensory appreciation to a given yield? Even for a single small vineyard with a single grape variety there will not be an immutable or precisely predictable figure for maximum quality, and even less will there be a necessary correlation between yield and quality from one year to the next. As Bruno Prats of Château Cos d'Estournel has pointed out, many of the best vintages in Bordeaux during the 1980s happened to be the highest yielding. Turn the coin over to the New World, and some of the worst vintages have been drought-ravaged, low-yielding years in which flavour is either diminished or over the top, with cooked, jammy fruit, excessive tannins, and so forth.

The focus returns to a vine in balance, both in terms of its architecture (the ratio of grapes, leaves, canes, wood and roots) and in terms of the growing season.

Plague and Pestilence

Enemies of the vine

Nature has a way of balancing things, and the attempts of the human population to interfere with its course can bring unpredictable consequences. Plants, animals, diseases and predators can live in perfect equilibrium in one environment; alter one element and the balance tips. As Australia's experience with the rabbit and the cane toad show all too clearly, some of the greatest dangers arise when a creature is introduced into a new country.

The rich family of American grape vine species evolved over the millennia in temperate climates which encouraged the growth of downy mildew and oidium (alias powdery mildew or *Uncinula necator*) and in soils which harboured large colonies of the microscopic louse called 'phylloxera'. In a Europe ever-curious about the exotic plants and animals of the Americas, Australasia and Asia, it was inevitable that American vines would be introduced as novelties. With the wisdom of hindsight, it was also inevitable they would bring with them the American

A coven of diseases, old and new

Most vine diseases need heat or humidity to flourish. They find both in New Zealand's northern vineyards, near Auckland. Mildew is a constant threat here, and spraying is routine.

diseases to which they had built up a near-total immunity. The European grapevine, *Vitis vinifera*, in contrast, had no such immunity, and fell prey with devastating rapidity.

Anthracnose

It is not easy to identify all the diseases of the vine which pre-existed the American invasion, or be certain when they first appeared. The most significant was anthracnose, which some observers have suggested was active in Roman times. It develops in conditions of high humidity and warm temperatures (21°C), and causes dark stains on the leaves, shoots and grapes. It seldom causes problems now because the treatment (spraying the plants with copper sulphate, lime and water, or 'Bordeaux mixture') is the same as that used for downy mildew, which is far more active.

Botrytis cinerea

Botrytis cinerea has been known since ancient times. Botrytis is a fungus which grows on the skin of the grapes. After several weeks of growth it punctures tiny holes in the grape skin which allow moisture (ie water) to escape. Under ideal conditions the mould does its work gradually, over a prolonged period, and as the water from the grape evaporates sugar and acid in the juice will increase until they almost double their original concentration. For botrytis to work in this way very precise conditions are required: cold and dry nights to slow down the growth of the mould, and warm, humid mid-day temperatures between 15 and 25°C to promote its growth. Under these circumstances what the Sauternais call '*pourriture noble*' and the Germans '*Edelfäule*' produces the great sweet table wines of the world.

The grapes of Château d'Yquem. Botrytis cinerea *rots their skins grape by grape, concentrating the juice to extraordinary intensity of sweetness and flavour.*

If conditions are too dry or too cold the mould will not develop. In Germany 1959 was such a year: it was certainly warm enough but in most vineyards it was too dry. Many *Beerenauslese* and *Trockenbeerenauslese* wines were made, but with minimal influence from *Edelfäule*. The concentrated sweetness came from the grapes singly dehydrating into near-raisins. If conditions are excessively warm, humid and wet, on the other hand, the mould grows too quickly, and rapidly degenerates into grey mould: *pourriture grise*. It may also be accompanied by black rot, a disease of American origin which thrives at temperatures of around 21°C. The result is total loss of the crop: nothing can be made of it.

Botrytis is included here as a disease because it is a major problem (if left unchecked) for makers of dry white and all red wines. What is more, it can (and frequently does) attack the vine at flowering, leading to the outright death of the bunch before the grapes have even begun to form. Systemic sprays therefore have to be used in the cool, humid regions which are prone to attack in spring. A small degree of botrytis in white grapes, however, may be no bad thing, even when making dry wines such as Chardonnay: it accentuates and adds to the complexity of the total flavour.

Prophylaxis in the vineyard

In red wine botrytis is always unwelcome. And the problem is that it will attack red grapes as readily as it does white, respecting neither plot boundaries nor the prayers of the vigneron. It is especially harmful to red wine colour, lightening it and leading to premature browning. European growers have to deal with a percentage of rot (noble and ignoble) in almost every vintage; sulphur dioxide added to the crushed grapes is the standard response, and where the level of infection is minor, all is well. Prophylaxis in the vineyard is the better answer. There is hope, but no certainty, that years such as 1963, 1965 and 1968 will never occur again. In these years the red wines of Bordeaux and Burgundy were all but totally destroyed by mould.

The golden years

Other pre-American diseases were relatively minor, and in 1850 the general health of European vines was excellent. The productive life of a vine was generally recognized to be 70 to 80 years, and regeneration was an easy matter: simply bury a cane in the ground, leaving its tip exposed, and a new vine identical to its parent would take root. This technique of layering (or *marcottage*) is still practised in those parts of the world where phylloxera and nematodes are yet to invade. Especially in a mature vineyard it was the most effective way of replacing a single vine, as, if a rootling was planted, the competition from the surrounding vines often severely stunted its growth. (It is for this reason that, in Europe, rather than replant on a vine by vine basis, whole sections of vineyard are removed and replanted together.)

The consequence of such good health was that the vine could ripen its crop fully in most years, and the vigneron could wait until late in the season until picking, without the threat of oidium and mildew. French viticulture was entering a golden age. In 1855 Napoleon III presided over the Paris International Exhibition which gave rise to the Bordeaux classification of that year. The 1858, 1864, 1865, 1869, 1870, 1874, 1875 and 1878 vintages were of such fabulous quality that well-preserved bottles still provide vinous nectar today; and between 1850 and 1875 France's total vineyard area increased in size by 202,500 hectares.

Further scourges

Around 1850 (some say 1845, others 1854) oidium, or powdery mildew, arrived from America. Alarming crop losses of up to a quarter of the potential harvest were the result. It took ten years to find the right treatment, but – once discovered – powdered sulphur dusted on the vines proved an enduring antidote. Oidium seemed to be a mere hiccup in a triumphant progress. But far worse was in store. In 1869 Professor Westwood of Oxford University was to write the following words:

Oidium

> 'In the month of June, 1863, I received from Hammersmith a vine leaf covered with minute gall-like excrescences, "each containing", in the words of my correspondent "a multitude of eggs, and some perfect Acari, which seem to spring from them, and sometimes a curiously corrugated coccus".'

This was the first description (in Europe) of *Phylloxera vastatrix*, the tiny louse which was to change the face of European viticulture forever, and many would say for the worse. And rather than leave that suggestion in the air, as it were, it is not for the reason that Professor George Saintsbury and others averred – namely that grafted vines per se were inferior to ungrafted vines. That myth is comprehensively answered by countries such as Australia, in which grafted and ungrafted vines exist side by side, and no-one believes or suggests there is any necessary quality differential. The causes of the change for the worse are far more complicated, as we shall see.

Phylloxera

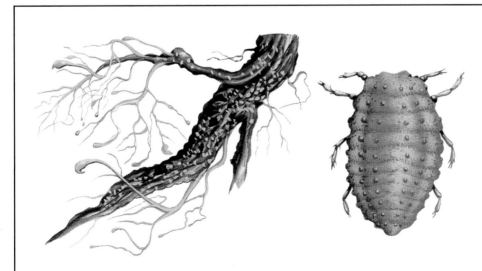

Phylloxera vastatrix

The effects of phylloxera eclipsed all other viticultural disasters when it arrived in Europe, doubtless carried in with botanical specimens brought from the USA by plant collectors. This tiny insect attacks the roots of *vinifera* vines, injecting them with poisonous saliva. With a healthy international trade in vine cuttings, and no effective quarantine, the insect found its way all over Europe, to South Africa, Australia, New Zealand as well as California by the end of the 19th century.

Downy mildew

The last of America's unfriendly contributions to European wine-growing was a new and aggressive form of mildew (known as 'downy' to distinguish it from the 'powdery' oidium) that appeared in 1878. By this time the chemists were alert. Within only four years Bordeaux University had brewed the cure, a bright-blue mixture of copper sulphate and lime, known to this day as 'Bordeaux mixture', and which is sovereign against fungus diseases of most kinds.

One might think this litany of afflictions was enough, but an even more sinister attack was being mounted against the vines of Europe. Vine viruses had been in existence for thousands of years: descriptions from Roman times leave no doubt of their existence. But it is clear that their incidence was not severe, nor is there any evidence of spread from infected to healthy vines.

Viruses in the vineyard

The need for universal grafting, to combat phylloxera, changed the situation radically. Many of the American rootstocks brought into Europe for this purpose were (and are) carriers of viruses without showing any symptoms. In their apparent innocence they introduced two devastating viruses – 'fan leaf' and 'leaf-roll' – to the vineyards of the world. Grafting onto infected rootstocks dramatically increases the risk of viral infection, and one of the main concerns of modern day plant-breeders is to ensure their rootstocks are virus-free.

If one takes the combined effect of oidium, mildew, viruses, young vines and some pretty indifferent weather it is hardly surprising that the average quality of French wine slumped between 1878 and 1899. To lay the blame at the feet of the American rootstocks, as many have done, is only indirectly justifiable. As for viruses, there is no cure: prevention through clonal selection and, perhaps, genetic engineering are the only answers.

Above: *American rootstocks have a variable but limited tolerance to lime in the soil. Too much prevents their uptake of iron salts, leading to chlorosis and yellowing leaves.*

Right: *Reddening vine leaves with green veins is a symptom of viral infection. Many old vineyards are infected without suffering unduly, but heat-treatment of propagating material to destroy viruses in new vines is now standard practice.*

There remains the threat of Pierce's Disease, yet another American harbinger of doom. Endemic throughout Texas and Florida it swept across the United States, over the Rocky Mountains, through southern California, to Anaheim in Los Angeles (it was originally called Anaheim Disease). The cause is a bacteria which is spread by small winged insects called 'sharpshooters'. The bacteria breeds in reeds and other stream-side vegetation. So three things are needed: water, the bacteria, and the vector (the sharpshooter). Perhaps for this reason it has not become a worldwide problem – although there have been suggestions that it has arrived in Europe. The implications (in Europe, as in California) are chilling, for – unlike phylloxera and nematodes – there is no known answer, other than the removal of the infected vines. The eradication of reeds and their attendant insects from all wine regions is a proposition that makes mere root-grafting look like child's play.

Pierce's Disease

The United States of America – California particularly – is currently the centre of renewed concern about phylloxera. Some research scientists at UCLA Davis believe that a new and potentially destructive mutant (they call it 'Phylloxera Type B') is destroying vines with more ferocity than the familiar form. Phylloxera travelled across the Rocky Mountains from the east in about 1870, only a few years after its appearance in Europe, at much the same time as it arrived in Australia. Given the complexity of its life cycle, it is hardly surprising that there should be different biotypes, and it is suggested that at this time it was a relatively mild version that arrived in California. Ignoring the experience of grafting gained in France, Californians adopted *Vitis rupestris* hybrid rootstocks (ARGI, AXR and 1202) to counter the first invasion, which the French had earlier discarded because of their relatively low resistance, and which now leave the vines once again vulnerable to attack. An alternative theory to that of the mutant development of Type B is that there has been a fresh infusion of phylloxera from the east, including the more active biotypes which had travelled to Europe a century before. What is certain is that in California today any ungrafted vineyard and any vineyard planted on low-resistance hybrid rootstocks is at risk. Indeed many vines are dying. The Napa Valley alone is faced with a cost of $1 billion over the coming years, to replant up to 80 percent of its vines, using more phylloxera-resistant roots.

California and Phylloxera Type B

Australia has been through it too. In 1875 phylloxera was identified at Geelong, just to the west of Melbourne, one of Victoria's leading wine areas. Notwithstanding that grafting had been identified as the solution, the Government of the day ordered the wholesale eradication of all infected vineyards. When the louse appeared at Bendigo in central Victoria in the 1880s, the same orders were made. Two flourishing wine regions disappeared overnight and it was almost 100 years before vines reappeared in these areas. The rationale was to protect the wine industry in northeast Victoria, but in vain. By 1900 it had taken a firm hold there. This time, at least, grafting was preferred to compulsory eradication.

The Australian phylloxera invasion

Phylloxera stopped at the Murray River. It has never penetrated South Australia, thanks to stringent quarantine precautions. And although it was active around both Sydney and Brisbane, it has similarly never affected the Hunter Valley. Even more surprising – and inexplicable – has been the escape of the isolated Chateau Tahbilk, in the Goulburn Valley of central Victoria, where Shiraz (Syrah) vines planted in 1860 remain defiantly in production, among adjoining plots long since devastated by phylloxera and replanted on grafted rootstocks. (You can purchase a special bin wine made solely from these vines.) Here, at least, there is an explanation: the old Shiraz is planted on sandy soil through which phylloxera cannot travel – it prefers rocky or clay soils which crack in dry weather.

The Chileans frequently like to claim that theirs is the only country in the world producing wine from 'pre-phylloxera' vines, which is actually untrue. It is certainly a viticultural paradise in which diseases of all kinds are virtually unknown. But others include the whole island of Cyprus, part of Hungary, sandy seaside

Chile: a vine-grower's paradise

When the vines have survived every threat, and are laden with ripening fruit, it is the turn of the birds and wasps to destroy the crop. At Coldstream Hills in the Yarra Valley, Victoria, vulnerable areas away from the winery have to be netted against attack.

vineyards at Colares in Portugal, and in the Midi, and a whole catalogue of areas, big and small, where phylloxera has not (so far) installed itself.

New Zealand and South Africa

New Zealand shows how vulnerable vineyards remain. Notwithstanding all the knowledge of quarantine procedures and of phylloxera's life cycle, and notwithstanding the watery barrier of the Cook Strait separating the North and South Islands, it took little more than a decade for phylloxera to arrive on the South Island, at Marlborough. Viruses, too, are endemic in New Zealand and South Africa, and it is only in the past few years that South Africa has had access to Chardonnay vines which are not heavily virus-infected.

If we are to return to a golden age similar to that of the mid-19th century it will be because we have eliminated viruses and (through genetic engineering) built in resistance to oidium and mildew. Whether this can be done without compromising varietal character nobody knows. What is certain is that it will not be through the development of more powerful fungicides; both past and present tell us that chemical control is not the way to go.

Irrigation

A necessary evil?

Irrigation is one of the more emotive words in viticulture, and hence one of the least understood: there is nothing like a touch of good old-fashioned prejudice to stand in the way of truth. The French ban its use in most appellations (it is permitted in parts of the Midi) and out of that ban stems a surprisingly widely held view that irrigation and quality are incompatible.

The vine, like any other plant, demands a certain amount of water during its growing season. How much will depend on factors such as growing season temperatures, wind speed, humidity, sunshine hours, and inherent vigour (influenced by clone, rootstock, variety, soil and cultivation), to name but a few.

A certain amount of irrigation is necessary for vineyards in all of Australia's wine regions. The only large vineyard established there in the last 20 years without it is in the Hastings Valley on the New South Wales coast. It must also be remembered that in a country such as Australia, wide climatic fluctuations occur. In wet years there may be little or no need for irrigation, but in drought years the need becomes acute. New World growers have therefore developed a simple litmus test: look at the grass by the roadside during summer: if it is green, there is no need of irrigation. In most of Australia you may be assured it is brown.

The situation in most French vineyards – certainly in Bordeaux and Burgundy – is entirely different. Ignoring some of the eccentric weather of the latter part of the 1980s, rainfall and humidity in the growing season supplies the vine naturally with most, if not all, of the moisture it needs. What is more, the structure of the soil and subsoil of areas such as the Médoc have excellent moisture retention capacity.

But as in all matters viticultural, there are no absolutes, no simple rules of thumb. The widely held theory is that if you deny a vine easy access to water it will send its roots deep in search of it and in so doing find flavour-enhancing nutrients which surface roots cannot collect. At best, this is a deceptive half truth. Conversely, no grower in search of maximum quality wishes to have to rely on irrigation. He or she will be more than happy to have it available as a fall-back, but would prefer the vine to find its water naturally. Nature, though, is unpredictable. Ask any farmer anywhere in the world about the weather and you will receive a long and detailed dissertation about the shortcomings of the current season.

Viticultural research has increasingly shown that the timing of irrigation is as important as its extent. Two of the most vulnerable periods are flowering and *véraison* (the time at which grape colour changes and cell division stops). Too little water during and immediately after flowering will result in poor fruit-set and in berry shatter (the tiny berries simply fall off), while too little water up to and during *véraison* will lead to reduced berry size.

As always, there are choices and there are consequences. Irrigation can be used to increase yields, by promoting growth of bigger berries, bigger bunches, and more bunches per vine, without any adverse effect on the crude chemical measurements of sugar, acid and pH. Indeed, these measurements may be better than those of grapes produced from vines with less or no irrigation. If the aim is to produce white wine for sale in cask, jug or flagon, there is no question: this is the way to go. But

Water of course – but how much?

The limestone soils of Jerez that produce the finest sherry are admirable sponges for winter and spring rains (there is none in summer) if they are tilled to open the surface. Water runs off compacted, untilled land.

Irrigation for yield

The aim and great advantage of drip irrigation is precision. Each vine has its own water supply and a measurable amount goes only where it is needed – drip by drip.

white wine is far less critical than red. Similarly, as the quality aspirations of the grower increase, the situation becomes more complicated.

God-like control

Most modern irrigation systems use drip feeders, one dripper per vine, emitting precisely controlled amounts of water, usually between two and four litres per hour. These saturate an inverted cone-shaped area directly under the dripper. Where irrigation is used simply to increase yield the vine will become entirely dependent on this supply and develops a compact root system confined to the area wetted (close to the surface). In consequence, it may be necessary to introduce nitrogen and other minerals needed for the balanced growth of the vine through the irrigation system. It becomes, if you wish, a kind of hydroponics (or water culture), as far removed from the romantic notion of the struggling vine as one could imagine, but allowing the grower an almost god-like control.

The poor quality of grapes grown under conditions of excessive irrigation is the indirect, rather than the direct, consequence of over-watering. The vine simply grows out of balance: the canopy becomes far too big for the crop; the fruit is then shaded, and the grapes ripen very late, if at all.

Furrow, flood and spray

Drip irrigation is the most controllable system, also the most efficient and the most sparing of water. But there are others. The most ancient form of irrigation – furrow or flood – is practised in countries such as Chile and Argentina, with the snow-capped Andes providing an inexhaustible (and essential) water source in a bone-dry summer. In the Langhorne Creek area of South Australia the Bremer River is deliberately diverted in late winter to flood the vineyards, providing subsoil water reserves which last right through the summer. Then there is overhead spray irrigation, particularly suited to very dry climates in which mildews are not a problem, but doubly useful in areas subject to spring frosts. If a frost threatens, the sprays are turned on and the ice forming on the buds will insulate them from temperatures below freezing point.

Laissez-faire

In regions where the growing season rainfall (and soil moisture reserves) is usually enough to keep the vines growing and ripen their fruit, there will inevitably be years with too much rain. In these vintages the crop will be diluted in flavour, will not ripen properly and will probably be affected by rot. Red wines will suffer most, and may be a far cry from the noble quality implied by the label. However, given

normal or below-average rainfall, and assuming frost or hail have not intervened, the classic regions of Germany, France and Italy produce wines of such quality that the ban on irrigation becomes irrelevant. If a continuation of the extreme weather patterns of the late 1980s were to occur attitudes might change, but it is unlikely.

Through empirical observation of vines, grapes and wines we have already arrived at the proposition that 50 hectolitres per hectare represents the maximum yield for red wines of the finest quality. The norm for irrigated vineyards is to exceed that level, in some instances by a wide margin. But reduced irrigation can restrict yield to almost any level one cares to choose. The real question is whether by so restricting yield, quality will be improved.

Irrigation for quality

To take an extreme example, vineyards in many parts of Australia (whether or not irrigation is available and used) suffer acute water-stress late in the growing season: the leaves dry up and fall off and the vine stops growing. Even where favourable winter and spring growing conditions and fertile soil have set the vine off to a flying start, things can go badly wrong. Despite a strong canopy and crop potential, if the water supply fails and no reserve is available, the vine's productivity will abruptly halt. The French call this condition 'apoplexy'.

Apoplexy

It takes a skilful grower, using irrigation, to balance quantity against quality. He must know precisely what is happening in the soil surrounding the root zone. Moisture measuring devices (tensiometers or gypsum blocks) give a fairly accurate picture. The grower's decisions then have to be carefully weighed, using his experience of the particular vineyard. By restricting water supply before *véraison* he can, if he judges correctly, advantageously slow down the grapes' growth. Similarly, it is possible to promote ripening and simultaneously limit the weight of the bunches by restricting water after *véraison*. 'Deficit-irrigation' can produce grapes of very high quality if skilfully used, but the risks of miscalculation are high, and the consequences entirely counterproductive.

In a perfect world irrigation would not be necessary. Exactly the right amount of spring and summer rain, followed by three weeks of warm, dry weather leading up to vintage, would produce grapes as good as the *terroir* and grape variety allow. In the real world there will almost always be too much or too little rain. There is not much the vigneron can do about too much, but if there is too little, irrigation is preferable to inaction.

66

Mechanization

Simply a question of time?

The Industrial Revolution of the vine

Gradually at first, then gathering speed, and now seemingly unstoppable, the Industrial Revolution has at last reached the vineyards of the world. There have been two dress rehearsals: first the introduction of the horse-drawn plough, second that of the tractor. These innovations had a radical effect on the way vines were planted, and in particular on the pattern and density of planting. But the mechanization of today and tomorrow is something far more fundamental.

There will always be pockets of resistance; indeed corners where not even the plough will reach. It is hard to imagine any form of mechanization (other than helicopters) coming to the near vertical face of the Berncasteler Doktor or the terraces of Côte Rôtie. How long it will take for the Industrial Revolution to cross the conservative thresholds of the Grands Crus of Bordeaux and Burgundy, though, is an open question. But a question of when and how far, not if.

No more cheap labour

In Europe, the pool of cheap labour provided by Portugal and Spain is drying up as surely as that provided by Mexico for California. In Australia equal pay for men and women, with peculiar irony, led directly to the development of mechanical pruning. For women are by far the best vineyard workers on time-consuming jobs such as pruning and summer training, and if wage justice were taken to its logical

The old adage was 'where ploughs can go no vines should go'. (It referred to such land as the astonishing terraced slopes of the Rhine and Mosel (right) – and the old belief that meagre soils meant better wine.)

conclusion they should have been paid more than men, not less. Equal pay was thrust upon them and thousands lost their jobs forever as a result.

If robots can build motor vehicles they can certainly perform the far simpler task of caring for vines. And just as with the motor industry, the cost-efficiencies of the automated producers sooner or later force change on the more conservative or force the less efficient out of business.

Is hand-made best?

Extending the motor car analogy, exotica such as the Rolls Royce and Lamborghini may well always be hand made – and sold for a price which reflects that care and cost. But what about the Mercedes Benz, BMW, Lexus and Cadillac? More and more automation; less and less need for hand finishing. This is the future for wine too. And at the so-called beverage end of the industry – casks, flagons, jugs, *vin ordinaire* – automation and mass production techniques have been in use since the days of Henry Ford and his model T.

Mechanization starts the day the vine is planted. Broad areas in the New World are planted by tractor-drawn devices which open up the soil, allow a seated operator to drop in the vine, and then close up the earth immediately afterwards. The time and cost savings relative to hand planting are huge, and the results are better because greater accuracy is possible. In fact, modern technology will have made its mark well before the vine was planted: lasers can be used to level the land with perfect precision, and vine rows established with equal care; computer-controlled drip irrigation will have been installed in advance, and the vines given an exactly measured quantity of water within hours of planting; the soil may have been fumigated against nematodes, and herbicides will ensure they begin life without any competition from grass or weeds.

The march of the machine

In its first and second years the modern New World vineyard may still need some hand labour. From this point on mechanization can take over. Not only can the vines be mechanically pruned but all the canopy training and trimming during the growing season can be mechanized too. To this end the machines of the future – being simultaneously developed in Italy, Australia and the United States – are designed on a modular basis: a single mechanized basic frame can be quickly converted by interchanging spray unit, pruning and harvesting modules, providing three machines for the price of two or less. There are also French-designed machines which lift up the foliage in summer by clipping the moveable foliage wires together, exposing the fruit underneath to sunlight. New Zealand has pioneered mechanical leaf-plucking machines to perform a similar task by removing excess leaves from around the fruit.

Mechanical pruning

Whether or not the vineyard is mechanically pruned is a decision taken on grounds of cost and quality. The options, including minimal pruning, have been considered in previous chapters, but it is hard to imagine the greatest vineyards, either in France or anywhere else, opting for anything so imprecise as a hedge-cutter. Pneumatic secateurs are their compromise with mechanization.

Mechanical harvesting

Mechanical harvesting is another matter. Used in conjunction with pruning it has few disadvantages. But when the vineyard has been mechanically (or minimally) pruned uneven ripening of the fruit is almost inevitable and a mechanical harvester cannot be selective between ripe and unripe bunches. Whatever the pruning system, the collection of material other than grapes (familiarly known as MOG) has been the main drawback of mechanical harvesting, and one which technical advances are only beginning to overcome. In some areas a peculiar leafy, gamey, meaty mélange of flavours in the wine – 'pie and peas' is one description – has been contributed by a percentage of very green and very overripe bunches, augmented by MOG – chiefly canes and leaves, but sometimes including large numbers of snails or insects.

. . . and MOG

Left: *Working in the cool of the night in the Napa Valley a mechanical harvester looks like a fire-breathing dragon.*

Below: *The antithesis of mechanical harvesting: stackable plastic boxes for hand-picked grapes. The fruit is not damaged even by its own weight in these de luxe containers.*

Cheaper, quicker, cooler

Cost is the most obvious advantage: a third to a quarter that of hand-picking if done by an independent contractor, less still if the grape-grower has a large enough area of vineyards to justify owning a grape-harvester. Speed is another: mechanical harvesters can operate 24 hours a day, ensuring that large areas can be harvested rapidly before a change in the weather (or after if rot is developing); and that in hot regions grapes can be harvested at night – taking advantage of cooler temperatures and lower grape-sugar levels. This makes processing – particularly of white grapes – very much easier, and significantly reduces the need for, and high cost of, refrigeration.

In large vineyards speed has a second implication for quality: reducing the time lapse between harvesting and the grapes arriving at the winery. The typical method of hand-harvesting in the New World is to pick into buckets; tip the grapes from buckets into a tractor-drawn skip; and then either tip this into a larger bin on a truck or lift several skips progressively onto the truck. Either way, there can be a

... or a long hot wait

long hot wait in the sun. The jostled and squeezed bunches break, their juice runs into the bottom of the containers, and oxidation gets to work. Mechanization of this process does not avoid breakage of the grapes, but significantly reduces the time over which oxidation can occur.

In the early days of mechanization in the vineyard, mechanical harvesting, according to conventional wisdom, was suited to red grapes but not to white. The assumption was that any oxidation of white grape juice caused by breakage of the grapes too long prior to fermentation was necessarily a bad thing. Obviously under hot and possibly dirty conditions it was and remains a serious matter. But

Controlled oxidation

nowadays it is, within limits, actually sought after: controlled oxidation is preached and practised by such as Zelma Long at Simi Winery in Sonoma, California, and by many leading Italian winemakers. They take no risks, though. They strictly limit oxidation to the level and timing they want by using field processing-stations or by rushing the grapes to the winery, protected by a dusting of ascorbic acid.

At most points from planting to harvesting choices exist: neither size nor commitment to quality necessarily preclude mechanical options. But certain grapes, and certain wines, do. In Champagne the bunches are always pressed whole; mechanical harvesters cannot cut whole bunches. Many Burgundians and other makers of Pinot Noir are equally adamant they must have at least a percentage of whole bunches and (or) stalks in the must, once again precluding mechanical harvesting. The selective picking of grapes with noble rot for Sauternes does likewise. In the press, moreover, unfermented grapes without stalks tend to become a congealed mass: stalks and stems keep the mass open enough for the juice to drain out.

There are exceptions

The most luxurious alternative to mechanical harvesting is the use of small stackable picking baskets usually containing between ten and 15 kilograms of fruit, which are filled by the picker and transported without further movement or decanting to the winery. White grapes in hot climates may be stored in their baskets in a cool room overnight and crushed the following morning when they are thoroughly cooled (to 5°C or thereabouts). This is the gentlest possible handling option, more gentle than one usually finds in even the greatest French vineyards, where the common practice is to pick into baskets; for the pickers to tip the grapes into an *hotte* on the back of a worker who walks through the rows, and for the contents of the *hotte* to be tipped into a tub, tray or other larger container which will be taken back to the cellar by tractor, or horse; finally to be tipped into the crusher or press.

The other extreme

Rapid transit from vineyard to winery is always important. In most small European vineyards this is an academic problem: distances are typically measured in metres rather than miles. In the New World distances can be, and frequently are, measured in hundreds of miles. In New Zealand many of the grapes grown in Hawke's Bay are machine-harvested and then transported to wineries in Auckland. The time from harvesting to processing may be over 24 hours, which is not of undue moment with sound red grapes free of rot, but can give white winemakers a serious problem. The delay in processing amounts to involuntary skin-contact with the juice. When used by choice in the winery this can be very beneficial. When imposed on the winemaker in an uncontrolled situation it can lead to some strange results. Hawke's Bay Chardonnay or Sauvignon Blanc fermented in Auckland can develop a strange mélange of jungle-like aromas and flavours as young wine, then go yellow rapidly in the next year or two, and finally taste coarse and oily.

From vineyard to winery

Anyone who has planted a vine, watched it grow, picked its crop and made its wine feels the deep satisfaction of the ancient craft. The more the process is mechanized, the less that personal satisfaction. But 95 percent or more of the world's wine has not been made traditionally for a long time. Much of it has become a mass-produced beverage, little different from beer or spirits. Quality, though, lies not in the facts of hand-craft or mechanization, but in their application. And, increasingly, in the sheer technical excellence of the machines themselves.

Ancient craft or technical excellence?

IN THE WINERY

Making the Wine

Winery equipment and how to use it

The line between the vineyard and the winery is not as absolute and clearcut as it might seem at first sight. The winery – and much of its equipment – is but a passing phase in the transition from grape to wine, and as demonstrated by the grapes stored in clay jars it is not even essential for that. The battery of equipment to be found there cannot of itself guarantee quality, create identity, or forge style. These things come primarily from the grapes and the winemaker's imprint on them: the skill with which he or she manipulates the winery tools and imposes his or her thumbprint is the key.

The first tool to be found in most wineries is the crusher, an invention of the late 19th century. It is sometimes called a crusher-destemmer, in deference to the two quite separate functions it performs: crushing or splitting the berries to liberate the juice and then removing the berries from the stem of the bunch. Most crushers pass the bunches through a series of rollers first (to crush the berries), then separate the stalks with beaters revolving within a slotted cage: the already-crushed berries drop through the slots and the stalks are ejected through the open end of the cage.

Some crushers destem first (and are known as destemmer-crushers) while most modern versions – in whichever configuration – have adjustable rollers which permit the winemaker to select anything from virtually whole berries to fully crushed grapes.

Sparkling-wine makers in many parts of the world (notably Champagne), and an increasing number of makers of high quality white table wines, by-pass the crusher altogether, placing the whole bunches directly into the press. The pressing process is much slower as a result but the juice yielded is clearer and finer.

Makers of certain red wines using carbonic maceration techniques may also wholly or partially by-pass the crusher – the most obvious examples being Beaujolais winemakers, who incorporate some whole bunches or use *pigeage* (foot stamping) for the entire *cuvée*.

A battery of tools

Crusher-destemmers

Opposite: *Most of the world's wine today is made in plants as romantic as an oil refinery. Grapes look vulnerable and out of place in such a harsh industrial environment. Yet nothing need necessarily be lost just because the scale is big.*

Cooling the must   New World makers of white wine who have chosen to crush the grapes may well pass the must through a device called a 'heat-exchanger' on its way to the press. The heat exchanger is an intestine-like contraption, with an inner tube (through which the must passes in one direction) and an outer tube (through which freezing-cold brine solution – methylated spirits and water – passes in the other direction) arranged in a series of folds, with a single entry and exit point for each of the two tubes. The effect is instantaneously to reduce the temperature of the must.

The press   It is the timing of the use of the next major piece of equipment – the press – which so differentiates the making of white and red wine. Red wine is 'made' – in the sense of the conversion of the sugar to alcohol, the transition from grape juice to wine – before the press is used; with white wine it is the other way round.

Whether or not a crusher is used, and whether or not skin contact is employed, white grapes will be pressed before fermentation begins. But with the exception of the unique, purpose-built champagne presses, the same press can (and probably will) be used for both red and white wines.

Méthode ancienne   These days there are several different types of press. The most numerous (particularly in small wineries) are the basket presses; the 20th century has introduced electrically driven hydraulics to apply the pressure, but the principle remains precisely the same as it was for the preceding 400 years. (The 'old press' at the Clos de Tart was built in 1570 and remained in use until 1924; and Robert Drouhin of Beaune has used a press of similar antiquity in the 1980s to make small quantities of burgundy using, in all respects, the *méthode ancienne*.)

The traditional basket press was built in an upright fashion, with a solid plate descending on the grape skins, forcing the juice between the slots or gaps of the vertically arranged (and bound) pieces of wood forming the circular basket or cage. (The champagne press works on the same principle, except that it is much shallower in proportion.)

. . . sidewards into the 20th century   The first major development of the 20th century was to turn the cage over on its side, allowing it to revolve, and to mechanize (and ultimately computerize) the whole process. Vaslin of France was one of the major developers of this system.

The pneumatic, or airbag, press is in a sense a further development of this configuration. Instead of a plate moving along inside the cage towards a fixed end,

Cooling can make a crucial difference to quality at every stage, from the grapes themselves (right, Chardonnay enters a combined crusher and heat-exchanger in Western Australia) to the fermenting must (above, passing through water-cooled pipes in the Rhône Valley).

or of two plates converging, a bag running along one side or section of the press is inflated, pressing the skins against the cage. Because of the larger surface area under pressure, the grapes are pressed more gently, with less mincing and little or no chance of breaking the pips or unduly compressing the stalks (in either case liberating undesirable forms of tannin).

A yet further development has been the tank press, in which the external barrel is enclosed, other than for exit ports for the juice, theoretically offering a fully enclosed vessel which can be filled with gas so as to exclude oxygen.

Making the pips squeak

The last type of press is found only in very large wineries, and then is only used to make lesser quality wine. It is the continuous press, which as its name implies extrudes the pressed skins (or marc) continuously from one end as fresh must is introduced at the other end. It is very efficient in terms of time, but significantly harsher than the 'batch' presses. If pips squeak it is in one of these machines.

The introduction of stainless steel has revolutionized the vessels in which fermentation takes place, particularly for white wines. The traditional vessels – still widely used in Germany and Italy, for example – were made of oak (or cherry, chestnut or walnut), with parallel sides and the planks running vertically. These vats were not intended to impart any wood flavour to the wine, and were used for many decades – if not hundreds of years – gradually building up tartrate deposits which should have been (although sometimes were not) cleaned off. In such open vats the red-grape skins can easily be 'punched' back into the juice on which they float – either by bare foot or by a disc on the end of a pole. This method of fermentation is only used for red (and fortified) wines and while labour-intensive and seemingly archaic, it is still strongly favoured by some excellent winemakers.

Fermentation vessels: from vat

With the 19th century came slate or cement vats, followed by enamel, glass or ceramic-lined vessels of similar shape, usually rectangular (or square) and installed in series in a permanently fixed position. Stainless steel is now replacing these world-wide. It introduces greater hygiene, facilitates in-place temperature control of fermentation, and allows for all sorts of automated or mechanized agitation methods – two of the last being the 'Autofermenter' (or Ducellier) of Portugal and the Potter Fermenter of Australia. The systems are many and varied, the least

. . . to tank

The Vaslin horizontal basket press (above) rotates while two metal plates repeatedly converge on the grapes. Chains break up the pulpy mass as the plates retract. More advanced is the Willmes 'bladder press' (left), in which a rubber bag (here deflated) is inflated to apply powerful but mechanically gentle pressure to the grapes.

Above: *Stainless steel vats in a Sonoma winery have their own lustre.*

Right: *Colour-coding could be a useful answer in this snakepit of hoses at Lindemans' Karadoc winery in Victoria, Australia.*

automatic being the simple draining off of juice from the bottom valve of the vat and pumping it back over the top of the cap.

The development of the sideways-mounted press almost certainly gave birth to the idea of the 'rotofermenter' (one of the proprietary brands being Vinimatic). Here the fermentation vessel is installed on its side and can be rotated to agitate the must: it is a potent piece of machinery, capable of quickly extracting massive colour and flavour of a certain kind. Used with sensitivity and discretion it is a valuable tool; used insensitively it produces curiously hollow, hard wines. A variation used in Burgundy (Drouhin is a major exponent) employs interior revolving paddles, with the drum remaining fixed.

Filters

Both before (in the case of white wines) and after fermentation there is a range of machines designed to clarify grape juice or wine. There are four basic types: first the centrifuge; second, pad or cartridge filters; third, earth and rotary filters; and fourth, cross-flow filters relying on osmosis.

Filtration is a highly technical affair. If this were not enough, it raises more emotion than almost any other aspect of winemaking, and is a subject we revisit later. The role (and use) of small oak barrels for fermentation and maturation is also discussed later, and so passed over here.

. . . and pumps

From this point the winery may contain numerous tools which are of interest only to winemakers and the technical journals – except for the ubiquitous must pump, which is considered essential by most but scorned by a few, who set up their winery so that they can rely entirely on gravity, and so return to the mists of winemaking time.

The basic process of present-day winemaking is explained by the diagrams on pages 88–89, 114–117, 140–141 and 176–177. At every stage of the process different options are available to the winemaker. Even given identical grapes it is these options that determine to a large extent the final quality, and certainly the individual style, of what is finally bottled.

In one sense it is easy to depict the winemaker as a mere quality control officer, whose job it is simply to protect the quality of the grapes while nature turns them into their predestined kind of wine. As we have seen, in the classic French view, *terroir* (first) and climate (second) determine character, and it is not for mere mortals to interfere with nature. Protect what it gives, by all means; enhance it with care and discretion, perhaps; but under no circumstances seek to change it. Grapes and wines have a preordained status in life, and it is a form of vinous blasphemy to challenge that established order.

The winemakers of the New World meanwhile exuberantly challenge that assumption, and all things implicit in it. That challenge, and increasing internationalism in all aspects of winemaking and wine marketing, have in turn led to a qualified reappraisal by the Old World of some of its cherished beliefs, and to a strong reaffirmation of others.

Out of all of this has come a much greater understanding, and deliberate rather than automatic use of the options available: devices which primarily affect character and style, and not necessarily quality. It is of course true that scientific knowledge greatly helps the winemaker in selecting options, for he or she does so fully understanding why the consequences occur rather than simply relying on empirical observations (possibly handed down over the generations).

Indeed, scientific knowledge has created many of those options. It ensures a measure of control over virtually all winemaking procedures undreamt of 50 or even 25 years ago, and is a powerful aid in the development of new techniques (and hence new flavours). Just as importantly, it all but eliminates the potential for the spoilage of wine in the winery, and equips the winemaker to deal effectively with poor grapes whether affected by rot, mould or simply lacking flavour.

With more thoughtful and precise vineyard management, the winemakers of the 21st century should have significantly better grapes to work with than their 20th-century counterparts. If this happens, it will facilitate a trend to natural winemaking, in which the role of chemicals of all kinds in vineyard and winery will be progressively diminished. This, at least, will be the path for fine wine, wine of the kind that most readers of this book will want to drink.

The making of jug wine or *vin ordinaire* may well go down a rather different path. Perversely, 'natural' winemaking can be much more costly than other methods, and certainly involves more sophisticated equipment. Manipulation may well become more important rather than less. One example is the making of wine with artificially reduced alcohol content. Heaven forbid that we should ever see a low-alcohol Corton-Charlemagne, but it seems probable we will see more and more low-alcohol jug wine sold in the supermarkets of the future.

Luddite views get one nowhere – even in winemaking. Modern technology will continue to produce better equipment. Membrane (pneumatic or air-bag) presses produce more and clearer white wine juice; computerized control of temperatures and sophisticated refrigeration equipment mean that the winemaker can perhaps even close the winery on Sunday; improving filtration methods are reducing the already-minimal use of chemical sterilants and anti-oxidants. And the list goes on.

If the term 'modern' suggests superiority or immutability, it has no place in the context of this book: all it can hope to do is provide a snapshot of the philosophies, practices and attitudes of winemakers and wine-drinkers at the end of the 20th century. These have no special status; they are no more correct than those which have preceded them or than those which will follow.

The winemaker's job

Conservative

Tactical

Reasonable

National Attitudes and Regional Characters

Jacques of all trades?

One of the immemorial cartoons shows the tubby, bereted Frenchman busy filling bottles labelled Beaujolais, Burgundy, Côtes du Rhône, Bordeaux and so on from a single cask in the back cellar, and out in front his wife offering the eager customers their choice (at suitably differing prices). It was born of an age in which there was a vast difference in the real articles, but not a great deal of knowledge about that difference, and when deceptive practices were a great deal more common.

Now there is ever-increasing knowledge about the actual (or theoretical) differences in character between the wines of the world, knowledge which raises one of the burning questions of our time. Are we in danger of moving towards universal 'styles' of wine which obliterate or significantly blur the all-important regional differences between otherwise similar wines? Will our French cartoon take on a new and altogether different meaning?

Chablis:

A test case

Chablis is a good example of the blurring of a distinct regional character. The classic description of Chablis likened its aroma to that of gunflint, the taste to sucking river pebbles. It was (and still is) regarded as the ultimate shellfish and seafood wine, austere, crisp, long-lived and bone dry; in other words, very different from the white burgundy of the Côte d'Or. Yet today it is sometimes not easy to tell the difference between a glass of Chablis and the majority of white burgundies. Is this a good or a bad thing, and why has it happened? And how does one relate it to the broader issue of wine around the world?

The differences between a Meursault or Montrachet, a Chablis, a California, an Italian, and an Australian Chardonnay are due to the interaction of *terroir*, climate, viticultural practice, winemaking practice and philosophy – the last a rather vague but nonetheless crucial factor partly reflected in viticultural and winemaking practices but also reflecting the tastes, and even the structure, of the society in which the wine is made and principally drunk. Of the interacting factors *terroir* and climate are largely (but not entirely) immutable: soil pH may be ameliorated by lime; soil structure may be improved by gypsum; soil drainage may be installed; trace elements may be added; and fertilizers are widely used. Climate may be softened by anti-frost devices; wind by the introduction of windbreaks; and canopy microclimate by sophisticated trellising and vine training techniques. But at the end of the day, and when the particular bottle of wine has reached the peak of its power, the *terroir* and climate will have placed their mark on the wine; and the greater the quality of that wine, the more pronounced will be its birthmark.

It is of fundamental importance to the French (and to a lesser degree the Germans, the Italians and the Spanish) that the influence of *terroir* be enhanced rather than diminished, for only in that way can the special monetary value attaching to their great appellations be protected and justified. The scarcity factor is vital in this context. But how much of the traditional character of Chablis is in fact due to *terroir* and climate, how much to the intervention of man?

The traditionalists of Chablis, with William Fèvre of the Domaine de la Maladière at their head, insist that the soil – the celebrated Kimmeridgian chalky clay – was (and is) crucial. They regard as dastardly upstarts the modernists, headed by Jean Durup of the Domaine de l'Eglantière, who over 20 years have

William Fèvre is Chablis' staunch conservative, insisting on the importance of geology to the flavour of the wine – but untraditionally ageing it in new oak.

successfully urged the authorities to redraw the Chablis map with far wider boundaries, well outside the Kimmeridgian zone. Fèvre blames the appellation authorities for any loss of true Chablis style.

Up to a point he must be right, recent though the changes are. One can, after all, taste the difference between the Grands Crus, the old-established Premiers Crus, and such newcomers as Vaudevey. But to put it all down to the *terroir* is plainly not right. In the past 20 or more years there have been major changes in the way Chablis is made. The majority of winemakers now ferment their wine in stainless steel with inbuilt cooling mechanisms, rather than the oak favoured by winemakers such as William Fèvre and François Raveneau. Deliberately induced malolactic fermentation is now par for the course, softening the naturally high acid, smoothing out the tart edges, and producing fuller wines. Better spray regimes, better viticultural practices and (particularly in the 1980s) a run of warm vintages have produced cleaner, riper grapes with higher alcohol levels – not that this, or apparently anything else, can dissuade the vignerons from their addiction to adding sugar. Chaptalisation is a religion in Burgundy. Most significantly, the levels of sulphur dioxide used in winemaking have been sharply reduced. The high levels, in excess of 200 parts per million, commonplace 30 or more years ago were responsible for stripping the wine's initial colour and preserving it as a pale, green yellow for decades; they inhibited or prevented the malolactic fermentation; they invested the wine with a Peter Pan quality which meant it often needed 20 years to reach its best; and they undoubtedly contributed a significant portion of those celebrated gunflint and river pebble characteristics.

The net result is that Chablis is now riper and softer, showing more pure fruit characteristics, cleaner, and less long-lived. It is in some respects less complex, and less aggressive, but is better balanced. If it is aged in new oak one would need to have a specialized palate to tell it apart from a Côte d'Or wine of similar age. One irony is that Monsieur Fèvre, who so passionately believes in the soil, is also the grower who uses most new barrels – with the consequence that some of his wines could almost be mistaken for Meursault. Nonetheless there are at least half a dozen growers – Raveneau, Michel, Fèvre, Dauvissat and a few others – who do make wines of distinctive character which are not pale imitations of Côte d'Or, and which show an individual and differing house style.

These exceptions apart, Chablis has indeed come closer to the Côte d'Or in becoming more user-friendly, requiring less patience, and developing into a technically much better wine. Whether it is better Chablis, and where the dividing line between anonymity and individuality should be drawn, is less clear.

Simply because the French have been more disciplined in their approach to making and marketing wine, they have long since out-distanced their most natural competitors, the Germans and the Italians. They have established a clearly defined and equally clearly differentiated appellation system which not only enshrines the varying types of wine, but also establishes a social structure extending downwards from royalty to nobility to bourgeoisie to peasantry – and woe betide any who seek to challenge their preordained status in life. The rigidity of the system has its dangers and shortcomings, but it has some potent advantages, not the least being stability. Wine can be a complex and intimidating subject for ordinary consumers, and a degree of certainty and predictability (be it real or imagined) is an obvious advantage.

That stability is built partly on history, partly on a clearly articulated philosophy – and the cynic would suggest on a presumption of inherent superiority. It also has – or had – an exceedingly narrow and parochial base, which has facilitated the most microscopic examination and exploitation of tiny pieces of land (obviously

Jean Durup embodies the progressive school in Chablis, pressing for wider boundaries and playing down the role of the soil.

Different – but better?

Appellation control: a sense of order

Quality: Divine Right?

The first-growth Château Lafite broke spectacularly with tradition in the '80s by building a magnificent circular underground chai for barrel-storage. The Médoc tradition is for long barns at or slightly below ground level.

beneficial) but inhibited a broader understanding of the world of wine beyond.

The emphasis has always been placed on *terroir*, which has justified a basically fatalistic approach to grape-growing and winemaking. A striking example of this attitude – striking because it is so recent and because of the château involved – is the story told of Château Margaux immediately after the great first-growth was bought by the late André Mentzelopoulos. One Sunday late in the 1978 vintage, while working in Paris, he telephoned the château to check on the progress of the fermentations. Receiving no answer, he chartered a plane and flew to the château, finding it indeed untended. His widow Laura recollected that '*He thought it was*

'Back on Monday' *inadmissible that employees closed on Saturday and came back on Monday during fermentation, which lasts only three weeks of the year.*' For his part the *maître de chai*, who was responsible, pointed out that the fermentations were slowing down with no risk of overheating, but admitted '*We weren't used to having a person of that calibre around, and we didn't follow the vinification as closely as we do now.*' Not only do the wineries of the United States, Australasia, New Zealand and South Africa routinely work a seven day week during a vintage, which will frequently extend for six to eight weeks, but they will equally routinely operate round the clock, night shifts taking over from day shifts, and senior winemakers accepting an

The 126 hour week 18 hour day as part of their job.

In France, though, the non-interventionist approach extends right through the winemaking process. Natural yeasts for both primary fermentation and malolactic fermentation are regarded as essential: they are an extension of the expression of *terroir*, providing subtle but palpable complexity in the wine, unlike the one-dimensional and 'foreign' character of a single cultured yeast (or so the French believe). The hot and super-abundant vintage of 1982 caused many Bordeaux châteaux to rethink their attitudes to cooling, however, as fermenting vats heated beyond control, but to this day opening or closing windows, louvres and doors is accepted as the natural way to control fermentation temperatures. Many Burgundians prefer to avoid filtering their wines. And the Burgundian (and Muscadet) practice of keeping the wine on its lees in the barrel (and even stirring up the lees at intervals) also has its genesis in the creed of non-intervention, or following nature.

Spain's most influential modern bodega is the house of Torres at Pacs near Vilafranca del Penedès in Catalonia. The Torres family has startled the world with wines unlike any Spain has ever made.

If all this paints a picture of France as a land of stubborn traditionalists it only tells half the story. The emblem and embodiment of scientific rationalism is Bordeaux's famous Professor of Oenology, Emile Peynaud. Peynaud has been characterized as hero and as villain, as saviour and destroyer. His critics tell the (probably apocryphal) story of the expert given an unknown wine to comment on, and whose response was: '*I can't tell you what the wine is or where it came from, but I can tell you it was made by Professor Peynaud.*' (Other countries have their equivalents: in Australia Brian Croser and Dr Tony Jordan have been accused of a similar Svengali-like influence.) The supporters of Professor Peynaud would simply say that all he sought to do was give the winemaker a better understanding of, and greater control over, all aspects of winemaking: if chemical and bacterial reactions take place in the course of making the wine (and they do) those reactions should be planned and their consequences understood. If there is a problem with this approach it is that it takes much of the mystique out of winemaking, and exposes impotence or incompetence for what it is. And by eliminating the chance consequences of bacterial contamination, oxidation, acetification or whatever, it is perfectly true that the wines made under Peynaud's control exhibit a degree of family resemblance: they are devoid of major technical faults.

Fully understood, science does not mean the end of individuality nor enforce the making of sterile, squeaky-clean wines. Giotto proved his skill by drawing a perfect freehand circle; Picasso showed in his early realist period that he had the ability to portray nature as precisely as any artist. Once winemakers have mastered the basic skills and techniques, then of course they may eschew them: it is an entirely different thing to ignore technique simply because it is not available in the first place – or because you do not understand it.

Almost as important as the Professor in shifting French thought has been the emergence of the cult of oak in Bordeaux and – to a slightly lesser degree – Burgundy. New oak barrels have always played a role, of course; the greater the estate, the greater the role. It was a wholly symbiotic if partially unconscious relationship: the highest quality grapes produced the most intensely flavoured wine, readily able to absorb the flavour of new oak without becoming in the least

Rationalism: Professor Peynaud

Svengali-like influence

The new oak syndrome

subordinated to it. The result was spontaneously recognized as exceptional, and commanded a price which amply repaid the proprietor for his investment in new barrels. Lesser wines were perceived as simply that: they were accorded hand-me-down barrels, and the price became suitably modest. In periods of decline, one of the things that typified a poorly performing classed growth château was that it spent less on new barrels.

The catalyst for change came largely from California. In the 1960s intelligent and active winemakers such as Robert Mondavi started visiting France regularly, tasting the wines of the great producers, watching their techniques and asking questions, and in particular asking questions about their barrels. Those early inquisitors must have concluded the French were being more than usually uncooperative for all but the most general questions went unanswered. Just as milk comes from bottles or cartons, oak comes from the cooperage. But which forest? If the winemaker knew, he was not about to tell. In truth, he almost certainly regarded the question as stupid and unnecessary: the barrels had been supplied by the same cooperage for generations, and they were always satisfactory because the cooper knew the style of wine in question very well. As for how the barrels were made – with low, moderate or high 'toast' – clearly these were the questions of a madman.

The kiss of oak   Since then the field of enquiry has extended to issues of air drying versus kiln drying; tight- versus loose-grained oak; and to a detailed correlation between those questions and toast, oak-type and wine-style. Look at any dissertation on the classed growths of Bordeaux today and you are certain to find reference to the amount of new oak used each year. Yet when Edmund Penning-Rowsell wrote his seminal work *The Wines of Bordeaux* in 1969, nowhere did he mention the use (or absence) of new oak. Quite modest châteaux have built high reputations by giving their wines the kiss of oak; not to mention regions whose wines a mere decade ago would have been sold anonymously in bulk.

Tastes in evolution

The French mainstream

But in a sense these are distractions from the main thrust of the great French wines. These are wines in which subtlety, complexity and typicity are accorded pride of place. Adornments of oak, the embellishment of fruit, and the sophistication of convoluted chemical adjustment come a distant second. Certainly changes have come, but they have come slowly, and not without great heart-searching, such as when, in the early 1960s, first Château Haut-Brion, then Château Latour, dispensed with their old oak fermentation-vats and installed stainless steel. The close bond between the winemaker, his *terroir*, his vines and his grapes – virtually unchanged for centuries – has built up an intuitive approach to winemaking which brash outsiders misunderstand, underestimate or deride to their peril.

Italian idiosyncrasies   The Italians have gone down their own idiosyncratic and at times undisciplined path. The noble growths of Italy were few and far between. Even more so than in France, wine was (and is) a simple necessity of life, made casually and consumed without introspection. Almost everywhere you go in Italy there is a flourishing regional wine industry (there are 232 officially recognized DOC and DOCG zones), many places using indigenous grape varieties of obscure history which grow nowhere else in the world. Winemaking in Italy is every bit as rich and ancient – indeed much more ancient – than that of France: the Frescobaldi family of Tuscany traces its wine lineage back to 1300 – and this is a relatively recent date in the full 4,000-year perspective of Italian wine history.

Despite – perhaps because of – the ubiquitous nature of winemaking across the country, certain patterns appear. Over a long period of time Italians have come to expect dry white wines which are exceedingly pale in colour, almost devoid of any aroma, and largely lacking any recognizable varietal flavour. Served fully chilled these are acceptable food wines: they perform the function of water, but have the advantages of being antiseptic and alcoholic. Looked at more critically, and compared to the white wines of other parts of the world, what aroma they have is not very pleasant, they are often exceedingly hard on the palate, and have a chalky or bitter finish. The reasons are: the preponderance of Trebbiano (there are 100,000 hectares of this high-yielding but eminently undistinguished variety); the surprisingly widespread lack of refrigeration for white wine fermentation; and a real dislike of the fruity flavours which can be obtained from any white grape variety. It is no coincidence that hyper-oxidation of white grape juice was developed in Italy; it is a logical extension of the juice oxidation which was already widely practised, though by accident rather than design.

This approach is popularly supposed to have been modified for varieties new to Italy – notably Chardonnay. Yet arrange a blind tasting of French, California, Australian and Italian Chardonnays, and the Italians will still stand apart. They will no doubt have their supporters – Angelo Gaja in Piedmont commands spectacular prices for his – but the majority of non-Italian judges would have no difficulty in spotting the difference.

The style and overall quality of Italian red wines is rather less challenging and, most would agree, decidedly more satisfying. Whereas gimmicky bottles (and some brilliant label designs) have made Frascati, Soave, Verdicchio and such wines commercially acceptable, if not entirely successful, red wines such as Brunello, Barolo, Barbaresco and Chianti Reserva need no apology. Tuscany and Piedmont *Leaders of modern Italy* are emerging as regions where Italian technological flair has finally got to grips with wine. But once again it is necessary to stress that these are the tip of a very large iceberg, still bearing no resemblance to the raw, often fizzy and rough reds consumed within a year of vintage and which will never be found more than 30 miles from where they were made.

Despite the differing climates, *terroirs*, and grape varieties lying behind the best traditional Italian red wines, there was a common theme: they were aged for long periods in large, neutral, wooden vats (cherry, chestnut, walnut or oak) and given further bottle-age before release, this approach being based on the need to overcome formidable tannins.

Over the past 15 years the already bewildering complexity of Italian wines has become tangled enough to drive a critic to drink. Enthusiastic planting of the classic varieties (notably the Cabernet family and Chardonnay) has been followed by equally enthusiastic use of new small oak barrels (the wooden '*barrique*' is enough to add several thousand lire to the price) and the emergence of several Italian equivalents of Professor Peynaud. The result was a profusion of non-conforming *vini da tavola* rejoicing under exotic names and frequently stunning packaging, selling for far more than the theoretically better DOC and DOCG *Revolution '92* wines, and tasting like a Franco-Californian hybrid. The Tuscan Cabernet Sassicaia started it all. By 1990 the situation was out of control. In 1992 the government had to rewrite the rulebook to contain the revolution.

Rioja is Spain's one classic red-wine region with an unmistakable style of its *Spanish parallels* own. Structurally Riojas are not dissimilar to the best traditional Chiantis, the main difference being that American oak casks give them their characteristic vanilla-and-lemon flavour. The winemaking methods and philosophies, however, also run on parallel paths – blending grapes, then softening their tannins and lightening primary fruit by maturing for several years in oak. In Rioja, as in Italy, the current trend is to shorten the time in barrel and to encourage fresher, crisper fruit flavours. Rioja's white wines rarely reach the standard of its reds.

The white wines of Germany, of Alsace and of the Loire Valley come under the *USA* microscope in the next chapter; for now the attention swings to the New World, and first to the United States of America (and thereby principally to California). Californian winemaking philosophy has passed through a series of metamorphoses since the repeal of Prohibition. Initially it was concerned almost entirely with fortified wine production, in precisely the same way as Australia was. Its next phase started in the 1950s with the emergence of table wine as a serious commercial category, but largely fashioned from the same ignoble grape varieties as had been used to make fortified wine. Then in the 1960s the classic varieties, now becoming the international varieties, were rediscovered. Cabernet Sauvignon, Chardonnay, Sauvignon Blanc, Chenin Blanc, Johannisberg Riesling, Pinot Noir, and Merlot changed the face of American winemaking forever. Rapid planting began in California, but soon spread – with varying degrees of success – to scattered regions right across the country.

From basic to classic

The initial response was one of wonder and adulation on the part of winemakers and consumers alike. The more powerful the aroma, the bigger the flavour, the higher the alcohol the better. These were strange wines, soul-mates of the waddling

Wine has not ceased to express the qualities of landscape because the scale has changed. It is easy to find in the bold fruit flavours of California a reflection of the rich ranchland that rolls down to the Pacific.

finned-monsters churned out by the Detroit carmakers, and of the society which nurtured Marilyn Monroe. America's crush on size continued well into the 1970s. Many attribute its demise to an article by New York Times wine critic, Frank Prial, but whatever the cause, the end came remarkably quickly.

Prial's (and many others') complaint was that these wines were clumsy, one-dimensional and just too darned strong; that they were varietal caricatures which could not be drunk with any pleasure, and least of all with food. So the era of 'food wines' was born; wines in which dominant fruit flavours were toned down in a search for subtlety and complexity. Part of the stimulus for change came from improved viticulture: the massive, heavily shaded, traditional Californian vine canopy had meant that flavour ripeness did not occur until very late in the season, by which time potential alcohol levels were 14 percent or more. For some growers at least, better canopy management meant better grapes at lower alcohol levels.

Just too darned strong

The changes in the winery saw the enthusiastic adoption of French (and Italian) winemaking techniques. Juice oxidation, barrel fermentation and full malolactic fermentation were adopted as normal practice for Chardonnay; the quest to tame the tart grassiness of Sauvignon Blanc adopting some of the same techniques, and blending it with Sémillon in imitation of white Bordeaux. The prime subject for postgraduate research at the Californian wine university, Davis, became the changes in Cabernet Sauvignon's tannin structure when macerated for periods of ten to 25 days after first fermentation. Then Merlot, followed by Cabernet Franc – and afterwards Petit Verdot – began to be blended with Cabernet Sauvignon, first experimentally, then as a matter of course.

The 'choices' and 'consequences' will be looked at in greater detail in the following chapters, but one is bound to ask whether the pendulum has swung too far. Has obsession with technique and theory, the quest for subtlety and complexity led to wines which have lost the ability to capture the attention of the drinker, to effortlessly beguile the tongue?

The Australian love affair

Australia's experience certainly suggests the answer is yes. Here there is an unashamed and uncomplicated love affair with primary varietal fruit flavour, augmented by sometimes profligate use of oak. Both white and red wines may be accused of simplicity, but above all else they are user-friendly. They are positive in their aroma and flavour, yet neither demanding nor intimidating. The white wines are spotlessly clean, and the majority of the Chardonnays are at their best within 18 months of the harvest. The red wines are soft, fruity and much, much lower in tannin than their Californian counterparts. While most repay cellaring, and a few demand it, they are nonetheless easily enjoyed when they are first released, usually at two to three years of age. In virtually every Australian-American blind tasting challenge conducted over the past five years – in England, Australia or America – Australia has emerged the clear victor. As the French (who had earlier received similar treatment at the hands of the Americans) would be quick to point out, such competitions have to be taken in context, but they cannot be dismissed.

Australian winemakers achieve their results by meticulous attention to detail (in common, it must be said, with their equally fastidious and technically skilled American counterparts). But Australian ideas are different. Rather than allow oxidation of the juice, for example, the usual Australian way with Chardonnay, Sémillon and Sauvignon Blanc is to extend their contact with grape skins, totally exclude oxygen from the juice by using sulphur dioxide and ascorbic acid, to cold ferment totally clarified juice, and also to carry out some malolactic fermentation. (These techniques are all explained in detail in later chapters.) With Riesling the aim is to reduce rather than enhance the flavour, but by ultra-careful handling of juice and fermentation, and allowing bottle-age to bring the wine to its peak.

The Australian approach to red wine making shows a similar emphasis on varietal and fruit flavour. Barrel-fermentation is almost as widely practised as extended maceration (after fermentation) and at no time has there been any concern about achieving any particular level of alcohol. Australia also has a wine mid-way in style between Pinot Noir and Cabernet Sauvignon: Syrah (or Shiraz or Hermitage as it is called there) gives wines diverse in style (according to climate) but which are mostly soft and round in the mouth.

New Zealand schools of thought

New Zealand's winemakers are in some ways caught between the Australian philosophy of today and the Californian of ten years ago. Particularly with white wines, winemakers and consumers alike appear convinced that more is better. This philosophy works well with Sauvignon Blanc, particularly when it is grown in Marlborough and made by Montana, Cloudy Bay or Hunters, but less convincingly with Chardonnay. A combination of high yields, rather more botrytis and other moulds than are desirable, extended skin contact (often imposed willy nilly on the winemaker as machine-harvested fruit is brought in from many miles away) and malolactic fermentation, sometimes contribute flavours so complex that they threaten to overwhelm one in a jungle-like web.

South Africa and South America – particularly Chile – have had to contend with a mixture of political and economic millstones which have checked their rate of progress. Chile's viticultural potential is apparently limitless; that of South Africa only marginally less so. Those who think that trade sanctions stultified South African winemaking should think again: the shadow of the KWV has not blotted out an ever-increasing number of superbly equipped, innovative and outward-looking small- to medium-sized wineries capable of producing wines to challenge those of Australia or California. Virus-infected vineyards have held back progress, and Chardonnay is still a newcomer (a highly successful one), but South Africans effortlessly produce excellent Sauvignon Blanc in various guises (from steel-fermented and matured to barrel-aged wines) and sturdy, ever-reliable, if rather dry, Cabernet Sauvignon. They struggle manfully with their indigenous Pinotage. But the most ambitious growers are more interested in Pinot Noir.

Millstones and milestones: South Africa and Chile

New Zealand provides the newest landscape for the vine. Within a single decade her Sauvignon Blanc has become the world's favourite. The Te Mata estate at Hawke's Bay on North Island has the longest history – over a century – but its stunningly original architecture expresses an entirely new ethic. Te Mata emulates California, specifically Sonoma, with one of New Zealand's most successful red wines yet – a Cabernet and Merlot blend.

Light-Bodied White Wines

Choices, consequences and techniques

One way of regarding the enormously wide spectrum of white wines, deriving from different grapes, different climates and soils, and different winemaking techniques, is to see Riesling as the epitome of the most aromatic, least full-bodied, most transparent and brilliant in flavour. Its great rival, Chardonnay (few people would deny that they are the world's two greatest white-wine grapes), then stands at the other end of the spectrum, epitomizing dense, full-bodied, multi-faceted wines that derive much of their personality and individuality from the way they are made and aged – and above all from the oak of their barrels.

A continuum of characters

In between lies a continuum of characters, from the lightly aromatic (close in style to Riesling), to the merely neutral, and onwards to the grapes that react in a similar way to Chardonnay to winery techniques.

The aromatic grapes and wines begin with Riesling, Gewürztraminer, Sylvaner, Welschriesling, Grüner Veltliner, Muscat Blanc à Petits Grains and Müller-Thurgau (along with the rest of the family of German-bred *vinifera* hybrids). Then there are a number of white varieties which, like the aromatics, are usually made without oak influence and bottled early in their life. These include Chasselas (the

From the Rudesheimer Klosterberg vineyards the view sweeps down towards Rudesheim, then on across the Rhine to the vineyards of Bingen and the Nahe Valley beyond.

principal grape of Switzerland), Chenin Blanc, Aligoté, Colombard, Marsanne, Roussanne, Melon de Bourgogne (better known as Muscadet), the Trebbiano of Italy and the Rkatsiteli of Eastern Europe.

Of all these, Riesling stands out as the classic variety. Yet its hold on the hearts and minds of the world's wine drinkers is curiously uncertain, and infinitely weaker than it was 100, or even 50, years ago. Rhine wines have a longer history in international trade than any other white wines. When, in the 18th century, almost all the best German vineyards were planted with Riesling, their quality soared, and they became eagerly followed by discriminating drinkers round the world. Even France acknowledged the unique qualities of the great Rieslings of the Mosel, and to the British, Hock (meaning Rhine wine) and Mosel were household words in just the same way as Chardonnay is today.

German Riesling

German wines of the 19th and early 20th centuries were intense, long-lived and basically dry. After World War II, and particularly the great 1959 vintage which produced many sweet wines, the taste for sweetness developed, and various technical means were found to keep German wines from fermenting to dryness, or to re-sweeten them before bottling. The 1970s, however, saw a powerful reaction against sweetness in the German domestic market. Suddenly 'trocken' or very dry wines were in vogue.

As the fashion for *trocken* and *halbtrocken* wines emerged, much was made of the suggestion that these dry or near-dry wines were merely a reversion to the style of the golden age of German winemaking. The flaw in this argument is the radically different nature of the grapes: 120 years ago the average yield was 17 hectolitres per hectare, compared to as much as 140 hectolitres per hectare today, and alcohol levels were significantly higher. So whatever the German enthusiasm for the modern *trocken* wines, it is not generally shared by the rest of the world, which sees most of them as charmless, thin and hard. The realization is dawning that German wines need to be of far-above-average quality to be balanced and satisfying without a little residual sugar. A dry *Spätlese* may well be highly enjoyable to drink, but a bone-dry *Kabinett* wine is usually a meagre creature. Better to add sugar, French-style, to make a plain 'Qualitätswein', which then at least has the substance to be satisfying.

Sweet or trocken?

The subject of German wine quality is a minefield of politics and paradoxes. The very selection of Riesling seems perverse: as a late-ripener it seems an illogical choice for the German climate. Early-ripening Chardonnay would have been more suitable, one would have thought. Yet Riesling's peculiarity is that it can, and indeed does, achieve intense flavour ripeness at as little as 10 percent alcohol – indeed, on occasions, as little as 7 percent.

The German approach to winemaking is based on the qualities Riesling can achieve in cool climates where full ripeness is the exception. Alcohol is regarded in a quite different light. The measure used to differentiate quality categories is 'potential alcohol' – which of course includes residual sugar.

Cool but ripe

The emphasis in German Riesling is all on freshness, on fruit and on a balance between sweetness and acidity. Alcohol imparts its own sweetness; if it is reduced, the logical result is unfermented sugar. For this reason many observers think German Riesling finds its ultimate expression in *Auslesen* (*see* page 228) from the Mosel (and its least expression in *trocken* wines). It is the fine Rieslings which we are concerned with here.

The winemaking options for Riesling, though, are limited: there are only minor differences in the way it is made in Germany, Alsace, South Africa, California or Australia, yet, as we have seen within Germany alone, the resulting wines differ from one another quite considerably. The reason lies partly in philosophy, but largely in climate and *terroir*.

Making White Wine

CRUSHING

The first stage of controlled vinification is to crush the grapes and release the pulp and juice, making them easier to press. A key decision at this stage is whether or not to remove the stems. Left with the grapes stems allow juice to drain more freely during pressing, but they also release tannins. For grapes high in fruit flavour, tannins may be desirable, adding complexity, but for more subtly flavoured musts they are a disadvantage and destemming is carried out at the crushing stage.

PRESSING

Cooling
Delaying fermentation until after pressing is essential. Where the ambient must temperatures are high the juice is cooled by pumping it through 'must chillers'.

Pressing
White wine grapes are always pressed. Better quality juice results when pressing is gentle. If too aggressive the pips and stems break and bitter astringent flavours, which overpower those natural in the grapes, are released. Good results are achieved with pneumatic presses, which are now replacing traditional vertical wooden ones. Both types yield juice of the highest quality and also enable the separation of different quality pressings.

Settling
The juice is drained from the press into settling vats where the skin, pip and stem fragments remaining in suspension after pressing will settle to the bottom of the vat. The clean juice is then racked into separate vats ready for fermentation to begin. Centrifuging can also be carried out at this stage to clarify the wine, but it is an aggressive process, removing all the larger particles in the must, even yeast cells. It is often carried out when cultured yeasts are to replace natural ones for fermentation.

FERMENTATION

Traditionally in oak casks (increasingly favoured for many high-quality wines) white wine is now more often fermented in stainless steel vats which enable easier regulation of yeast activity through temperature control. Prolonged fermentation at cool temperatures protects primary fruit characteristics and ensures the conversion of all the sugar to alcohol. After fermentation some winemakers chose to leave their wine in contact with its lees (yeast sediment) which adds both flavour and freshness to the wine, retained by bottling it without delay.

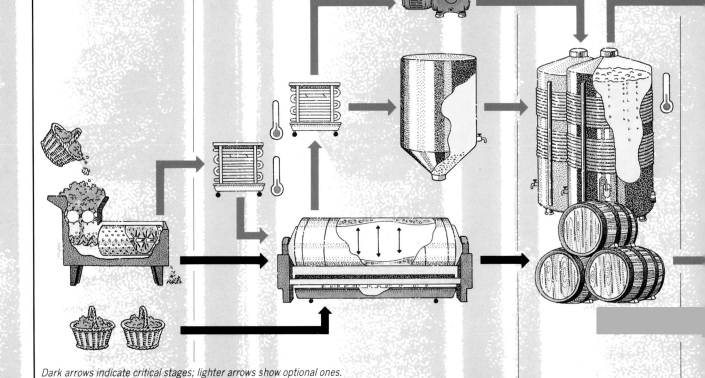

Dark arrows indicate critical stages; lighter arrows show optional ones.

MALOLACTIC FERMENTATION

To soften astringent acidic flavours and to add complexity, a second or malolactic fermentation can be encouraged (it may occur quite naturally or be brought about artificially). This converts harsher malic acids to softer lactic ones. Where retaining acidic qualities in the wine is important (eg in warmer climates where the grapes gain greater sugar and fruit flavours at the expense of their natural acidity) this second fermentation is prevented by removing the yeasts and proteins needed to initiate it.

MATURING

Clarification
Filtration, centrifuging or fining with bentonite clay (which 'collects' remaining yeasts, proteins, grape skin particles etc, and precipitates them to the bottom of the vat) are used to prevent unwanted malolactic fermentation and any further yeast acitivity once all the sugar in the wine has been converted to alcohol. It also removes substances leading to 'off tastes'. With clarification the wine gains stability; the processes used for this stabilization, however, are quite aggressive and many believe they lead to flavour loss. Clarification is completed by removing tartrates from the wine. Modern wineries now use thickly insulated stainless steel vats for cold stabilization. By cooling the wine to around −4℃, tartrate crystals, which may otherwise form in the bottle, precipitate and fall to the bottom of the vat. In Germany this process traditionally occurred in large oak *Füders* situated in cellars cool enough for tartrates to precipitate out at ambient temperatures.

After stabilization the wine may be bottled immediately or matured first in oak barrels.

Maturing in oak
Maturing white wine in new oak imparts flavours which can overpower wines of more subtle character, but add depth and complexity to others. Older barrels give more moderate flavours and are an option often favoured in Burgundy.

FINISHING

Bottling
During bottling cleanliness is essential; any bacterial activity, which may be encouraged by warm temperatures – especially when the wine is later transported or shipped for sale – is prevented by passing the wine through a fine filter. Some producers bottle the wine straight from its lees after fermentation to retain yeast character and freshness (even a slight spritz). Others, particularly in the New World, inject CO_2 at the bottling stage for the same effect.

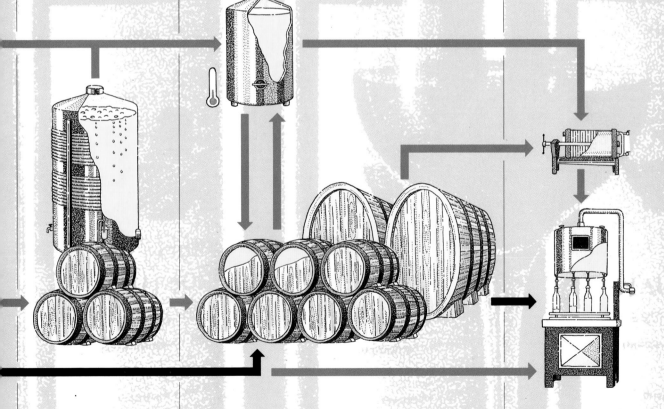

The grapes come first   The German attitude to winemaking is very simple and straightforward, ever emphasizing the grapes, ever downplaying the role of the winemaker. Grapes from Germany's Riesling vineyards (the best of which are often on steep slopes) are almost invariably hand-picked, and those from better estates are hurried to be processed with as little damage to their skins as possible: freshness of juice is seen as crucial. On less perfectionist properties a certain amount of maceration of skins and juice in the collection-containers is not uncommon, due to tight packing or even semi-crushing. The crushed must is taken directly to the press (pneumatic presses are now standard) and subsequently care is taken to select only free-run and light pressings for the better wines. Levels of sulphur dioxide are more moderate than in former years, as the usually low ambient temperatures of both the grapes and the cellars give a measure of protection against oxidation at this stage. Most winemakers are unconcerned about slight yellowing (or even browning) of juice, indicating a touch of juice oxidation. They are wary though, of the implications of botrytis in dry or semi-dry winemaking – in particular its tendency to bind sulphur and thereby neutralize its protective function.

The juice is cold-settled overnight. Centrifuge pumps are sparingly used; filtration of the juice is even rarer. Because of the minuscule lots which the fine estates are often dealing with (for example the famous house of J. J. Prüm of Wehlen in the Middle Mosel released 60 cases of its 1975 Auslese Long Gold Cap, 225 cases of its 1976 and 30 cases of its 1982 – with none at all made in the intervening years) fermentation vessels (usually stainless steel, sometimes old oak) are small, and the low cellar temperatures mean that fermentation usually proceeds quite slowly at 12 to 15°C, initiated by either cultured or wild yeasts. While this last choice is very personal to the winemaker, the very top estates almost invariably allow their 'wild' yeasts to do the job.

Harmony and charm   Frequently, particularly in the typically German, small oval casks called *Füders*, and in cold damp cellars (which are the rule rather than the exception) fermentation peters out before all the grape sugar is converted to alcohol, leaving the slight degree of natural sweetness which gives the wine great harmony and charm. To preserve the sugar at this level, the wine is racked and sulphured immediately at the end of fermentation, and may be sterile filtered. It will be fined (if necessary) with a variety of fining agents, and racked once again. The former German custom of keeping the wine for two, three or even far more years in cask to soften their harsh acidity has all but disappeared with current methods of acidity-adjustment. Where once Rieslings were prized for savoury, sappy intensity and almost limitless endurance (they withstood even quite severe oxidation – some were prized for brownness and almost sherry-like qualities) today what is asked of them is bouquets of floral perfumes, and palate-tingling freshness.

Süssreserve   Perhaps the most contentious German practice is the use of *süssreserve*: sweet unfermented must added after fermentation and immediately before the final filtration and bottling. This 'back-blending' (as the Australians describe it) is legal for all grades of QmP wines, on condition that it is made from grapes grown in the same vineyard or region, and which are of the same grade, as the wine to be sweetened. In other words, *süssreserve* of *Spätlese* quality must be used for *Spätlese* wine, and so on. The level of addition is also limited by reference to the natural alcohol of the wine. But while much German wine, from slightly to moderately sweet, is made with the help of *süssreserve*, the finest estates refuse to use it; much preferring the fermentation to remain just short of complete, and then stabilizing the wine as necessary.

The great German Rieslings have exceptional intensity of fruit flavour, deriving directly from the vineyard. Yields for these wines (when made as *Kabinett* or *Spätlese*) seldom exceed 60 hectolitres per hectare (with much lower yields for *Auslese* and the sweetest wines). They are intensely aromatic and flowery, with a little botrytis frequently adding complexity, their sweetness (be it slight or marked) combining with the always perceptible acidity to give impact to the fruit flavour. In no other wines is the nature and degree of their acidity so essential to quality. The Germans distinguish between 'Weinsaüre' – tartaric acid which stimulates the palate attractively – and 'Apfelsaüre' – harsh-tasting malic acid. It is the difference between these two, and the vineyards – sheltered and south-sloping, or wind-chilled and shady – that create the crucial difference that provides the fundamental criteria for quality in German Riesling.

The nature of acidity

Alsace Riesling

The Alsace winemaker consciously endeavours to make a Riesling as different from that of Germany as the laws of chemistry and biochemistry will allow. The German strives for fruit and finesse, the Alsace for power and strength. To the former alcohol is unimportant, to the latter it is all-important. Sweetness is almost an embarrassment, however high the price the top growers seek for their luscious Vendange Tardive and Sélection des Grains Nobles. The amount of sweetness tolerated in such wines is a mere fraction of that which a German winemaker looks for; the amount of alcohol correspondingly much higher. A 'Grains Nobles', the sweetest category of Alsace wine, is much more like Sauternes in strength and body than anything made in Germany.

Alsace lies in the rain-shadow of the Vosges Mountains, where summers are typically long, sunny and dry, with France's second-lowest average rainfall. Riesling makes the greatest wines, but not by the margin it does in Germany. The

Dark clouds over the Vosges mountains contrast starkly with the sunny vineyards of Alsace. The vineyards of the whole region are protected by the peaks and forests of the Vosges. They provide the rain-shadow which gives Alsace its hot dry summers.

Jean Hugel with a glass of Pinot Blanc from the St Catharine cask in the Hugel cellars in Riquewihr. Built in 1715, it is the oldest cask in the world still in continuous use.

grapes will usually be picked at higher sugar levels: to qualify as a *grand vin* (or better) the wine must contain 11 percent alcohol (although chaptalisation is permitted – and practised – whether the wine needs it or not). One feels that the Alsace Riesling is being brought up as a man – a Spartan, even. One of the few concessions to modern technology is the centrifuge, used to clarify the juice after 12 hours or so of rough settling. From this point on the aim is to subjugate the pretty, flowery characters of Riesling and to invest it instead with a dry, steely strength.

In such traditional family houses as Hugel, fermentation takes place in ancient wooden casks; in banks of towering stainless steel fermentation vats in the cooperatives. Fermentation temperatures are nominally held at 20°C but in practice go higher; particularly where precise temperature-control facilities are not available. These temperatures are much higher than those which (for example) Australian winemakers would use (12–15°C), and burn out many of the fruity esters and flavours of the grape. In 1981 Marc Hugel (son of Jean Hugel) worked a vintage in Australia, and returned determined to experiment using much lower fermentation temperatures (around 14°C). His results yielded a wine which was incredibly aromatic and intense, a kind of perfumed essence which was unrecognizable as a wine of Alsace. Rumour has it that small percentages are from time to time blended into the wines of the house, but – with good reason – Jean Hugel, who is regarded by many as a spokesman for the whole Alsace wine industry, has not allowed any overt change.

Once fermentation has finished, and the wine racked off its lees, the Alsace approach is strictly non-interventionist. Filtration, fining, even pumping, is kept to a minimum. The one enemy the winemaker is concerned about is oxidation (*see* page 214), one which is comprehensively defeated. Fresh, bracing, firm and aggressive in their youth, Alsace Rieslings need time in bottle; the greater the vintage, the longer. Just as the finest 1971 German *Spätlesen* and *Auslesen* were reaching their peak in 1990, so were the top Rieslings of Alsace. And if one were to give those wines another 20 years, it is arguable Alsace would better stand the test of time.

Elsewhere in Europe true Riesling is far outnumbered by its ignoble namesake, Welsh or Italian Riesling. Where true Riesling is found – in northern Italy, Czechoslovakia, Slovenia, a little in Austria and Hungary (and a very great deal in Ukraine and Russia) – local tastes divide between the German and the Alsace approach to winemaking. Italy is more Alsatian; Austria (and even more Czechoslovakia) incline towards the riper German style typical of the Palatinate.

Australian Riesling

Until the still-recent arrival of Chardonnay in Australia, Riesling was the country's best-loved white grape by far. It remains the most widely planted, high-quality white grape – above all in South Australia, where the Barossa Valley is its original headquarters. Australia traditionally adopted the Alsatian philosophy of fermenting to dryness, and – courtesy of its climate rather than any particular philosophical conviction – achieved equal or higher alcohol levels to those of Alsace without the aid of chaptalisation. The curious feature of Australian Rieslings is that the greatest wines have so far come from the relatively warm regions of the Clare and Eden Valleys in South Australia, and the much cooler regions of far southeastern Australia, southern Victoria and Tasmania produce wines of less character and interest; high in aroma but often rather hard and thin on the palate.

The aim is to produce a wine which is highly aromatic and intensely fruity, but which has minimal reliance on sugar. In general terms, the Australian (and now New Zealand) approach is strictly to protect the juice before fermentation, keeping it at 0°C; to 'cold-settle', centrifuge or filter it to absolute clarity; to ferment it in stainless steel at precisely controlled temperatures; to arrest fermentation with a barely perceptible (to the palate) level of residual sugar, achieved by bringing the

temperature of the wine down to 5°C and sterile-filtering it; and to bottle the wine as quickly as possible, usually within three months of the end of fermentation. At no time will it be put in oak, new or old, large or small. The sulphur levels will be kept as low as possible. The only chemical adjustment will be to the acid, with tartaric (and possibly a little malic) acid added during fermentation and adjusted (if necessary) at bottling. (In the cooler parts of Australia and New Zealand it may be necessary to go the other way, and reduce natural acidity by chaptalising, as in Germany, but this is not common.)

One characteristic of Australian (and indeed all warm-country) Rieslings which has yet to find a full explanation is the relatively rapid onset of a singular aroma of maturity that in German (and Alsace) wines usually takes several, even many, years to develop. The smell is variously described as petrol or kerosene. A suggestion of it, combined with a lemon- or lime-like smell, can be teasingly delicious. Too much is like a taint; it makes a dull drink.

The Riesling-scape of the United States is changing day by day as the winemaking map extends. California's earlier (post-Prohibition) efforts with this grape resulted in dry wines, not unlike the Australian version of the period. Later, some wineries elected to use Riesling (or Johannisberg Riesling, as it is called) as what might be called a beginner's wine. It was made to a Liebfraumilch-type or 'Fanta' formula of moderate sweetness, mild flavour and the lowest possible price; the antithesis of the early Chardonnays. Half a dozen wineries continue to produce very-near-dry Rieslings of impeccable mouth-watering freshness, despite their Alsace-like alcohol content. Interest has ebbed from them, though, with the discovery that the Napa Valley is as good a place as any to make *Beerenauslese*. Today Riesling, to any well-heeled California wine-lover, means luscious dessert wine.

Other states are according the variety rather more courtesy. Washington State Riesling is a promising adolescent, although some observers see the wines as living off their flowery aroma and failing on the palate, with the hard, slightly green, herbaceous flavours which seem to be associated with unripe pips. Those of Oregon are quite different; the more humid and slightly warmer growing conditions produce grapes with high sugar levels and balanced acidity. The result is wines with lime-juice aroma and flavour, off-set by the suggestion of bath-powder that certain German wines evoke, and frequently enriched by a light infection of botrytis. There should be a future for these wines – as there should for the burgeoning Rieslings of regions as disparate as New York and British Columbia.

Above left: *The development of modern presses (these are airbag presses at Stag's Leap in the Napa Valley) is towards gentler, more controlled but if possible faster pressing.*

Above right: *Refrigerated tanks at Montana's Riverland winery. In New Zealand (as in Australia) the approach with Riesling is to ferment under strictly controlled temperatures to produce aromatic and fruity wines.*

Riesling in the USA

From 'Fanta' . . .

. . . to lime juice and bath powder

Aromatic white wines

This choices and consequences chart illustrates those stages in the winemaking process in which the options chosen by the winemaker will fundamentally influence the taste and individuality of the final wine. The example is of light-bodied, so-called aromatic wines, epitomized perhaps by Riesling. Not every stage of the process is indicated: for that the reader is directed to the white-wine process chart on pages 88–89.

Aromatic wines strive for finesse. They are deliberately made light in flavour, relying on fruit in the absence of oak overtones, and balancing sweetness with acidity. An important decision is whether to blend several grape varieties or produce a single-grape, varietal wine. Beyond the broad division of sweet or dry, there are discernable regional differences in varietal character, reflecting the climate and soils as well as the vinification methods. Changing tastes also lend their weight: the trend in recent years has been towards drier, fresher wines. All of these factors need to be taken into consideration when choosing grape varieties and winemaking techniques.

1
IN THE VINEYARD

Choice of grape variety
(a) *Single variety*
(b) *Blend*
The choice of grapes largely turns upon the decision whether or not to blend. Riesling, the finest of the aromatic varieties, is seldom blended with other varieties, although Riesling-Traminer blends had a brief period of popularity in Australia. Simply because of the style of the wines – aiming at finesse, elegance and clarity – the complexity offered by blending is only rarely regarded as important.

2
CRUSHING AND PRESSING

Juice handling
The very name 'aromatic' means that apart from certain countries such as Italy, the usual practice is to protect the juice from oxidation by the addition of sulphur dioxide, which may be added in the crusher, in the press or as the juice is placed in the vat for settling.

3
FERMENTING

Right: Hunawihr's most famous vineyard, Ste-Hune, grows particularly fine Riesling. Alsace is the only wine region in France in which the Riesling grape is permitted.

Far right: Temperature control in the fermentation vat is more essential than ever for aromatic wines as grapey aromas are easily lost as the temperature rises.

Method of picking
(a) *By hand*
(b) *By machine*
The initial belief that delicate white wines could not be made from machine harvested fruit has long since been proved false. In California and Australia, speed of harvesting and the ability to harvest during cool night-time temperatures have more than compensated for damage to the grapes. In Germany and Alsace almost all the grapes are picked by hand because of the limitations of steep slopes and the need to be selective.

Left: Growers aiming for high quality wine use a very sparing hand in applying fertilizers.

Crushing and pressing
For almost all aromatic white wines grapes are pressed immediately after crushing. For top-quality wines only the free-run or lightly pressed juice is used.

Juice clarification
Juice must be clarified before fermentation and this can be achieved by natural cold settling, by filtration or by centrifuging.

Left: Centrifugal clarifiers are frequently used in modern wineries usually to clean the must before fermentation and sometimes as a rapid form of filtration.

Yeast choice
Because of the absence of skins and therefore the absence of natural yeasts, cultured yeasts are almost always used.

Choice of fermentation vat
Old oak vats are still widely used in parts of Europe but the advantages of stainless steel (sterility, temperature control) are increasingly recognized. If oak is used, it does not impart any flavour to the wine.

Fermentation timing and temperature
The length of fermentation directly relates to fermentation temperature. In the New World it may last one month at temperatures of 9–10°C; Old World fermentations tend to be much warmer and quicker.

Termination of fermentation
For most aromatic white wines the fermentation is stopped while there is still a little unfermented sugar left in the wine. This is achieved by chilling the wine, racking it and adding sulphur dioxide. Others – typically in Alsace and Italy – are fermented bone dry and others still are sweetened after being fermented dry by the addition of grape juice (*süssreserve*).

4
FINISHING

Filtration
In the New World aromatic white wines are almost invariably filtered. In the Old World filtering tends to be kept to the minimum.

Cold stabilization
This process involves chilling the wine to just above freezing point in order to prevent the risk of tartrate crystals forming after the wine is bottled. This is standard procedure in all larger wineries.

Bottling
In most instances the wines are bottled immediately or shortly after the end of fermentation; by and large, nothing is to be gained by storage in tank.

Gewürztraminer

It seems that the Gewürztraminer is as difficult to vinify well as it is easy to recognize and remember. It is an early-ripening variety, prone to spring frost damage, yielding much less than Riesling, and demanding nice judgement to pick it at the right moment when its aromas are ripened, but before its acidity drops (as it does, rapidly). Alsace has the climate and its growers know the secret. It is a pink-skinned grape that needs quick but gentle pressing to keep the juice white and clear: any turbidity results in almost unpleasantly aromatic wine.

In other parts of the world winemakers find themselves between the devil and the deep blue sea in handling this variety. If they are too restrained in their approach – picking the grapes a little too early is a prime cause – a pale, faintly spicy but rather anaemic wine results. If they leave the grapes on the vine a little too long and lower the temperature of the fermentation vat a little too far, an oily, pungent, coarse, tannic wine with a particularly aggressive finish and aftertaste is the consequence. On balance, though, it is better to wait for full ripeness and risk having to boost the acidity artificially than to pick too soon. The aim should be a lively, fresh, rose-petal scent leading to a clean, refreshing, lychee-like finish. The Alsace version is most convincing fully dry; the German is softer, fainter, sweeter and rarely as memorable. Few New World winemakers seem to have the temerity to offer it without a little residual sugar to mask a tendency to coarseness. If any region shows the potential to challenge Alsace it is probably New Zealand.

New Zealand has the potential to challenge Alsace with its Gewürztraminer. Here in the Wairau Valley near Marlborough more of the land is being turned over to vineyards every year and fewer sheep graze.

Pinot Gris rejoices in more actively used synonyms than any other important grape variety, even since one of its most important *noms de verre*, Tokay d'Alsace, was outlawed by the EC mandarins. It is known as Ruländer in Germany, Pinot Grigio in Italy, Pinot Beurot in Burgundy, Fromenteau in Champagne, Malvoisie on the Loire, and Szürkebarát in Hungary. A comparative tasting of Pinot Gris from these countries will emphasize that it is versatile enough to produce light, dry wines (especially in northeast Italy), or wines as dense, broad and mouth-filling as any white grape can produce. That seems to have been the significance of its now-outlawed name 'Tokay' in Alsace, where it achieves an almost oily, unctuous richness. This led a number of winemakers to bring in new oak in an effort to show the Burgundians what a real white wine should taste like. So far, at least, the Burgundians do not seem unduly worried, which simply reinforces the Alsatian view that the Burgundians know nothing about wine anyway.

If there is to be a newly fashionable white wine variety for the next generation it could boil down to a choice between the erratic Viognier and Pinot Gris. (Australia might contribute Verdelho as a long-shot challenger.) Of the three, Pinot Gris has the best credentials: in countries as far apart as Hungary and New Zealand it makes a wine full of character, a wine which does not need new oak – and usually does not receive it, hence its inclusion in this chapter – but which can react synergistically with it, given the chance. Because of its robust, mouth-filling flavour

Pinot Gris

it is one of those varieties which winemakers class as forgiving – a feature which they promptly take advantage of. For the reality is that if you see a wine labelled Pinot Gris (or one of its synonyms) be prepared for any possibility: it may be a little sweet, it may be bone dry; it may have a little oak, but by rights should have none; it may be succulent in flavour and texture, or it may be oily and bitter, or thin, hard and chalky; it may be white, yellow, bronze-copper or delicately pink in colour; it may be very good or very bad.

Chenin Blanc

Chenin Blanc is a more predictable grape and produces a more predictable wine, but is very nearly as variable in style and quality as Pinot Gris. In South Africa (where it is very widely propagated as 'Steen'), in the United States, Australia, New Zealand, Argentina and Chile, it usually makes a blandly fruity wine which is as inoffensive as it is unremarkable. When handled intelligently, as it often is in South Africa, it keeps a lively zing of acidity – but many versions are simply dull semi-sweet middle-of-the-roaders. In utter contrast, along the Loire Valley, in Vouvray, Montlouis, Anjou, Bonnezeaux, Coteaux du Layon and Quarts de Chaume, it produces wines of at times Olympian quality but which are understood and appreciated by only a few, and which are grossly underrated in consequence.

Longevity on the Loire

The most striking quality of Chenin Blanc wines is their longevity. A vertical tasting of Vouvrays of the famous house of Marc Brédif, spanning 18 vintages between 1911 and 1970 – with more than half falling before 1950 – will not only graphically demonstrate that longevity, but also a most curious phenomenon. Alone among the white wines of the world, they become sweeter (rather than drier) with age. The explanation is that their acidity in youth is so high that it completely masks what can be a formidable amount of sugar, which time slowly reveals. A supplementary explanation emerged in a lengthy correspondence with Monsieur Jacques Cartier – then owner and manager of Marc Brédif – which brought forth charming analogies to the difference between eiderdown, swansdown and feather-down pillows, before hinting at the unromantic explanation that changing tastes resulted in the wines being made progressively drier over the years in question.

The making of Chenin Blanc in the great cellars of the Loire Valley is exceedingly simple: crush, press, partially clarify the juice, ferment in an assortment of stainless steel, fibreglass and ancient wooden vessels with no more than a chilly autumn for temperature control, a limited degree of lees-contact, and unhurried (but not particularly early) bottling. No oak, no artifice, no sophistication. The magic lies in *terroir*, climate, *pourriture noble* (for the sweet versions) and, perhaps above all else, time in bottle.

The result is a wine which emerges like a butterfly from its chrysalis. It is hard, slightly chalky and obviously acidic when young; with time it achieves a honeyed complexity with all manner of flowers and fruits hovering in the background. No other region where Chenin is planted is as marginal, on such a high latitude, as the Loire (where the harvest is often the latest in France). And once again it seems as though New Zealand is the likeliest candidate to reproduce a singularly French phenomenon. It is always difficult to know where to place such wines in a food context (particularly when they fall in the *demi-sec* to *moelleux* range) but for many the solution is the terrace, the apéritif role.

Muscadet

The role of Muscadet (alias Melon de Bourgogne) is altogether easier to define. It should be served as cold as possible with fresh oysters. If it is a good Muscadet the aroma will be similar; if it is not so good, just leave the oyster shells in the sun for a few hours. From a winemaking viewpoint (if not all viewpoints), the chief interest of Muscadet lies in the fact that it popularized lees contact: the best Muscadets are invariably bottled straight from unracked barrels, or '*sur lie*'. Lees are principally composed of the dead yeast cells which have multiplied in their millions during fermentation, and which settle as a creamy mud at the bottom of the fermentation vat once the process is over. The lees are a potent natural anti-oxidant, and there is no question that they have a real role in keeping the wine fresh and crisp (and equally no question that they can contribute to some of the smelly off-odours in some of the more forgettable Muscadets).

Muscadet takes the process of lees contact further than in the making of any other wine except champagne (where the use is different but essential, nonetheless). It is of great importance, too, in the fashioning of great Chardonnay, but only for Muscadet do the winemakers dare bottle the wine, unracked and unfiltered, direct from its lees. Muscadet therefore begins its maturation in a reductive environment, undisturbed by dissolved carbon dioxide, and its slight *pétillance* stems directly from this. (In the New World such *pétillance* may come from zealous protection with gaseous carbon dioxide designed to prevent any possibility of oxidation, and – in many cases – deliberately to provide a touch of spritz on the tip of the tongue.)

By no means does this end the list of white grapes whose winemaking is, or should be, a simple and rapid, if not hurried affair; where the essence of the matter is to preserve the fruit from oxidation, ferment clean juice, stabilize it if need be and bottle it early.

The same rules apply to some extremely aromatic grapes and some almost scentless ones. The most aromatic are Germany's *vinifera* crosses such as Sieggerebe, Scheurebe, and all the younger -rebes that threaten the integrity of German wine. England's vineyards may well benefit from the work of German vine-breeders: Germany's definitely do not.

The list of more or less neutral varieties is endless: the best that can be hoped of most of them is enough sugar and extract to make them taste and feel vinous, and enough acidity to give them the power to refresh. The archetype of such grapes is the grossly over-planted Trebbiano of central Italy (which answers the Italian demand for a cold drink with some strength but no flavour to wash down seafood). Just how fine a 'neutral' wine can be is, however, illustrated by the best Swiss Chasselas (or Fendant), which offer texture and a most delicate hint of fruit.

On the fringes are such varieties as the Marsanne and Roussanne of the Rhône Valley; the Marsanne fat and weighty, the Roussanne more fragile but an excellent lively leavener of a blend. The two together, under the ideal conditions of the hill of Hermitage, can make a monument of a wine that slowly deepens in flavour over decades while remaining almost unbelievably fresh. Though barrel-flavour does not usually enter into its composition, in truth this is the sort of full-bodied, multifaceted wine that is closer to the subject-matter of the next chapter.

Vinifera crosses

German vines for English vineyards

Wooded and Full-Bodied White Wines

Choices, consequences and techniques

Sauvignon Blanc

Sauvignon Blanc is a grape open to even more differing interpretations than most. At one end of its spectrum it makes featherweight aromatic wines, rather like those that are particularly sharp and grassy from Germany. Lesser Loire Valley versions such as Sauvignon de Touraine are like this in moderate vintages. At the other end, ripened to almost tropical fruitiness and aged in oak, Sauvignon Blanc can play the role of the poor man's Chardonnay. Some would not even regard it as a quality grape, let alone as a classic variety. Viticulturally, it is much more temperamental than Chardonnay, tending to produce tiny crops one year, excessive crops the next. In the winery winemakers can find themselves between the devil of excessive, rank, herbal varietal character and the deep blue sea of bland, oily mediocrity.

Where the Pouilly is Fumé

Few would disagree that Sauvignon Blanc finds its greatest expression between the towns of Pouilly sur Loire and Sancerre at the eastern end of the lower Loire Valley. Here ground-hugging vines planted at very high densities produce wine almost painfully crammed with flavour and intensity (to some it is indeed exceedingly distasteful). The magic occurs entirely in the vineyard, the benefits of *terroir* culminating in fine, chalky soils.

Sauvignon Blanc's singular flavour is at its most powerful in Sancerre. The vineyards rise on all sides of the village of Chavignol, one of the most sought-after in the region.

Winemaking methods and equipment vary from extremely primitive to adequate: hard pressing of the grapes, rough juice settling, minimal temperature control of fermentation, minimal post-fermentation handling, and bottling when it suits the work pattern in the vineyard are the order of the day. Rarely would you find a single stick of oak – until recently, that is, for the new-oak disease is a highly

contagious one and the scene is now changing. But with exceptions – the large firm of de Ladoucette and a few cooperatives – most of the producers are small, and the money for expensive items like new barrels, or more sensitive equipment such as membrane presses, is simply not there.

In its contribution to the great sweet wines of Bordeaux (which we visit in due course) the role – and stature – of Sauvignon Blanc is undoubted. Its support role to Sémillon in producing the dry white wines of Bordeaux has been rather less distinguished – not through any fault of either Sémillon or Sauvignon Blanc, but simply through what could often only be described as diabolically bad wine-making. These were white wines made (apparently reluctantly) by red winemakers using red winemaking equipment and techniques to produce what everyone knew was second-class wine.

The most immediate and catastrophic consequences of such perfunctory winemaking were averted by massive doses of sulphur dioxide. Young white Graves used to reek of nothing but sulphur (and perhaps a little cabbage) for the first ten years of their life; thereafter the poor or mediocre vintages would simply rot away. Happily, the great vintages can slowly throw off the chains which bound them for so long and at 30, 40 or 50 years of age become fine wines. There was one winemaker, though, Claude Ricard of Domaine de Chevalier, who went to great pains, clarifying the juice before fermenting it by laborious barrel-racking. His wines were (and still are) splendid. But he was alone.

Strange as it sounds, it was an Australian initiative that changed this gloomy picture. In 1978 Len Evans from the Hunter Valley headed the team which bought Château Rahoul, an unknown property in the village of Portets in the Graves region. Their first vintage, 1979, was made by Brian Croser of Petaluma (South Australia) assisted by a Dane, Peter Vinding-Diers.

Croser applied his New World technology, cleaning the juice by cold-stabilization, chilling it at 0°C until all solids were precipitated, and then fermenting at a moderate temperature. He also used indigenous yeasts, rather than a 'safe' cultured strain, which imparted what Vinding-Diers calls 'the signature of the farm'. (Vinding-Diers has since carried out remarkable experiments with yeast-strains.) The immediate result was a cleaner, fruitier and altogether more attractive young wine than any Graves property had ever made.

In 1980 Denis Dubourdieu of the Barsac château Doisy-Daëne followed suit, soon joined by the *négociant* Pierre Coste of Langon, in this new wave in wine-making. Bordeaux's dry white wines had been given new life from the Antipodes. The 1980s saw 'flying winemakers' bringing Australian technology to more and more areas of southern France to make young wines which tasted frankly of fruit.

Gone now is the sulphur dioxide; in its place is selective use of skin contact; the cold-fermentation of relatively clear juice, and the judicious use of new oak, together with lees contact and many of the New World Chardonnay techniques. Wines of great fragrance, suppleness and intensity are the result; wines which produce a very credible alternative to those of the Loire Valley, particularly for those who prefer complexity to instant stimulation.

California instinctively emulates the white Bordeaux style. It shies away from the aggressive, almost 'wild', Sancerre flavours. Nowhere is the American diffidence about full-frontal fruit flavour more apparent than with Sauvignon Blanc. A society that drinks swimming pools of Coca-Cola every hour, that indiscriminately throws fruit, waffles and maple syrup on the breakfast bacon and eggs, studiously avoids salt and substitutes sugar, takes all the flavour out of coffee, and that invented the Waldorf Salad, is inherently unlikely to enjoy the tart, herbal, gooseberry flavour of untamed Sauvignon Blanc. Robert Mondavi had the answer when he coined the label 'Blanc Fumé' for a slightly oak-aged version that avoids all extremes. It has been widely and industriously imitated.

White Bordeaux

'Flying winemakers'

California's 'Blanc Fumé'

New Zealand   New Zealand, in contrast, emulates the Loire and – most would say – takes its flavours to another dimension. Sauvignon Blanc is given free reign in a manner identical to the Australian approach with Chardonnay. The Marlborough district of the South Island is one of the few clear-cut examples in the New World of a region with a homogeneous *terroir* and climate, which are ideally suited to a particular variety – Sauvignon Blanc – and which could satisfy in all respects the French Appellation Controlée system. Other parts of New Zealand produce Sauvignon Blanc of quality, but none of it with the consistency or the panache of that of Marlborough.

Like California, New Zealand's winemaking techniques cover the full gamut from simple vat-fermentation through to cool-room barrel fermentation. The differences lie in the vineyard, in the growing techniques, and in the climate. On an issue such as this, there is no right or wrong: the Californians make one style, the New Zealanders another. On the evidence to date, the world at large strongly prefers the New Zealand version.

Other varieties

Sémillon   Sémillon, Pinot Blanc and Viognier complete the transition to the market-leader among full-bodied white wine varieties. Only in Australia does Sémillon make a great dry white wine on its own; traditionally in an unoaked form but increasingly treated as if it were just another clone of Chardonnay. Its epicentre was and is the Hunter Valley, whence 20-year-old Sémillon without any exposure to oak whatsoever assumes a honeyed, nutty, toasty richness which suggests total barrel fermentation in 100 percent new French oak of the highest quality. The problem is that it takes this many years; a luxury not permitted in today's market (although one producer – McWilliams in the Hunter Valley – is gallantly, and largely successfully, swimming against the tide). So most producers are bowing to the inevitable, either using oak or abandoning Sémillon in favour of Chardonnay.

Viognier   Viognier is a wonderful eccentric, producing wines in the northern Rhône which taste as if a truck-load of children's gum sweets had been emptied into the fermentation vat. Here and there across America and Australia a few brave souls are seeing whether they can work something of the same magic with this, a notoriously awkward grape to grow, using a variety of winemaking techniques ranging from the deliberately rustic (Rhône) approach to ultra-sophisticated barrel-fermentation. While the novelty remains the wines are assured of a ready market; their long-term future beyond Condrieu and Château Grillet remains to be seen.

Pinot Blanc   Pinot Blanc has long been taken for a first cousin of Chardonnay, and in parts of the Côte d'Or treated as such. Monsieur Ponsot, the Mayor of Morey St-Denis, makes a Pinot Blanc of enormous power and strength, using precisely the same methods as he would if it were Chardonnay. Perhaps the flavour is slightly less fruity and lingering, but it would take an ace taster to spot it. Odd vines and patches of Pinot Blanc persist in many old Chardonnay vineyards. And yet it is no relation. Pinot Blanc is a white mutation of Pinot Noir, thus a cousin (or sister) of Pinot Gris. Chardonnay comes from another 'bloodline' altogether.

The great majority of the world's Pinot Blanc wines come from Alsace and (as Pinot Bianco) from northern Italy. Neither region treats it in the Chardonnay manner; instead it is used as a rather high-yielding, gently fruity but generally rather neutral grape for quick-drinking wine. That of Alsace is attractively soft (without the steeliness typical of the region), while most Pinot Bianco is just Bianco. Picked early with high acidity it provides the base for many Italian sparkling wines. But mention should be made of some growers in the northeast, particularly in Collio, who do make the most of its character.

In Germany Pinot Blanc, known as Weissburgunder, has been used (in such warmer regions as Baden) mainly to make a softer and less aromatic alternative to Riesling, or to blend with over-aromatic hybrids. Recently more free-thinking

German winemakers have given it a brief spell in 'barrique' (the French term is modish) to produce something very distinctly alternative and almost shockingly un-Germanic; an excellent table wine nonetheless.

One hears little of Pinot Blanc in the New World. Chalone Vineyards in California makes the most upper-crust example, treating it like Chardonnay. As yet Australia does not grow it. New Zealand has a little, and wishes for more.

Chardonnay

And so we come to the grape which has forged such a close bond with oak that it is no exaggeration to say that a substantial percentage of regular wine drinkers have little idea where the flavour of Chardonnay stops and that of oak starts. The more skilled the winemaker and the better the wine, the more difficult it will be to make the distinction. It has to be said that the winemaker has an unfair advantage with the extraordinary range of options available in handling this most flexible (and forgiving) of varieties; the selection of which will fundamentally affect the ultimate style of the wine (and the apparent role of the oak).

White burgundy

Anyone who has shared a bottle of one of the very best white burgundies (1978 Le Montrachet of the Domaine de la Romanée-Conti comes to mind) has tasted such perfection that it brings a touch of sadness: a feeling that one will never taste a greater white wine. (A feeling which a privileged few have periodically experienced ever since Claude Arnoux wrote his panegyric for Montrachet in the early 1700s, so the sadness is quite illogical.) Complexity is the keynote of white burgundy; complexity deriving from a series of fortuitous and planned inputs, which may be totally convincing and satisfying, or flawed and unsound – but it will be burgundy.

Viewed in contrast with the convolutions and sophistications of New World winemakers, the traditional Burgundian approach to Chardonnay was simple, if not downright rustic. There was a conviction that they (the winemakers) were correct in everything they did; a Gallic confidence born of centuries of experience, and an indifference to what others may be doing, because those outsiders did not share their *terroir*. We use the past tense, for the younger generation of Burgundians – encouraged by such patrician figures as Vincent Leflaive – are now travelling, working and comparing notes in California, Australia and elsewhere.

The result is that the face of white burgundy is changing. Just as in Chablis (*see* page 76), care and attention to detail are making the traditional recourse to heavy doses of sulphur dioxide unnecessary and, importantly, unfashionable. The wines are becoming cleaner, softer, more forward and – some would say – more anonymous. The majority would say they are also distinctly better wines, and that bottle-age will allow their *terroir* and true quality (or lack of it) to be expressed.

Chardonnay grapes arriving at the Robert Mondavi Winery in the Napa Valley. After being tipped from the 'gondola' in which they are transported, an Archimedean screw moves the grapes into the winery.

A greater threat to clear-cut vineyard identity comes from increasing yields. Astute judges have for long pondered about the extraordinary concentration and flavour of Le Montrachet: specifically, how much of this derives from *terroir*, and how much from the lower-than-usual yields? But all things are relative. First, Chardonnay suffers far less from the effects of increased yield than does Pinot Noir (as indeed does any white grape compared to any red). Secondly, the Burgundians have certainly been blessed with a superb combination of *terroir*, climate and (by and large) clonal selection. The overall quality of the raw material – the grapes – is better than that of any other region in the world.

The winemaker using Chardonnay grapes can be likened to a sculptor: he starts with a mass of raw, moist clay. The greater the mass, the more profligate can be the sculptor in shaping his work: great chunks may be carved away without undue concern, for there will always be enough left to allow the last shaping and chiselling as the work takes its final form. It is something which many New World winemakers should realize, but do not. Blissfully unaware, it seems, that their mass of clay is very much smaller, they use Burgundian methods and thereby threaten (and sometimes altogether destroy) the integrity of their raw material.

Chardonnay

This chart illustrates those stages in making wine with Chardonnay in which the options chosen by the winemaker will fundamentally influence the taste and individuality of the final wine. Not every stage of the process is indicated: for that the reader is directed to the white-wine process chart on pages 88–89.

Chardonnay's varietal character is expressed in many forms: as the steely acidic wine of Chablis; as a fuller-bodied more buttery wine in southern Burgundy (gaining warm fruit characteristics in New World regions); and as a base wine for champagne, to name a few.

Geographical variation in style is influenced by vinification techniques, but of key consideration everywhere is the emphasis placed on either simple primary fruit structure or on secondary fruit characteristics, that develop as the wine matures. Balance of the two is very important. Using wood for fermentation or maturation, and malolactic fermentation, are also key influences on style, as is 'tradition': should Chardonnay be vinified to emulate a classic burgundy or should varietal character be expressed according to the region?

1
HARVESTING

Method of picking
(a) *Picking by hand*
Definitely preferable if the grapes are not going to be crushed before pressing. Only economically viable in smaller-scale vineyards such as in Burgundy.
(b) *Picking by machine*
Almost a necessity in the grand-scale New World vineyards. Enables night harvesting when it is cool – a great advantage in hot regions.

2
CRUSHING AND PRESSING

Juice and must handling
(a) *Protective handling*
Adding a small dose of sulphur dioxide to the crushed grapes and cooling the juice protects it from oxidation and results in more colour and primary grape flavour.
(b) *Unprotected handling*
Oxidation can be deliberate, to produce more complex, fuller wines. These age more slowly, but loss of primary fruit flavour must be accepted. This option eases the onset of malolactic fermentation. Cooling optional.

Above: *Loved by growers and winemakers alike, Chardonnay is one of the most popular grape varieties – here growing for champagne production in the Côte de Blancs.*

Right: *Chardonnay grapes destined for Robert Mondavi's winery in the Napa Valley, California. Chardonnays from this region are said to rival even top-quality white burgundies.*

Far left: *Contoured vineyards in Napa Valley, California's most concentrated and prestigious wine county, now home to all the best grape varieties.*

Left: *Chardonnay grapes from the Santa Maria valley region are trucked to the Tepusquet crushing plant in Santa Barbara, California's southern central coast county.*

Crushing
The decision whether to crush or not depends on pressing decisions (*see* pressing).

Skin contact
Will only follow protective handling. Increases phenol extraction from grape skins leading to a more robust Chardonnay with fuller flavour. Extended contact (up to 30 hours) deepens colour prematurely and flavours may break up and become oily.

Pressing
(a) *Whole bunch*
Whole bunch pressing is traditionally used for sparkling wine, increasingly used for table wine. Leads to juice with lowest possible phenol levels, very clear juice and very finely flavoured and structured wine results.

(b) *Crushed fruit*
A better option if full-flavoured table wine is required or if grapes are relatively low in flavouring phenols in the first place.

Juice clarification
(a) *Nil*
(b) *Partial*
(c) *Total*
Normally nil or partial in Old World. If followed by cool fermentation should lead to a richer wine. This option followed by ambient fermentation is only possible with a huge amount of flavour in the grapes or where a neutral wine is desired. Normally total in New World, followed by cool fermentation. Clarification can be achieved by holding in a settling tank, filtering or centrifuging.

3
FERMENTING

Choice of fermentation vat
New oak can dramatically influence quality and taste. Usually limited to great wines because of the difficulty of sterilizing oak vats and keeping them watertight. Stainless steel is usually preferred because of the ease of cleaning and cooling.

Fermentation temperature
In the eyes of New World makers, the single most critical factor in determining style. Modern practice is to ferment Chardonnay very cool – at about 15°C – to produce fruitier wine. Uncontrolled fermentation in a hot climate can rise above 30°C. Classic burgundies are fermented in small barrels that maintain the cool temperature of the cellar.

Malolactic fermentation
Significantly softens and adds to the complexity of Chardonnay. It will be encouraged in cool-climate wines that might have excess acidity. Generally avoided in warmer regions where acidity tends to be low.

4
MATURING

Maturing in oak
Thanks to Robert Mondavi the importance of oak selection is now widely understood. The options are between type of oak, new or old, and the degree of toast. Maturation in oak gives a radically different effect from fermentation in oak.

Lees contact
Originally a French technique but now being widely used. Lees is a powerful anti-oxidant and adds a creamy complexity to the wine. Some prefer it to skin contact though care must be taken to ensure lees remains sweet. *Battonage* (stirring) will accentuate the effects.

Maturation time before bottling
Ranges from 3 months to 2 years – the former if no oak is used or if wine is oak-fermented and a delicate wine is required. Temperature and humidity of barrel storage room are critical factors.

Picking and crushing

The initial handling by the Burgundian is gentle and sensitive; while mechanical harvesting is on the increase, it has not yet reached – and may never reach – the great estates. The highly fragmented pattern of vineyard ownership in Burgundy, the relatively ready availability of labour, the sheer conservatism of the average Burgundian, and the need to selectively discard mouldy grapes in poorer years, all tell in favour of hand-harvesting and against the use of machines. The very small distances between vineyards and cellar, and the generally low ambient temperatures of autumn also help the grapes reach the winery in prime condition.

New 'high-tech' crushers such as the Demoisy – developed in Burgundy – give the winemaker many choices enabling great control over the must. While whole-bunch pressing, retaining the stalks (the grapes in this instance bypass the crusher and are taken direct to the press), is very rare in Burgundy, so, happily, is skin contact: usually the must is taken direct from the crusher to the press, and then pressed without delay.

Sulphur dioxide may be added at the crusher, at the press or as the juice is passed into the vat for settling, although the later the addition, the more the juice will have oxidized. Only a few winemakers are experimenting with wholly oxidative (unprotected) juice handling, a technique we look at in detail later in this chapter.

Barrel-fermentation

The must is allowed to settle overnight, during which time most of the heavy solids (chiefly minute pieces of grape pulp) will fall to the bottom of the vat. The standard procedure is then to rack the still-cloudy juice into the barrels, and wait. If the weather is particularly cool, the juice may have to be warmed: ideally it should be at around 15°C for fermentation to start. Although most Burgundian winemakers prefer to rely on wild yeasts, they may resort to cultured yeast if there are problems with the fermentation getting started. Once it does, it creates its own heat, and there is no further need to warm the cellar – indeed the reverse. White wine fermenting in barrel will readily reach 22 to 25°C of its own accord; anything higher or lower than this will be due to the ambient temperature. While the typical Burgundian cellar may naturally be very cold, if it is filled with fermenting *barriques* of wine, that ambient temperature will rise considerably, and wine temperature likewise. Refrigerated cool rooms are unheard of in Burgundy, so if winemakers want to reduce the fermentation temperature they must pump the wine out of the barrel and pass it through a heat exchanger – or possibly empty a number of barrels into a temperature-controlled stainless steel vat.

Wild yeasts

Barrel-fermentation of partially clarified juice at moderately high temperatures leads to a suppression of primary fruit aroma and flavour in the wine, although these will recover to an extent over a period of time, both before and after bottling. The texture and structure will be complex, although once again it will initially be hard and rough. For the system to work well two preconditions must be satisfied: there must be a tremendous depth and intensity to the flavour of the grapes, and the wine must be given time in bottle (a minimum of three years, sometimes much longer) for the component parts to marry, soften and evolve.

Wine made in this way from this type of raw material has the capacity to swallow the aroma and flavour of new oak. It is exceedingly rare to find a white burgundy with the type of overt oak influence regularly encountered in the New World (or in the new-wave Italian Chardonnays). One is tempted to instance Louis Latour's invariably outstanding Corton Charlemagne as an exception, but it is highly likely that a significant portion of its toasty, nutty aroma and flavour comes from the wine rather than the oak.

Lees contact is widely practised in Burgundy; indeed the lees are so highly prized that those from a great wine (such as Montrachet or Bâtard Montrachet) may be transferred to a lesser wine to enrich or ennoble it (only, of course, once they have done their work with the parent). Regular stirring of the lees – known as *battonage* – is practised weekly in the first few months, less regularly thereafter. With luck, a naturally occurring malolactic fermentation will then start shortly after the primary fermentation; with a great deal of luck it will finish before the onset of winter takes the temperature of the wine down to levels (5–15°C) at which the malolactic bacteria cease their activity. In this last event they appear to go into hibernation, and will spontaneously resume their activity the following spring as cellar temperatures rise once again. It was this observation without any understanding of its chemical and biochemical origins that caused winemakers well into this century to claim that the wine in the cellar stirred and came to life in response to the sap rising and buds bursting in the vineyard.

Lees contact

Burgundians do not like filtration, and practise it sparingly. It is perhaps less of an issue with Chardonnay than Pinot Noir, since the alleged colour and flavour loss due to filtration is less apparent, and the risk of bacterial activity in the bottled – and unfiltered – wine is also substantially lower.

Filtration

The traditional white burgundy was an extremely powerful, complex and long-lived wine. The relatively high levels of free sulphur dioxide early in its life gradually diminished and became bound, actually contributing to its complexity. The lush fruit, tamed by the winemaking methods, needed years to reassert itself. For the New World winemaker, smelling these wines could be an unnerving experience, with all sorts of sulphide, malolactic and botrytis influences at work. The modern style of white burgundy is much cleaner: the juice has been clarified to a greater degree, sulphur levels reduced, fermentation temperatures lowered and

White burgundy then and now

(particularly with the malolactic fermentation) cultured micro-organisms used. The time in oak, too, may have been shortened; and, although it is hard to draw any particular conclusion from this, the winemaker following this path will quite probably filter the wine.

New World Chardonnay: California

If Burgundians are finding new excitement and possibilities in the winery, their New World counterparts are finding many (though not all) of them in the vineyard. Two of California's top winemakers are at the fore of a new approach to, and respect for, *terroir*. Tim Mondavi, of the Mondavi Winery in Napa Valley:

> '*Philosophically I think it's extremely important to recognize that we are beginning to understand we are raising a natural beverage from the soil and the climate we have; we are interacting with these, and pursuing the soil just as the Burgundians are pursuing the textbooks. The polar opposites of* terroir *and technology are coming together.*'

Zelma Long, winemaker at Simi Winery in Napa Valley, echoes this thinking:

> '*If you choose to do so, winemaking technique can entirely screen out the influence of* terroir; *and California has historically engaged in the cult of the winemaker, so much so that it is still very hard for the winemaker to get himself out into the vineyard and truly start making the wine there. There is no question that is the trend, but I still see the idea having really taken hold with only five percent to ten percent of the winemakers. Yet there are enormous quality and style competitive advantages for those people who get out there: that's where the excitement of California in 1990 really is.*'

Right: California's pioneering winemakers have been experimenting with Burgundian methods since the 1960s. They include barrel fermentation and consequently higher fermentation temperatures. The barrels in the foreground hold fermenting wine.

Below: *The mission-inspired Robert Mondavi Winery.*

The Californian approach to Chardonnay has undergone several profound changes since the variety became popular in the 1960s. The style of the early wines was massively alcoholic and strong, but monolithic in flavour and structure, with the characteristic hot, sweet, burn of any high-alcohol white wine.

By the mid-1950s, though, a few producers were asking searching questions – and sometimes stumbling on the answers. Fred McCrea at Stony Hill began as early as 1951 taking infinite pains to make balanced Chardonnay. In 1956 Brad Webb, winemaker at Hanzell Vineyards in Sonoma, introduced French barrels for ageing for the first time. His assistant Bill Bonetti, now making top-line Chardonnays at Sonoma-Cutrer, recalls *'our surprise when a barrel of Chardonnay must was left unattended, I confess by mistake, and fermented in the barrel and turned out the best lot of all'*. Hanzell was the moment of discovery: the mysterious essence of burgundy lay in marrying Chardonnay with new oak. But it took years to find out exactly how much – and we are still learning.

A revelation: oak

In most wineries the emphasis was on new oak, the winemakers arguing that such a strong and forceful fruit base as theirs could support a high level of oak – and indeed needed it to provide complexity. The result was a massive assault on the senses: such wine was an exhilarating experience for the wine lover who had not encountered it before. The difficulty lay in drinking a whole glass: the flavour built up and up. No-one could actually drink the wine; least of all with food.

The standard approach in making these wines had been to use no skin contact; to carry out temperature-controlled fermentation in stainless steel vats, followed by sterile filtration. Brilliantly clean wines were then taken to barrel, with no possibility of either lees contact or malolactic fermentation, and were bottled six to 15 months later. The result was wines as far removed from those of Burgundy as one could possibly fashion.

By the second half of the 1970s the winds of change had started to blow, and they intensified in the 1980s. Winery practices changed first: barrel fermentation of cloudy juice, total lees contact, partial or total malolactic fermentations (increasingly the latter) and higher fermentation temperatures – indeed the full gamut of Burgundian practices, with only the high sulphur levels absent (and in fact reduced to an absolute minimum). In more recent times, some Californian winemakers have gone even one step further with the deliberate use of juice oxidation.

Change in the wind

Much of the pioneering work was done at Simi Winery in 1981, and since that time all Simi Chardonnays have been made using juice oxidation. Specifically, the use of sulphur dioxide (and to a lesser degree ascorbic acid), usually added to the juice before and during fermentation, has been stopped and is only used once the malolactic fermentation is complete. Parallel with this approach, the use of protective inert gases (carbon dioxide and nitrogen) has also been abandoned until the fermentation is finished. After this point one or other of these gases are always used to protect the wine while it is moved around the winery.

Juice oxidation

The resulting wine has a lower content of flavouring phenols, lighter and fresher colour taking longer to deepen, lower sulphur dioxide levels, and ages more slowly. The question remains, of course, whether reduced phenols (and hence modified and reduced fruit flavours) are a desirable aim. As Zelma Long herself readily concedes, they may not be desirable for all wines (particularly where the starting levels of phenols are in any event low) and may not be philosophically desirable for winemakers who place special value on primary Chardonnay fruit flavour.

Racking Chardonnay at Heitz Wine Cellars in the Napa Valley.

Lower phenol levels are also the consequence of another trend – the pressing of whole bunches, stalks and all. This technique, borrowed from sparkling winemaking, works well with high-flavoured grapes, less well where flavour is naturally delicate. Once again, it developed in California, but has since been taken up by Australia.

Growing wine in the   As the 1980s got underway a few of the more perspicacious winemakers started
vineyard   thinking about their vineyards, adopting the catch-cry 'growing wine', an upbeat
version of the old aphorism that 'great wine is made in the vineyard'. By the end of
the decade, it was clear that progress had been slow in the Napa Valley –
'California Sprawl' (*see* page 49) was still evident everywhere: large undisciplined
vines surrounded by masses of dark green leaves, cascading to the ground from the
relatively low, single-wire trellises. But in Oregon, as in Sonoma and Carneros, far
more sophisticated viticulture was already the norm, and it is only a question of
time before the main body of the Napa Valley follows the direction indicated by
Tim Mondavi and Zelma Long.

The aim of the new viticulture is simple: to grow a vine which is in balance,
producing a modest crop of grapes which have been adequately exposed to the
sunlight, and which reach full flavour ('organoleptic ripeness' – to use the jargon)
at 12.5 to 13 degrees Baumé. The aim of the new winemaking is to produce wines
with elegance, complexity, subtlety and – above all else – good 'mouthfeel' (the last
a predictable reaction to the sledgehammer wines of the 1970s). 'Harmonization',
according to Tim Mondavi, is the key:

> '*We as a winery were once appropriately criticized for having too much
> oak in a number of our wines. All that has changed, with far less use
> of new oak and much more use of two-, three- and four-year-old oak.
> And it is not just the amount of oak, but the way the oak is used which
> has changed incredibly and led to much more subtle integration.
> Diminished sulphur and lees stirring have also helped produce a
> brighter coloured wine, more fragrant, with more honey in the aroma as
> well as suppleness in the mouth.*'

As Zelma Long puts it:

> '*Winemakers still want power, but they are more interested in finesse
> and balance; they still want aromatics, but they are more interested in
> how the wine feels in the mouth; they are looking for wines that are
> more multi-dimensional, in which wood and fruit are integrated.*'

> '*Most California Chardonnays are distinguished by tropical fruit
> flavours – pineapple, banana – and some apple. I am trying to look for
> something beyond that, to get away from what is not only simple fruit
> but what is always the same kind of fruit. I am trying to find the other
> nuances of Chardonnay flavour – more of the stony/gravelly flavours –
> to bring another dimension, while still looking for concentration of
> flavour, and of course complexity.*'

Chardonnay in Australia   These issues come into even stronger relief when the typical California
Chardonnay is compared to the typical Australian version. Here there is an
unrestrained focus on simple, primary fruit flavour, on softness, on accessibility –
on simple pleasure, on wines which appeal to the heart (and the stomach) rather
than to the mind. Australia may be said to be where California was 20 years ago,
which, looking at the pattern and rate of introduction of Chardonnay and the other
classic varieties, is a not unrealistic view. There is, however, one critical difference:
the Australian wines do not have that hard, alcoholic burn, and the fruit flavour –
while soft – does have intensity and reasonable length.

Taste in flux   Quite apart from the intrinsic qualities of the various Chardonnay styles,
common sense would suggest that Australian wine will become more similar to
that of California (and hopefully that California Chardonnay will revert in style
towards that of Australia). In fact, there are signs of movement in Australia.
Thanks to such viticulturalists as Dr Richard Smart, to a number of strongly

California has few vineyards more ideally sited or better-maintained than the Joseph Phelps estate in wooded foothills on the east side of the Napa Valley at St Helena.

motivated growers and to a small band of highly experienced consultants, Australian viticulture is in the vanguard, even if it is obsessed with economics. In the winery, the more intelligent and skilful winemakers are making moves to pull back on fruit and introduce more complexity. Skin contact times are being reduced or eliminated; oxidative juice handling is being selectively used, as is whole bunch pressing; barrel-fermentation is employed wherever economics permit; cloudy-juice fermentation followed by some malolactic fermentation is giving greater complexity; and oak flavour is being more subtly incorporated. The pendulum seems to be not so much swinging as going round in circles.

Two styles are emerging: there are the super-rich, relatively high alcohol (12.5–13°), warm-climate wines made with some skin contact, lots of oak and tasting of honeyed, peachy fruit. Variously likened to peaches and cream or Dolly Parton; they bloom lusciously but briefly, passing their best within two to three years. This is the Chardonnay style which has captured most attention overseas and – surprisingly – in the United States in particular. The other style is far less obvious: usually cool-grown, with highly disciplined and selective winemaker input (little or no skin contact, careful pressing, and so forth). The wine takes three years to begin showing its potential, and evolves fully over a much longer period of time.

Chardonnay is grown almost everywhere *Vitis vinifera* will grow and ripen. To discuss all of its styles is not practicable in anything other than an entire book on Chardonnay (of which there are a number). Suffice to say its current popularity will not be a seven-day wonder: it is a superb grape capable of producing superb wine in an almost infinite number of guises; and to hope that the combined influences of *terroir* and healthy parochialism will defeat the dark forces of universalization.

'Dolly Partons'

Sparkling Wines

Choices, consequences and techniques

Champagne

Its history

Of the great wines of France, champagne is the newest arrival. Champagne as a district has been making wine since early Roman times, and by the 9th century it had become sufficiently well established as a high-quality region for a distinction to be drawn between the wines of the Vallée de la Marne and those of the Montagne de Reims. From this time on it went from strength to strength: by the early 16th century the wine of Aÿ had become so highly prized that it was said to be '*the ordinary drink of kings and princes*'.

It was not until the 17th century, however, that the first sparkling wines made their appearance, and not until the early 19th century that champagne came to be synonymous with sparkling wine. Nor were the numerous special techniques essential for making champagne all discovered by one person (notwithstanding the extraordinary feats popularly attributed to Dom Pérignon) nor at any one time. The evolution of the present-day method of making clear sparkling wine using the second fermentation took over 200 years.

Its image

From the outset, champagne has been blessed with a superabundance of extraordinarily talented and energetic marketers. Small wonder that so many books have been written about the subject, so rich is its anecdotal history. Those marketing and promotion skills remain undimmed to this day, making truly objective assessment or criticism of champagne extremely difficult. On the one hand there is the knowledge that if one does a blind tasting of champagne under neutral 'scientific' conditions, comparing 20 or 30 champagnes, what appear to be some quite unpleasant aromas and flavours will be detected in a few of the wines, while others free from fault will nonetheless fall well short of the top-ranked wines. Yet on the other hand, ask a wine judge when he or she last found fault with a glass of champagne proffered in ordinary social surroundings and the answer is very likely to be 'hardly ever'.

Made to be drunk

Part of this stems from the fact that champagne is made to be drunk. Now that may seem a banal statement of the obvious, but not so much so when you realize a dedicated wine-drinker might savour the bouquet of a great burgundy for ten minutes before taking a first sip and if sharing the bottle with a number of others might take 30 minutes to consume a single glass. Champagne, even extremely rare and old champagne, will seldom be treated like this. It will be uncommon for its bouquet to be given more than cursory acknowledgment, while to swill it ruminatively around one's gums is to turn one's mouth into a mini washing machine. Champagne is a wine which appeals to the broadest senses, rather than to the particular: it is the overall impression it leaves in the mouth after it is swallowed which matters most.

Its style

It is true that the greatest champagnes are wines of extraordinary finesse, balance and above all else length of flavour; the intrinsic quality of these wines is on a par with the greatest of the still white or red table wines. And just as the Burgundians place special emphasis on the bouquet, the Bordelais on the palate and structure, so the Champenois claim the finish and in particular the aftertaste as the special feature of their wine.

Not that all champagnes taste the same: there is a world of difference between a Pol Roger and a Krug, a Taittinger and a Bollinger, let alone between a vintage

champagne of one of the *grandes marques* and a non-vintage 'buyers own-brand' from one of the cooperatives. Yet the overall consistency of the quality and style of non-vintage champagne from the *grandes marques* exceeds that of any other category of wine in any other region; an astonishing achievement, given the marginal climate in which the Champenois grow their grapes, and the fluctuations in supply and demand which they so skilfully manage from both marketing and making viewpoints.

Assemblage (blending) is the most critical stage of the long and convoluted process which makes the finished champagne. It is the art that made Dom Pérignon the most famous oenologist of his day; indeed perhaps the first famous winemaker in history.

Blending involves a detailed knowledge of the past, present and future of the materials, and requires highly specialized tasting skills which can see beyond the often hard, acidic, thin and chalky base wines which give only a barest glimpse of how they will taste once they have been blended, undergone the second fermentation, benefited from contact with yeasts during years of maturation on lees, and been adjusted for sweetness using *liqueur d'expédition*. The task demands the mental skills of a chess grandmaster as the literally endless permutations and combinations are considered. The blenders at Moët & Chandon typically have 300 different base wines from any one vintage to deal with. The possible permutations are beyond calculation.

Champagne is France's northernmost vineyard region. Without the special properties of its chalk soil, free-draining and sun-reflecting, it would be a very doubtful area for ripening grapes.

Assemblage

Making Champagne

PRESSING

Making the finest champagne depends first on attaining the purest possible must. This is achieved by harvesting the crop by hand, gently pressing grape bunches whole and ensuring that the contact between juice and broken grape skins is minimal. Many champagne houses believe the traditional basket presses to be the gentlest method of pressing. The large surface area of the press and small fruit loads ensure that must does not drain over crushed grapes, absorbing tannins en route. Pneumatic or bladder presses are also commonly used. They are much faster.

The juice is released from the press in order of quality. The more the fruit is pressed the greater the tannin, pip and skin content. Better-quality wines are made from only the free-run and first pressings. Second pressings may be used, but for lesser wines.

Cooling

From the press the must is pumped to small vats, each containing only one press-load of juice so that the choice in the final blend can be as precise as possible. En route the must may be chilled to prevent any bacterial activity and to stop fermentation beginning before *débourbage* (clarification) can take place.

FIRST FERMENTATION

Débourbage

Skin and other impurities, especially yeast sediment, can be settled out of the wine at ambient cellar temperatures, but a quicker and more thorough clarification is achieved by chilling to −5°C. Purity, and therefore stability, can be increased by fining with bentonite clay. Many winemakers argue that if clarification at this stage is too thorough the complexity of flavours in the wine will be reduced.

Fermentation

Once clarified the wine is racked into clean fermentation vats. The size and composition of the vats are of key importance: small vats enable greater control of the fermentation and stainless steel ensures cleanliness. However, two of the best champagne houses, Krug and Alfred Gratien, still prefer to ferment their wines in oak barrels.

Other important considerations at this stage include choice of yeast, chaptalisation and malolactic fermentation. 'Cultured' yeasts will usually be used, their effects on the wine being more predictable. The use of 'wild' yeasts can be a gamble, though they may increase a wine's complexity. The wine's potential alcohol almost always needs raising and it is invariably chaptalised. Malolactic fermentation is encouraged as it softens and rounds the wine and adds to its stability.

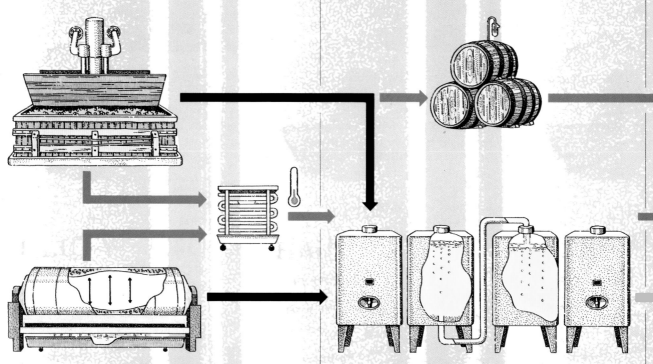

Dark arrows indicate critical stages; lighter arrows show optional ones.

ASSEMBLAGE

After fermentation the wine is once again stabilized before *assemblage* (blending): the most important stage of the *méthode champenoise* process.

Cold stabilization

Suspended matter is precipitated out of the wine by cold stabilization, preventing both the formation of tartrate crystals and any unwanted yeast or enzyme reactions which may impair the wine. It is then racked off the deposit and further clarified by filtering and fining.

Blending

Great skill and experience are required to create wine of a consistent and fine house style – non-Vintage champagne. Tasting after tasting will be set up, some wines of which will go in various proportions into the final blend. In years where the quality of the harvest is particularly high, a certain proportion will be used to make Vintage blends (from only one year). In other years 'reserve wine' is of more importance, and is blended in to maintain the house style – a closely guarded secret.

Blending together numerous wines of different chemical properties encourages the presence of unwanted matter and the wine must again be clarified. Producers aim to maximize purity and stability of the blend by a further period of cold stabilization, filtering and fining. Gelatine is the most common fining agent used in Champagne. The wine then undergoes its third and final racking.

Liqueur de tirage

After the final racking the wine is transferred to the bottling line. But before being bottled a mixture of reserve wine, sugar and selected yeast culture is added to the base wines to simulate a second alcoholic fermentation. Sugar is necessary in the blend because all base wines for champagne are dry, and devoid of fermentable sugar. The type and amount of yeast used will vary according to the style of the champagne.

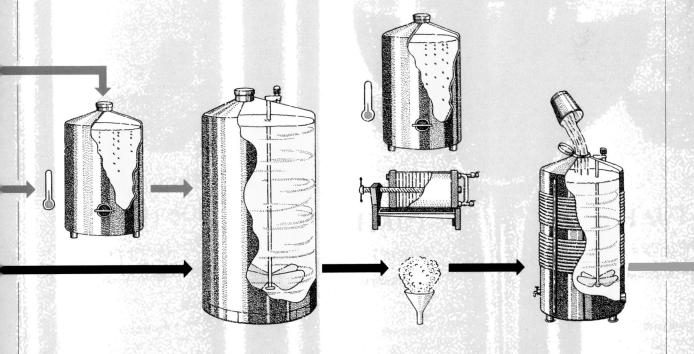

Making Champagne (CONTINUED)

SECOND FERMENTATION

Champagne gains its sparkle by undergoing a second fermentation, this time in the bottle. As the sugar in the *liqueur de tirage* is converted to alcohol, CO_2 bubbles dissolve in the wine, completing the transformation from still to sparkling. The thickness of the glass can withstand the pressure which builds up as CO_2 is produced. Metal crown caps are used to seal the wine during the fermentation. Keeping the temperature low slows down this process and results in smaller bubbles in the champagne – one indicator of good quality.

Storage 'sur lattes'
In most top champagne houses the second fermentation and subsequent maturing of the bottles takes place in deep cool chalk cellars. The ageing period may last as long as 20–50 years. During this time the wine gains in creaminess and complexity through contact with its yeast sediment (lees). The bottles are stacked, separated by laths (*lattes*). The care in their stacking is to ensure that should one bottle explode during fermentation, the others will be disturbed as little as possible.

Re-stacking and shaking of the bottles at intervals is carried out so that the sediment does not stick to the bottle, which would complicate clarification.

CLARIFICATION

Remuage
When secondary fermentation is complete the lees remaining in the bottle must be removed. The bottles are transferred to wooden racks, then each bottle must be gradually riddled (tilted from horizontal to vertical) to encourage the sediment down into the neck of the bottle. Performed manually this is painstaking work: skilled *remueurs* are employed to rotate and fractionally tilt the bottles until they are fully perpendicular and ready for disgorgement. The operation may last several months.

Gyropalettes
Using gyropalettes shortens the period over which clarification occurs to as little as a week. The principle is the same as *remuage* but mechanized and far more efficient. The bottles are stacked upside down on palettes and mechanically rotated every eight hours, which causes the sediment to spiral down to the neck.

Alginate beads
Current experiments with tiny porous beads may eventually render both *remuage* and gyropalettes obsolete. These beads actually contain the yeast. At the end of fermentation they fall to the neck of the bottle without urging and are easily removed.

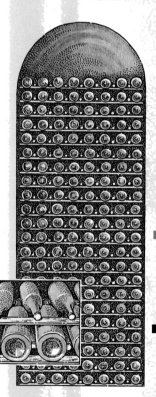

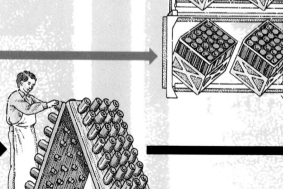

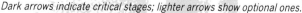

Dark arrows indicate critical stages; lighter arrows show optional ones.

MATURING

Once the yeast sediment has settled, finer champagnes are matured for up to 5 years *sur pointes* (upside down). The flavour is further enhanced by contact with the sediment in the neck of the bottle. The disgorging process to remove the sediment is delayed as long as possible.

DISGORGING AND DOSAGE

Disgorging is essential but disruptive because it briefly exposes the wine to air, increasing its natural oxidation rate and thus (perhaps) reducing its ageing potential. It requires extreme dexterity and speed to remove the crown-cap and quickly dislodge yeast sediment from the bottle without losing any wine. Freezing the sediment in the neck of the bottle provides a much tidier and more efficient method. The pressure from the champagne forces rapid ejaculation of the sediment when the crown cap is removed.

Dosage, sweetening with *liqueur d'expédition* (wine and sugar) is essential for most champagnes, which at this stage may be quite acid. Those which have undergone a long maturation will have been softened by contact with yeast sediment and may not need *dosage* – eg Brut Sauvage or very old RD – but they will need topping up with wine to fill the bottle after the removal of the sediment.

FINISHING

Immediately the *liqueur d'expédition* has been added, the bottles are corked, automatically shaken to distribute the *liqueur de tirage* and then labelled.

At this stage some wines will undergo additional 'cork age'. This is not encouraged by most champagne houses but old champagne does have a specialist (largely English) market. This process will change the style of the wine quite considerably, as the alcohol combines with various acids to create esters, which introduce scents of coffee and caramel, even hints of mushrooms.

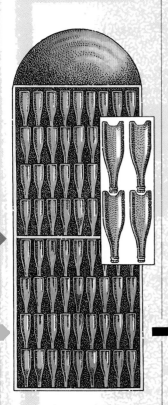

Reserve wine One of the most fascinating, important yet shadowy aspects of champagne is the use of 'reserve' wine held from earlier vintages. It may be held in magnums (under slight gaseous pressure), in stainless steel or (less commonly) in oak. Houses such as Krug have reserve wines of up to 20 years old, although in diminishing quantity with age. They will usually be held over from vintage years, and, tasted on their own, can be superb. A 60-year-old magnum of Bollinger reserve wine (made from 100 percent Pinot Noir) tasted in the 1980s, was a memorable experience: nothing to do with champagne, and more like an old (yet Peter Pan fresh) white burgundy – it had acquired the nutty creaminess of mature Chardonnay.

Reserve wines can be used at three stages in the making of champagne: they can be incorporated in the primary ferment; then, most commonly and importantly, at the time of blending or *assemblage* along with the *liqueur de tirage*; and least importantly (because of the tiny volume) with the *liqueur d'expédition*. All the champagne houses privately acknowledge that the quality and style of their reserve wines has a powerful influence on their overall house style, but tend to downplay this importance publicly.

Vintage champagne: a shadow of doubt Where, you may ask, is the mystery, where are the shadows? It lies with vintage champagne: under EC legislation, 85 percent of the wine must be from the stated vintage year, which would allow generous incorporation of reserve wine. Under the Appellation Contrôlée of Champagne, the wine must be 100 percent from its stated vintage. It is a situation which one can imagine the Italians finding themselves in, and runs entirely counter to the precision with which so much of the affairs of Champagne is run. No one will officially admit it, of course, and strict proof of any breach would be very difficult to obtain, but Reserve wines are customarily used in the blending of vintage champagne – and to its great benefit – just as much as with non-vintage wines.

Making champagne

The basic steps of champagne-making appear on pages 114–117. Rather than repeat that explanation here, we shall focus on those aspects which affect the style of champagne, and differentiate it from all other sparkling wines.

Terroir and the échelle des crus The Champenois and the Comité Interprofessionnel du Vin de Champagne are ever alert to emphasize their unique combination of *terroir* and climate. However much the cynics or the jealous may seek to dismiss this as an empty piece of propaganda, there is something very special about the grapes grown in Champagne. Others may point to the progressive upgrading in the *échelle des crus* system (which classifies every tiny part of Champagne on a percentage basis from 80 to 100 percent) and to the extreme concentration of *échelles* at the top of the scale rather than the bottom. Cynics may scoff at the story that Dom Pérignon could tell from which vineyards otherwise unidentified grapes came merely by tasting them, and that he decided his blends by an early morning tasting of grapes left on his window-sill overnight. The fact remains that over the centuries the Champenois have decided which plots should be planted with Pinot Noir, which with Pinot Meunier and which with Chardonnay and have then graded each vineyard or *cru* in the most detailed fashion imaginable. The ultimate fascination is that having so minutely detailed their *vignoble*, they proceed to blend white and red grapes from across its length and breadth – although wines such as Moët & Chandon's luxury *cuvée*, named after Dom Pérignon, are made entirely from grapes with an *échelle*-rating of 100 percent.

Whole bunch pressing The champagne practice of taking whole bunches direct to the press goes back to the 17th century. The strict limitation of the yield of juice per tonne of grapes, the shape and size of the traditional press, and the low pressure under which it operates all pre-date scientific analysis (which totally supports the belief of the Champenois that these methods and controls produce juice of higher quality). We now know that free-run or lightly-pressed juice is likely to have higher acidity, lower pH,

Left: *North- as well as south-facing slopes in Champagne produce grapes for the finest sparkling wines in the world.*

Below: *The seemingly contradictory term 'Blanc de Noirs' is just that: champagne made from the very gentle pressing of black grapes.*

fewer solids (particulate matter from the pulp of the grape) and lower phenols (flavour compounds) than juice from grapes which have been passed through a crusher or been more rigorously pressed to produce a higher yield.

The advantages of fermentation in oak as opposed to stainless steel are still hotly debated, although only two houses (Krug and Alfred Gratien) ferment entirely this way, and only one (Bollinger) does so partially. These three houses produce particularly big, rich and complex champagne, and part of their style must derive from fermenting in oak. Oak barrel-fermenting is far more costly and time-consuming than fermentation in steel; it may help induce malolactic fermentation; but since the barrels are all very old there is no possibility of the pick-up of any oak flavour per se, nor is there any likelihood of greater oxidation (fermenting wine protects itself under its natural blanket of carbon dioxide). The obvious difference is the inability to control fermentation temperatures precisely, as can be done with stainless steel, and the probability that these will exceed the 18–20°C range normally found with stainless steel fermentation.

Fermentation vats or barrels

The paramount importance of *assemblage* (or blending) is not in dispute. However, the synergy achieved by a master-blender has its limits: the quality of the individual base wine components inevitably places some limits on what can be achieved. But given top quality base wines, and a skilled blender, a quite miraculous transformation takes place in the one to three years the wine matures in its bottle on yeast lees after the addition of the *liqueur de tirage*. It is customary in the New World to talk of the effect of 'yeast autolysis', and in particular about the flavour of yeast. The French disparage such talk: quite correctly, they say that the aroma, flavour and texture changes which occur during the period of lees contact are not due simply to the presence of the dead yeast cells, and in particular that one cannot smell or taste yeast per se (or at least the dead yeast we are talking about here). What one is observing is a complex change in aromas, esters and flavours, partly due to the ageing changes in the base wines, and only partly to the process of autolysis. While the changes are continual, and start soon after the end of the second fermentation, the effects on the aroma and flavour become progressively more apparent with time. Chemical analysis also shows that after an initial burst of activity, a slowdown is followed by a build-up, giving technical strength to the appellation requirement of at least 12 months on the lees.

The taste of yeast?

Dom Pérignon developed the art of blending in Champagne – now carried to such lengths that one of the finest brands, Krug Grande Cuvée, is a blend of between 40 and 50 different wines.

Recently disgorged   Champagne is kept fresh by its high concentration of carbon dioxide, but the yeast lees (so long as the wine has not been disgorged) bolster that freshness. It is this capacity (and the ever-continuing gain in complexity) which has given rise to the super-luxury class of wines which have spent an abnormally long time on their yeast lees. Traditionally, these were curiosities reserved for special guests in Champagne: anyone who has been privileged to taste a 1921 Pol Roger disgorged that morning will need no persuasion that they take champagne into another dimension. Bollinger, however, decided to commercialize such wines (albeit on a tiny scale), and to register a trade mark 'RD' which stands for *récemment dégorgé* (recently disgorged). Like Xerox, the expression RD has passed into general verbal usage to describe a product (or a process), but can only be used on the Bollinger label. The label always states the precise date of disgorgement.

Partly because recently disgorged wines are served in Champagne within hours or days of disgorging, partly perhaps because Bollinger specifies the disgorgement date, a myth has grown up that these wines suffer some magical but evil decay once they have been disgorged. This is nonsense: any champagne is (in a sense) at one point in its life recently disgorged. If the wine is extremely old when it is disgorged it is most unlikely to have any need or capacity for further improvement; and if it was cellared in Champagne, it will have been stored under perfect conditions. The natural conclusion is that it should be drunk before movement, inappropriate storage or other misfortune can occur. But it will not decay: other things being equal, a 50-year-old champagne disgorged ten years ago will be much fresher than the same wine disgorged at its normal time, ie 47 years ago.

Very large machines   The *méthode champenoise* has continually evolved over the centuries. Its recent developments have included the increasing use of automatic 'riddling' machines called *gyropalettes*, which agitate and tilt the bottles, in place of the stoical *remueurs*, whose daily round of shaking and turning interminable bottles was the most laborious part of the whole champagne process.

Moët & Chandon have meanwhile developed an ingenious means of enclosing the yeasts in little double-walled '*billes*', or beads of alginate, which may one day make the whole riddling process obsolete. The yeasts appear to perform their duties as well as ever, but being in the form of beads they need no patient coaxing towards the cork. The bottle is simply up-ended and they are ready to be disgorged.

Cava   The Spanish *cava* wines made in the Penedès region of Catalonia are the most widely known around the world after champagne. The reason is very simple: with a production of some five million cases each, Cordoníu and Freixenet, the two largest houses, are both over three times larger than Moët & Chandon (with a mere 1.5 million cases). In the wake of a controversial EC ruling banning the use of the term *méthode champenoise* on wine labels, *cava* as a name has become even better known, and (somewhat cynically) has been given the trappings of an Appellation Contrôlée. It has nominal geographical boundaries (conveniently drawn around all the *cava* producers), prescribes the making methods (almost identical to those of champagne), and prescribes the grape varieties.

Spanish investment in the latest winemaking technology means more cava *is produced than any other sparkling wine in the world.*

The *cava* producers spare no effort, time or expense in making their wine. Their cellars are massive and massively impressive; their technology is excellent (Cordoníu invented the *gyropalette*); and the packaging of the wine leaves nothing to be desired. The wine, unfortunately, does — and not merely in comparison to champagne. Its problem is that where champagne is delicate, *cava* is (with rare exceptions) leaden-footed. Certainly it has great complexity and abundant flavour, but that remarkable combination of intensity and elegance which is the hallmark of champagne is nowhere to be found.

The reasons lie partly in the climate (and possibly soil), partly in the grape varieties, and partly in that indefinable pulse which beats in the heart of

Champagne. The climate is simply too warm: lying on the same latitude as Tuscany. The three principal authorized varieties, Xarel-lo, Macabeo and Parellada, are beloved of the Spanish and well suited to the climate, but they will never produce a wine in the style of champagne.

Italian bubbles

Nothing could be less like Italy's usual ascetic style of dry whites than Asti Spumante: this is grapes in a bottle, with the fruit flavour intensified by the bubbles. For the dust-dry, chalky quality of Italy captured in bubbles you must go to the Veneto, where Prosecco is a venerable tradition. Both Asti Spumante and Prosecco are usually vat-fermented. Altogether more serious are the new generation *méthode champenoise* wines made from the 'right' varieties (Pinot Noir and Chardonnay) by winemakers such as the Trentino-based Ferrari, Ca' del Bosco in Lombardy or Villa Banfi in Piedmont. The Italians are exceedingly proud of their achievements, which are technically excellent. But seriousness alone does not make a wine great, and some find more charm in the frivolity of Spumante.

German Sekt

A challenge to the prodigious volume of the *cava* producers comes from the German producers of Sekt, a logical development for a country best suited to producing wine with low natural alcohol, high acidity and a modest level of fresh fruit. Small quantities of the best Sekt are made using the *méthode champenoise*; most is made by the Charmat process in vat. The top Sekts from 100 percent Riesling are thoroughly enjoyable: cheerfully fruity not at all too sweet, entirely natural and there is no pretence that these wines emulate champagne.

France's other fizz

Blanquette de Limoux

France has other sparkling wines of some class and interest. Blanquette de Limoux lays claim to being the first sparkling wine of modern times: its history begins over 100 years before champagne. Originally it was a *pétillant* wine made by the *méthode rurale* – in essence the first half of the *méthode champenoise* (it does not go to the trouble of removing the yeast lees). It is now made by the *méthode champenoise* – and in substantial quantities. The grapes are the local Mauzac, Chenin Blanc and (increasingly) Chardonnay, grown in the hills behind the Corbières above Carcassonne. For New World palates used to clean and clearly delineated styles the history of the wine is of greater interest than the wine, which tends to bitterness and a hard, chalky, lemony cast. Adding Chardonnay has changed the style considerably, and it will presumably continue to evolve.

Crémants

Other wine regions, notably Burgundy and Alsace, are also making sparkling wines, known as *crémants* to set them apart from champagne.

The Loire Valley

The sparkling wines of the Loire Valley – based primarily on Chenin Blanc, although Chardonnay is of increasing importance – were almost as famous as those of Champagne in the latter part of the 19th century. Three Champagne houses (Alfred Gratien, Bollinger, and Deutz and Geldermann) have significant operations there, although the major production comes from a number of cooperatives. A few *pétillant* wines continue to be made and, like the *mousseux* versions, can be quite superb with 20 years or more bottle-age. Some of the *mousseux* is made by the *méthode champenoise*; most, however, is produced by the Charmat process (*see* page 227).

New World sparkling wines

The old style

The importance of the right varietal base (Chardonnay, Pinot Noir and less convincingly Pinot Meunier) has been handsomely demonstrated in California, Australia and (albeit on a tiny scale so far) in New Zealand.

Both California and Australian sparkling wines have gone through several phases of development. Until the 1970s in California and the 1980s in Australia, base wines were fashioned from everything and anything other than Pinot Noir or Chardonnay. In Australia varieties typically used for better wines were Ondenc,

Sémillon, Chenin Blanc, Colombard, Trebbiano and Rhine Riesling, with the red
component usually absent but extending to Shiraz (Syrah) and Cabernet
Sauvignon when present. The approach was to pick at sugar levels similar to those
of champagne grapes; but because of the warm climate, they were harvested while
very green, with distinctly lower acidity and most significantly much less flavour
intensity. Winemakers found themselves in a cleft stick: if the grapes were allowed
to become too flavour-ripe, the finished sparkling wine became very coarse and
rank in flavour. If the winemaker judged his material to perfection, and if the wine
was given three or four years on yeast lees (and extra bottle-age thereafter), it could
attain a balance, a rich complexity similar to that of the best *cava* wines: a glowing
colour and a nutty, biscuity flavour which certainly filled the mouth, but which
could never claim elegance or finesse.

The next phase was the discovery (in both California and Australia) that Pinot
Noir grown in warm climates produced execrable table wine. By default, as it were,
it was diverted to production of sparkling wine, although it was noticeable that the
much more compliant Chardonnay did not initially accompany it: the Chardonnay
was in too much demand for table wine, a fact saying much about the attitude to
sparkling wine which prevailed at the time in both countries.

The new wave   Change came with the third phase and the development of vineyards purposely
established for sparkling-wine production: Chardonnay and Pinot Noir in cool
climates, such as those of Carneros and the Central Coast of California, southern
Victoria, the Adelaide Hills, far southeastern Australia (Coonawarra and
Padthaway), Tasmania and more recently the South Island of New Zealand. This
led to a further discovery about Pinot Noir: whether climate, *terroir*, the particular
clone or a combination of all three is the cause, it performs less well and less
predictably than Chardonnay in fashioning top-quality New World sparkling
wines. Pinot Noir seems to engender a certain toughness; one might expect it to
blend synergistically with the far softer, creamier Chardonnay, but it has tended
not to. Pinot Meunier is even less successful and is sparingly grown: its tendency to
rapid development in sparkling wine is even more pronounced, with a strong
yeasty, beef-tea aroma and flavour developing within 18 to 24 months.

California   The style of the best California sparkling wine is arguably closer to that of
Champagne than are Australia's versions. The differences between Australian and
California sparkling wines track those of their table wines. Domaine Chandon in

the Napa Valley is widely recognized as being the most reliable large producer, and manages to make wines with length, flavour and good mouthfeel. The long-established (indeed pioneering) Schramsberg maintains a rich (though dry) style which seems to express Napa values perfectly, while Iron Horse, lean and racy, seems to do the same for cooler Sonoma. Others can have aromas just as strange and off-putting as the less convincing efforts of Champagne: in the mouth they tend to be rather ungenerous, hard and chalky. Once again, it seems at least some of these deficiencies stem from inappropriate viticulture in inappropriately warm areas: the French-owned wineries have been surprisingly slow in moving to the cool climate of Carneros, although Taittinger has left no-one in any doubt about its views with the establishment of Domaine Carneros and its unfortunate 'château'.

Australia

Australia has been more content to make sparkling wine in an Australian idiom, with emphasis on clean, soft, crisp fruit flavours and less immediate concern with complexity and structure. There is a range of styles, with Croser (the premium sparkling wine from Petaluma) at one extreme (super-elegant, refined and understated) and Seppelt's Salinger at the other (opulent and full blown). The tendency has been to protect the juice against oxidation, to ferment at lower temperatures than are usual in Champagne, to be less concerned with blend complexity and to disgorge after only 12 to 18 months on yeast lees. There are exceptions: Domaine Chandon Australia, based in the Yarra Valley of Victoria, takes a French approach to fermentation and to *assemblage* complexity (its grapes come from right across southern Australia and New Zealand), while the Seppelt and Seaview wines can spend far longer on yeast lees. Greater finesse and complexity are perceived desirable, but not at the expense of fruit and only once all of the quality and potential of the base wine is fully understood.

Moët & Chandon in Victoria

Domaine Chandon Australia uses methods which closely track those of Moët & Chandon, and *assemblage* is strongly influenced by input from the Moët & Chandon chief blenders. The main difference is that Domaine Chandon puts only a small proportion of its wine through malolactic fermentation; Moët uses this process for all of its champagne. Yet there is no possibility of confusing the wines of the two companies; the distinction lies – obviously enough – in the flavour and to a minor degree in the chemical composition of the grapes, and in the incomplete knowledge as to how and where those grapes should be grown, when they should be picked, how they should be handled in the winery, and how they should be blended.

124

Sweet Table Wines

Choices, consequences and techniques

Ancient sweet wines

Sweet wines have a very much longer history than dry ones. The wines of the ancients, of the Near East, of Egypt and classical Greece were almost certainly made as sweet as possible – and as concentrated. The Greeks, at least, always drank their wine diluted with water (sometimes seawater), hot or cold according to the season, and usually flavoured with herbs and spices. Under these circumstances it may seem surprising that they made such fine distinctions between the qualities of the various regions of Greece, and especially of the Aegean Islands.

What vines Italy grew before its colonization by the Greeks were probably all high-trained up trees. The grapes could rarely have ripened enough to give sweet wine. Hence the ancient tradition in Italy that low-trained and staked vines were a Greek importation, and that sweet or strong wines were in the Greek style.

Madeira Fumé?

The Romans resorted to concentrating their grape juice by boiling it before fermentation. They also frequently 'smoked' their wines by stacking the amphoras in a loft above a furnace. The result must have been a sort of 'Madeira Fumé'. Certainly it indicates that they accepted (even encouraged) oxidation. Once oxidized under the right conditions the wine was stable (no wine is more stable than madeira) and could be kept indefinitely.

But another reason emerges for their liking for sweet wines, as concentrated as possible (and frequently laced with pepper, spices and honey). They were the traveller's insurance policy against wines too foul to drink, or vinegary 'posca', at inns along the road. The Romans were indefatigable travellers, and it was their custom to carry their own additives to make tavern-wine more palatable.

Keeping it sweet

Today there is no problem in adjusting the sweetness of any wine, strong or weak, to any desired level. Fermentation can be stopped before the natural sugar is exhausted by a number of methods. The two most common are adding sulphur dioxide and 'fine filtration' to remove the yeasts. Sweet must can then be 'back-blended' into dry wine with no risk of refermentation.

The ancient civilizations of the Near East and the Mediterranean fermented their wines in earthenware jars, usually buried to the neck in the ground (a practice still common in Georgia and just surviving in Cyprus). Sweetness and strength were the qualities they looked for.

Before the age of technology the only natural method was to ensure such a high degree of sugar that the yeasts suspended activity. This was achieved either when the fermentation produced about 14 percent of alcohol, or, in intensely sweet must, long before. In Greece and similar climates super-sweet grapes were easily achieved. The simplest methods were either to pick them and leave them piled in the sun to raisin, or to hang them under roofs to shrivel with a similar effect, or, more painstakingly, to go round the vineyard twisting the stalk of each bunch to restrict the circulation of sap, and then wait for the juice in each grape slowly to concentrate. There are examples of these methods still in use today (*see* page 136).

These warm-climate methods are not possible in cooler and more humid regions. Grapes left on the vine to over-ripen will simply rot. But there is more than one kind of fungus that makes a meal of a grape. One in particular has an entirely benevolent effect. How this 'noble' rot, the celebrated *Botrytis cinerea*, was first discovered and put to use is the subject of various legends (*see* page 130).

None of the stories is very convincing; the last least of all. For a start, *Botrytis cinerea* was known and described in Roman times, and in all probability goes back further still. Secondly, anyone who has grown grapes in a region in which botrytis occurs knows it is an ever-present phenomenon. In some years the level of infection

will be minor, in other years quite high, and in others still it will totally invade the crop. Thirdly, while the vignerons of 200 or 300 years ago may have lacked microscopes and a knowledge of biochemistry, they were acutely observant, and it seems very unlikely they would not have made the connection between botrytis and a wonderful rich flavour in their white wines. Finally, all are agreed its effect was known in Hungary since the mid-17th century. Why would that knowledge have remained a secret?

Besides, the Loire Valley, Bergerac and Sauternes had made celebrated sweet wines since the mid-1600s at least. In a 1666 court case, involving the then owner of Château d'Yquem and several of his tenants who wished to pick their grapes too soon, it was noted that '*it is not customary in Bommes and Sauternes to begin picking before 15th October*'. In most years botrytis must have taken a firm hold by this time. In those years when botrytis laid low (it depends on a degree of humidity) they probably tried to make similarly sweet and concentrated wine by leaving the grapes to over-ripen, 'Greek-style'. The recent vintages 1970 and 1978 are examples of Sauternes being denied the benison of botrytis. You can taste the difference – but not so clearly that the wines are not obviously Sauternes.

The benison of botrytis

To present-day eyes grapes heavily infected with botrytis are not exactly attractive. A heavy web of greenish-grey mould, with short hairs growing outwards, covers the grapes; each grape has partially or totally collapsed, and, if handled, readily exudes sticky juice and a cloud of mould spores. Extracting the juice from the crusher and press can be exceedingly difficult because the high juice-viscosity and sugary-slippery nature of the skins makes pressing difficult and the jam-like consistency of the must almost impossible to pump. What is more, the must has an evil-looking, murky black colour: the brilliant green-gold colour which emerges at the end of fermentation is scientifically explicable but to the eyes of the layman, like those winemakers of former centuries, it seems a miracle.

Château d'Yquem represents perfectionism on a scale not even attempted in any other vineyard. It can take ten 'tries' around the 250-acre vineyard to pick the vintage. Each vine produces only one glass.

Sweet Table Wines

This choices and consequences chart illustrates those stages in the process for making sweet wine in which the options chosen by the winemaker will fundamentally influence the taste and individuality of the final wine. Not every stage of the winemaking process is indicated: for that the reader is directed to the white-wine process chart on pages 88–89.

Sweet table wines are made from grapes that have dehydrated and the juice concentrated sufficiently for sugar and acid levels to rise significantly above normal. This might occur naturally in the vineyard or can be induced artificially in the winery. Other methods of producing sweet wine are to concentrate the juice after crushing and pressing or to add grape concentrate to dry wine to sweeten it.

1 IN THE VINEYARD

Botrytis cinerea
A cryptogamic fungus which occurs under warm and humid conditions. The spores settle on the skin of the grape which exudes moisture and shrivels and the juice becomes more and more concentrated. This has the effect of producing intensely sweet juice. Sauternes and German *Trockenbeerenauslese* are produced from botrytized grapes.

Freezing
Partially botrytized grapes are left on the vine until the December or January frosts occur then they are picked at dawn while still frozen. As the water in the grapes turns to ice, sugar and acidity in the juice that remains become increasingly concentrated. This method is used principally in Germany to make *Eiswein*.

Raising
Super-sweet grapes can be achieved by twisting the stalk of each bunch of grapes to restrict the circulation of sap and concentrate the juice. Rarely carried out now but was popular in the 18th century in Italy and Provence.

2 IN THE WINERY

Concentrating whole grapes
(a) *Freezing*
Partially botrytized grapes are frozen to produce an *Eiswein* variant in California and Australia.

(b) *Artificially induced botrytis*
Grapes picked at normal maturity are placed on racks in a temperature-controlled room then sprayed with botrytis spores. Alternating cool and warm air is blown over the grapes to simulate ideal conditions in the vineyard. After two weeks the grapes shrivel, leaving concentrated juice.

(c) *Raising*
Grapes are picked and left in the sun on straw or wooden trays to raisin or hung under roofs to shrivel. In the Jura in France the wine is called *vin de paille*, in Italy *passito*, in Germany *strohwein*.

Concentrating crushed and pressed grapes
(a) *Osmotic concentration*
An experimental technique which is being used as a means of by-passing the need for chaptalisation.

(b) *Freeze concentration*
This commercializes the principles underlying the production of *Eiswein*. A coil or hollow plate through which chilled brine is continuously pumped is placed into the vat. An ice-block gradually forms which is then lifted out of the vat or the concentrated juice is pumped out leaving the ice to melt.

Adding grape concentrate to wine
In this instance the wine is fermented dry and then *mistelle* (grape concentrate) is blended in to sweeten it.

Above: *A glucometer – an instrument for measuring the sugar concentration in sweet wines.*

Left: *Harvesting nobly rotted grapes at Château d'Yquem. It takes several passes through the vineyard to select completely rotten grapes. Pickers may use scissors or just forefinger and thumb to coax off individual berries, leaving others to become more concentrated in sugar.*

In Greece grapes are spread out on sheets to dry beneath the hot sun – a raisining technique that goes back to classical times.

Roller-coaster   Attitudes to sweet white wines have fluctuated wildly, especially in the 20th century. Having been extremely popular in the 19th century and the early decades of the 20th, the status of these wines declined precipitously in the years after World War II. By the end of the 1950s demand for Sauternes had diminished to the point where Sauvignon Blanc, Sémillon and Muscadelle were pulled out and replaced by Cabernet Sauvignon and Merlot; and even a château as famous as Château d'Yquem was compelled to introduce a near-dry white wine, which it calls simply 'Y' (pronounced 'Ygrec').

Glorious wines;   Such lack of interest – and such prices – underline the fact that the greatest sweet
fabulous prices   wines of the world have almost always been made because of the owner's (or the winemaker's) passion, rather than for a reasonable profit. A brief period of glory in the 19th century saw the Russian Tsars pay fabulous sums for Château d'Yquem, while the Austro-Hungarian, Russian and Polish nobility did the same for Tokay essence. Once the sharply diminished yield and the ever-present risk of the partial or total failure of the vintage are taken into account, the seemingly high price per bottle shrinks alarmingly. Château d'Yquem is not for sale, but if it were it would bring a price which would make a share market analyst shake his head in disbelief: the return would be a tiny fraction of that obtainable from Government Gilt Securities. A mortgage would be out of the question. (The same may currently be said of any of the classed-growth châteaux of Bordeaux, but nowhere near to the same degree.) The 90 hectares of vineyard produce 5,500 cases on average – if one ignores the years in which no wine at all is made under the Château d'Yquem label. A 90-hectare New World vineyard would routinely produce 45,000 cases of premium wine, perhaps more. Or, to look at it another way, the maximum permitted yield under the Appellation Contrôlée for Sauternes is a very low 25 hectolitres per hectare; that of Château d'Yquem is only nine; one-fifth of a classed-growth Bordeaux château.

Making Sauternes

Thanks in part to the lustre of Château d'Yquem, Sauternes has usually been acclaimed as the greatest of the sweet wines, whatever the merits of German *Trockenbeerenauslesen* or Tokay essence may be. As the chart shows (*see pages 126–127*), sweet white wine can be made in many different ways: here we will follow that of Sauternes, with Château d'Yquem as the model.

'Tries'   There are multiple choices at the time of picking. The traditional, time-consuming and very costly pattern of multiple passes through the vineyard, or 'tries', is still practised to the full at Château d'Yquem. The number of *tries* will depend on the vintage: in 1972 11 *tries* over a period of 71 days failed to produce any wine worthy of the name d'Yquem; in 1976 two *tries* over 22 days were sufficient to produce a classic wine; the average is eight to ten *tries* over 60 days. If quality is the prime concern, repeated *tries* are mandatory. The object is to harvest
Grains rôtis   only those grapes which are fully affected by botrytis, known locally as *grains rôtis*. Those affected by grey or black rot are cut off and discarded. Those still unaffected or only partially affected are left for a later pass – and so on, for however long and however many *tries* are necessary.

This is not only highly skilled work, but exceedingly slow. As few as two or three berries may be removed from a bunch, dislodged by a finger or with the closed tip of the secateurs. The picking rate is one-twentieth of that for dry white wines, where whole bunches are picked with virtually no selection involved.

Under the relentless pressure to control costs, multiple passes are steadily becoming less frequent in Sauternes. The least-satisfactory short-cut is to restrict the harvest to (say) two *tries*, for no further selection to be made, and to rely on chaptalisation to increase sugar levels. An optional approach is to sort the harvest on tables in the *chai*: the 1979 harvest at Château Padouen in Barsac (then owned by the Australian Len Evans and managed by the Dane Peter Vinding-Diers) was

Left: *Hand-made wine begins in the vineyard: botrytized grapes at Yquem are picked one by one; extracting juice from them is exceedingly difficult. Less oozes from a modern press than the old basket press* (below).

dealt with this way. Every bunch was cut with (of all things) nail scissors, the botrytized grapes going into one *cuve*, the unaffected grapes going to another (to make a dry white wine). There is evidence this method was used in bygone days: its disadvantage is that it reduces the amount of sweet wine which may be made from any given vintage because the unaffected berries are not given the chance to develop botrytis on the vine.

Pressing

At Château d'Yquem the grapes are crushed but not destalked, using gentle wooden crushers which discharge directly into the press cage – traditionally the wooden-slatted, upright hydraulic press found in small wineries all over the world. The stalks and stalk fragments perform a valuable role, providing some stability to the otherwise very slippery consistency of the crushed grapes. These are gentle presses, but are extremely slow and not terribly efficient in dealing with white pomace of any kind, let alone Sauternes. The pomace has to be pressed three times, and broken up in a crumbler in between each pressing, a process which can take six hours from start to finish. The modern air-bag press, no less gentle but more efficient in terms of both time and juice recovery, is inevitably taking over from the old basket press – even at d'Yquem.

Fermentation

The combined juice of the three pressings is run directly into barrels without clarification or settling. The only quick method of clarifying juice of this density is by a device known as a 'rotary drum vacuum filter', and Château d'Yquem finds no need of such gadgetry. Fermentation of extremely sweet musts can be very difficult: stories are told of German *Trockenbeerenauslesen* taking two years to partially ferment, and of Tokay essence not fermenting at all. This is not what one would expect, because sugar is a food which yeasts devour with gusto; however, at extreme sugar levels (35 degrees Baumé or above) fermentation is to all intents impossible, while even at 25 degrees Baumé it proceeds slowly, and will necessarily leave around 10 degrees Baumé of unfermented sugar.

In fact Château d'Yquem aims to harvest its grapes at 20 degrees Baumé which, at the end of fermentation leaves about 14 degrees of alcohol and around 6 degrees Baumé residual sugar unfermented. Normally fermentation will continue until the alcohol level reaches 16 degrees, but a combination of the high background sugar, a substance called botryticine (a form of antibiotic), and the addition of sulphur dioxide act together to limit the alcohol to 14 degrees.

New oak   Château d'Yquem uses 100 percent new oak every year for barrel ageing, and the wine remains in wood for three and a half years before it is bottled. During this time it will have been racked 11 times, and fined once or twice, but never filtered. During the spring of the following year the process of *assemblage* will commence, and will continue through the summer. During this time every cask will be evaluated: depending on the success of the vintage a considerable number (never less than 10 percent, often much more) will be declassified and either sold in bulk, or (in the case of semi-dry Sauvignon Blanc) used in making the dry white wine 'Y'. The *assemblage* will also have to arrive at the right balance between Sémillon (usually 80 percent) and Sauvignon Blanc (20 percent), the latter usually having much lower residual sugar.

Good new: Because of the extraordinary care Château d'Yquem takes at every stage of its
wonderful old winemaking it is not surprising that the resulting wine swallows up both the new oak and the sulphur dioxide, with the consequence that even a relatively young d'Yquem is a totally enjoyable experience to drink. A 1983 tasting in Australia of 50 vintages from 1899 onwards (the event spanned an entire day) simply proved what anyone with any experience of the wine already knew: even the weakest vintages improve for ten to 15 years, the good vintages for 20 to 30 years, while the great years can live (if not improve) for a century or more.

Sauternes below   What may be called good Sauternes from the other *crus classés* of the region are
d'Yquem   made in similar fashion. Less *tries* in the vineyard, lower starting degrees Baumé, a little more sulphur, some chaptalisation, increasing use of cultured yeasts, vat- rather than barrel-fermentation, and rather less new oak are to be expected. The wine is still very complex, and only in odd vintages will it be at its best within ten years. With cheap Sauternes you get what you pay for: grapes picked with a single pass, the maximum chaptalisation permitted by law (2 degrees of alcohol), a finished wine with an alcohol content of around 12 degrees alcohol, 3 to 4 degrees residual sugar, and no new oak. These are bland, soft, tropical (pineapple and apricot) flavoured wines at their best; thin and awkward at their worst. No fine Sauternes is ever inexpensive; no wine in the world is more costly to produce.

Edelfäule   Sauternes is challenged by Germany's *Beerenauslesen* and *Trockenbeerenauslesen*: the peak of the pyramid of wines, starting with *Spätlese*, from selected riper grapes in which botrytis is fully developed. A unique comparative tasting of Château
Trockenbeerenauslesen d'Yquem and Schloss Vollrads' *Trockenbeerenauslesen* in the late 1980s demon-

Botrytis legends

The first concerns Tokay. In 1650 the vintage at the Castle of Tokaji was delayed on the pretext of an expected Turkish attack; by the time they were picked the grapes were rotten on the vine – revealing the extraordinary effect of botrytis. For their part, the Germans have always regarded the discovery of botrytis as theirs, and typically are able to pinpoint the date (1775), the place (Schloss Johannisberg) and the people (J M Engert, the vineyard manager, and the Prince-Abbot of Fulda). Mr Engert always had to obtain the permission of the Abbot before starting the harvest, but in 1775 his messenger was inexplicably delayed between Fulda and Johannisberg. By the time he returned with permission to pick, the grapes had all become mouldy, but with nothing else to do, they were harvested – and produced a miraculous wine, allegedly unlike anything previously encountered.

Another legend relates how the German-born owner of Château La Tour Blanche (a Sauternes château) brought back the secret of botrytis from the Rhine in the 1830s and showed the then Marquis de Lur Saluces of Château d'Yquem how to recognize and handle botrytized grapes to make the great sweet wine for which Château d'Yquem promptly became famous.

strated that the two have virtually nothing in common except sweetness. It is simply not meaningful to compare them side by side: all it does is demonstrate that some tasters will prefer Sauternes, others *Trockenbeerenauslesen*, and that in any given vintage, one may excel, the other may disappoint.

The differences are all too obvious. The grapes in Germany are grown in a much colder climate, in places on near-vertical slopes of schist rock; a single high-yielding variety (normally Riesling) is used, rather than a blend of low-yielding grapes; the clarified juice is fermented exceedingly slowly; and new oak (or even near new) is never used. *Trockenbeerenauslesen* must be made from grapes *TBA* harvested with a potential alcohol of 21.5 degrees (more than all but a handful of exceptional and rare Sauternes ever attain) yet the chemical analysis of the two styles could hardly be further apart: Sauternes will typically have 14 degrees alcohol, 5 degrees Baumé residual sugar, and six grams per litre of acidity, for *Trockenbeerenauslesen* the figures will typically be 6.5 degrees alcohol, 14 degrees Baumé residual sugar and ten grams per litre of acidity. The structure of the Sauternes, in other words, rests on alcohol and sugar; the *Trockenbeerenauslese* on sugar and acidity.

The grapes, principally Riesling, are hand-picked in much the same way as in *Grape by grape* Sauternes. A grower making *Spätlese* and *Auslese* wines does not normally make any ripeness selection in the vineyard: it is the average 'must-weight', or degree Oechsle (the German version of Baumé) that categorizes the resulting wine. For *Beerenauslese* and *Trockenbeerenauslese* wines the regulations speak of the picking of individual berries. Whether it is berries or bunches that are picked depends both on the state of the grapes and on the perfectionism of the grower. But laborious, repeated pickings of the vineyard are essential, even though the extreme case, where (in the Rheingau) 100 pickers took two weeks to gather enough grapes for 300 litres of juice, is very unlikely to happen today.

The grapes are crushed and pressed (with the usual difficulty), and the juice clarified by chilling (and sometimes the addition of enzymes); sulphur dioxide is added at the crusher and at the press. Because the climate is so cold, no cooling of the fermentation is ever required; on the contrary, it may be necessary to slightly warm it. Tales are told of winemakers taking their treasured little barrels of *Trockenbeerenauslese* into their bedrooms – if not actually their beds – to keep the *Barrels in the bedroom* fermentation going. The sweeter the must, the slower and more reluctant the fermentation; since an active fermentation generates its own heat (and thereby, metaphorically, adds fuel to the fire) a slow one will not generate any significant warmth, and the winter may virtually stop it until the following spring. As with Sauternes (and indeed all sweet wines) malolactic fermentation does not occur – and just as well: depending on the bacteria, malolactic fermentation in a wine full of sugar can be quite disastrous, producing extreme levels of volatile acidity.

Fermentation will be stopped at the chosen time by cooling and by adding sulphur dioxide. The wine will then be racked and after fining, racked again. In past times German wines, both dry and sweet, were matured in large oak casks for exceedingly long periods. Now the practice is to bottle them as quickly as possible to minimize oxidation; and to 'sterile filter' to ensure subsequent stability.

Eiswein is made from grapes which have been frozen on the vine, and are picked *Eiswein* at dawn while still frozen – a picturesque scene involving mufflers, fur boots, lanterns (or car headlights) and many a draught of hot white wine and sugar from a kettle. Failing the onset of botrytis in his vineyard, a German grower has one last chance to salvage his remaining unpicked grapes and make sweet wine. He has to wait for them to freeze solid.

There are some who believe these are the finest of all the German sweet wines. Botrytis will have played a much lesser role; if all the water-content in the juice has been removed by botrytis, the grapes will have been picked before the deep

December – occasionally January – frosts which trigger the making of *Eiswein*. If there is little or no water, there is nothing to be gained from the freezing. So the Riesling flavour is usually much purer; and a feature of all great *Eisweins* is their superb, tingling acidity and extraordinary length of flavour.

Since 1982 an *Eiswein* has had to be made from must (or juice) with the same degree Oechsle as a *Beerenauslese*, and is labelled simply as *Eiswein*. Before 1982 there were grades of *Eiswein*, the most common being *Spätlese Eiswein* and *Auslese Eiswein*. *Beerenauslese Eisweins* were known but were uncommon, *Trockenbeerenauslese Eisweins* exceedingly rare. The 1982 regulation was much criticized at the time. Many growers felt that *Auslese Eisweins* had the best balance, and many also feared that the new mandatory must weights would seldom be achieved in practice. By chance, 1983 produced an unprecedented quantity of high-quality *Eisweins* which easily complied with the regulations, and the criticisms were silenced.

Frozen grapes   Little has so far been written about the making of *Eiswein*, and one account (suggesting that the grapes are crushed and pressed and the ice skimmed of the top of the vat) is patently wrong. In fact the grapes are simply pressed as whole bunches, and the ice remains with the skins in the press. Some secondary skimming could take place in the unlikely event of ice re-forming in the vat; although as freezing the juice (a method used in the New World) is forbidden, the amount of ice collection will be minimal. From this point on the winemaking practices will be the same as those used for *Trockenbeerenauslesen*, *Beerenauslesen*, and so on.

Tokay

If there is little comparison between Sauternes and the great German sweet wines, there is even less with Tokay. This quintessence of Hungarian taste has suffered severely from 40 years of Communist mismanagement, so there are few modern examples of top quality to make comparisons meaningful. Many pre-Communist bottles survive, however, as witness to its former greatness – 300-year-old bottles have been reported magnificent.

There are three separate types of (sweet) Tokay, increasing in sweetness: Tokay Aszú, Tokay Aszú Essencia, and Tokay Essencia – all made from the Furmint and Hárslevelü grape varieties. The last two are made from berries heavily infected with botrytis which are left on the vine until they are extremely desiccated. Picking is by bunches (with a single pass through the vineyard), although bunch selection in the cellar is used in making Aszú Essencia.

The grapes are (or used to be) picked into a *putton* (plural *puttonyos*) – a wooden tub which holds 25 kilograms of fruit. And there they remain for six to eight days. During this time a tiny amount of juice will exude from the grapes. This is 'Essencia'; a must so treacly-rich in sugar that it ferments with the greatest reluctance, if at all. Essencia may take years to achieve any measurable degree of alcohol. So strictly speaking it is not wine. One analysis reports a 13-year-old Essencia at two percent alcohol, 640 grams per litre residual sugar, and acidity at 38 grams per litre. The sugar content, in other words, amounted to nearly three-quarters of a pound in each half-litre bottle. Little, if any, of such Essencia was sold. It was too valuable as blending material for the less rich grades of Tokay. New legislation, though, will mean that in future Essencia must ferment enough to achieve about 5 percent alcohol. The goal-posts, in other words, have been moved.

Shrivelled grapes for making Tokay Azsú Essencia yield a minute amount of juice, concentrated to the consistency of treacle.

After the Essencia has been drawn off, the grapes are mashed into a form of porridge. A dry white wine made the previous year from the same vineyards, but before the onset of botrytis, is placed into a 140-litre cask called a *gönc* (plural *gönci*). It is only partially filled, thus allowing space for the addition of mash from the *puttonyos*. To make a three *putton* Aszú, 75 kilograms of must will have to be added to 136 litres of dry base wine. For a five *putton* Aszú, 125 kilograms of mash will be added to 136 litres of wine. The mixture is then stirred for 24 to 36 hours, and the wine racked off its solid lees to other *gönci* or larger casks.

Here the second fermentation takes place. For how long will depend on the number of *puttonyos* added, but it will only boost the alcohol content of the wine by between one and two degrees. Thus a very high level of sugar remains as sweetness in the wine. At the appropriate time the wine is sulphured, fined, racked and filtered before being transferred to other *gönci* to mature in the extremely humid (85 to 98 percent) underground cellars for many years. Some of the cramped little cellars of Tokay were dug in the 13th century. Their walls, ceiling, and everything in them are coated with a thick black mould (*Clodosporium cellare*), which, as well as helping to maintain the humidity, influences the flavour of the wine – beneficially, and without introducing the taste of mushrooms sometimes induced by mould (especially in sparkling wine cellars).

Puttonyos and gönci

Left: *Bottles in Tokay cellars are stored upright, not horizontally. Their corks are replaced every 10–15 years. Bottles have survived from the 17th century origins of Tokay in extraordinarily good condition.*

Below: *Fermentation in the presence of such intense sugar concentration is slow, if it starts at all. The best Tokays spend more than 10 years in cask.*

The casks are only topped up once a year. The extremely high humidity reduces evaporation to a minimum, but the winemakers not only tolerate the development of some ullage (or air-space) but actually welcome it. From the time botrytis has finished its work, and before the grapes have even left the vine, oxidation helps shape the wine. When first bottled, Tokay Aszú is already a golden brown colour, and this deepens progressively in bottle; Aszú Essencia is an even deeper, browner colour and ultimately acquires the black-olive aspect of an old wood-aged Muscat from Australia. The combined effect of the oxidation and extreme botrytis infection give the wine its plum-pudding, toffee apple aromas and flavours, and the oxidation also helps to mute what might otherwise be piercing sweetness and intensity.

East meets West   Now that the barriers to Eastern Europe have come down, several French winemakers have established working relationships in Tokay. While respecting the winemaking methods developed over more than 400 years, and not denying that oxidation makes a positive contribution to the inimitable style of the wine, some wonder whether an equally distinctive wine might be made with little or no oxidative influence. Clearly, the feeling is that the wine could be greater still. It will be fascinating to watch developments over the next decade.

Austria

For many years the world at large has undervalued all dessert wines except (but even sometimes including) Sauternes and the great Rhine and Mosel wines. This can be the only explanation for the general neglect of Austria's potential. In the Burgenland, lower Austria, *Beerenauslesen* and *Trockenbeerenauslesen* (and *Ausbruch*, which is somewhere in between) are regularly made with relative ease and in prodigious quantities. If most of them lack the celestial finesse of the greatest German Rieslings, they are nonetheless dessert wines of superb quality.

The Loire Valley

It is also true that the makers of the sweet wines of the Loire Valley might equally well claim that their wines are not given the recognition that is their due.

The sweet wines of Anjou, Bonnezeaux, the Coteaux du Layon, Vouvray, Montlouis and Quarts de Chaume can be absolutely superb. The 1921 Marc Brédif Vouvray Liquoreux ranks with the other monumental sweet wines of that extraordinary vintage (notably Château d'Yquem and various *Trockenbeeren-auslesen*). In more recent times 1947 and 1959 have produced unctuous Loire wines of great power, breed and longevity. Properly cellared, the sweetest *liquoreux* wines of those two years will live for at least another 30 to 40 years from now. Loire sweet-wine terminology is sometimes in dispute, but the long time cellarmaster and owner of Marc Brédif gives five grades (in descending order of sweetness), namely *liquoreux, doux, moelleux, demi-sec* and *sec*, with the sweetest two exceedingly rare, and the distinction between *moelleux* and *demi-sec* nebulous in the extreme.

The making of these wines is almost Germanic in its simplicity. Multiple passes through the vineyard are necessary for *moelleux* or sweeter wines. After crushing, pressing and clarification through either settling or filtration, the wines are fermented in stainless steel, enamelled vats (or, rarely these days, old oak) at moderate (18–20°C) temperatures. They are racked, fined and (usually) filtered before being bottled in the following spring, normally in April. It is left to bottle-age to work the miraculous transformation from a rather chalky, hard youth with a layer of simple sweetness superimposed, to the supple, complex and lingering flavour of maturity. The fruit flavours which then emerge range the full gamut from apricot to lime to peach to pineapple, but with no one character dominating, and with a honeyed envelope tinged with a touch of *crème brûlée* suggesting that these wines are almost a meal in themselves. Most agree that their predestined role is as a privileged apéritif.

In the last 20 years both California and Australia have produced some startlingly good 'botrytized' Riesling up to levels of sweetness equivalent to *Trockenbeere-nauslesen* – though in both countries winemakers have come to realize that wines of *Beerenauslese* must-weight are likely to be far better-balanced and show their varietal character more clearly. These wines have been achieved using a variety of techniques: naturally occurring botrytis on the vine; induced botrytis (by spraying inoculum on the vine); botrytis inoculation of grapes picked at normal maturity and then placed on racks in an air-conditioned room, with varying but regulated temperature and humidity; and freezing of partially affected grapes to produce an *Eiswein* variant.

Botrytis in the New World

The same applies to sweet wines made from grapes left to raisin in the sun. The abbé Bellet, writing between 1717 and 1736, reported that in Italy and Provence sweet wines were made from grape bunches, the stems of which were twisted, and which were then left to ripen on the vine. This labour-intensive technique was the

Wine from raisins

Warm airy lofts provide the means to achieve super-concentrated grapes, whatever the weather. Italy's vin santo *is a product of grapes raisined by this method.*

same as that used for the legendary Constantia of the Cape in the 18th and 19th centuries. Cane-cutting is the modern-day equivalent: the fruit-bearing cane is cut near the trunk or old wood, and left on the vine until the grapes shrivel.

The principal wines made by drying grapes today are *vins de paille* and *vini passiti* (notably *vin santo* and Amarone red wines from Veneto, Italy). The *vins de paille* of the Jura are not unlike Tokay Aszú: the grapes are air-dried on mats or trays in lofts for three months, then crushed, pressed and fermented in oak casks. They are matured in wood for at least two years, and just as with Tokay, oxidation plays an important role in producing a golden-brown coloured wine with a honeyed, toffee-like mid-palate, finishing off with a tangy bite.

Scant respect is paid to Commandaria, the liqueur wine of Cyprus, today, but few wines have such direct links with the ancient world. The grapes, black Mavron or white Xynisteri, grown in gritty sand in the foothills of the Troodos Mountains above Limassol, are picked onto mats (or sheets of plastic) and laid out beside the vines. One or two weeks of September Cyprus sun is enough to shrivel them. Donkeys are still used to carry the fruit-laden mats down to the press-house, where black and white grapes are pressed separately. A minority still ferment in rotund earthenware jars buried to their rims in the ground.

There is little Commandaria made to a high standard, but samples of fresh wines from Keo in Limassol have proved to be intensely sweet and clean with 14 percent of alcohol. There is real potential for quality here. The usual practice is to age them for some years in old barrels in the open air until they are thoroughly oxidized.

Sweet Sémillon

Australia also contributes two entirely different sweet white wines made from Sémillon. The traditional method of making these was to take a dry base wine (usually full-bodied) and then add concentrated grape juice to bring the wine to the desired level of sweetness. It would then be sterile-filtered and bottled immediately to avert the risk of refermentation. Prolonged bottle-age (ten to 15 years) can result in a quite distinctive aroma and taste: a mixture of camphor, eucalypt mint and honey unlike any other sweet wine. The other style dates from 1982, when a grower named de Bortoli in the irrigation area of Griffith, New South Wales, startled Australia with a marvellous 'botrytized', wood-aged Sémillon. He soon had imitators – in California as well as Australia. Once again the point is proved that (as Commandaria-growers will ruefully agree) a winemaker can only propose: it is the market that disposes.

The winemaker proposes; the market disposes

Light-Bodied Red Wines

Choices, consequences and techniques

The idea of lighter-bodied and fuller-bodied red wines is familiar to every drinker, even if he or she has never tried to pin down exactly what it means, or which wines fall into which categories.

For the purpose of this book three categories of 'body' are proposed. The first and the last should be more or less self-explanatory: clearly a Beaujolais *primeur* is a far lighter wine (though not necessarily a less alcoholic one) than a classed-growth Bordeaux. What lightness means here is absence of solid structure, of tannins and 'extract', the flavouring principles that give depth and longevity. The more of these elements a wine contains, the fuller-bodied it is deemed to be.

The medium-bodied category is possibly the most contentious, since wines from any of the groups will fall naturally into it under certain conditions. Bordeaux of a cool wet vintage will belong here (or may even be light-bodied) while outstanding Beaujolais from a great year will certainly have enough extract and ageing potential to be classed as medium-bodied. Thus the quality of individual wines and vintages will often displace them from their 'typical' categories.

Most difficult of all to place are burgundy and other wines made from Pinot Noir. They regularly run the gamut from near-rosés to full wines with both flesh

Beaujolais, the quintessentially light-hearted red before it was launched into international stardom, was bought by the barrel by the bistros of Lyon and Paris. It is prized for its softness of flavour, sappy smell and thirst-quenching appeal. Chiroubles (below), is one of the 'crus' of Beaujolais.

and muscle on their bones. They are placed in the medium-bodied category, the subject of the following chapter, because, while a Richebourg or a Chambertin may have great intensity of flavour and bouquet, it will not have the strong tannic structure of the full-bodied group. That is the grace and mystery of Pinot Noir.

The obvious profundity, complexity and longevity of the full-bodied red wines (chiefly but not entirely fashioned from Cabernet Sauvignon and its relatives) leads one to think that light-bodied reds are somehow inferior; or, if not inferior, certainly less serious. With that impression goes the assumption that it is easier to make a light-bodied red wine. Both impressions are incorrect: making the wine is every bit as challenging, and – if the winemaker surmounts the challenge and has started with the appropriate grapes – its quality can be every bit as good.

Types of light-bodied red wines: Rosés

Rosé wines could either be classified as tinted whites or very light-bodied reds, depending on their origin and vinification. They are something of a hybrid, borrowing part of their vinification technique from standard red winemaking, part from white. In terms of style and weight in the mouth they are commonly closer to white wine than conventional red. Although made in many parts of the world their popularity is waning in most markets – somewhat surprisingly in view of the worldwide swing towards white wine. Logically, one would have expected their consumption to increase, particularly as a warm-climate summer drink.

Choice of methods

Rosé wine can be made in any one of five different ways, or variations on them:

(i) White and red wines are blended: the usual method of achieving the colour in rosé sparkling wines (even champagne), in some European *vins gris* and occasional cheap New World rosés.

(ii) Red grapes, crushed or (better) uncrushed but broken, are chilled and allowed to macerate for between 12 and 48 hours before the juice is drawn off (by static draining rather than by pressing) and then cold-fermented in the same fashion as a white wine. With broken or barely crushed grapes this is known as the bleeding or *saignée* method. The pressings (after run-off) are diverted to other winemaking uses. With variations in timing and precise handling methods, this is the most commonly used method in the New World. With crushing but very little maceration it produces America's 'blush' wines.

(iii) Whole bunches of red grapes are pressed and the free-run and very lightly pressed juice is fermented without the skins. This is essentially a European method which gives rise to a very pale coloured wine, or *vin gris*.

(iv) Crushed grapes and juice are fermented together for one to three days before the juice is run off. The pressings are not used for the rosé. A traditional European method.

(v) Red wine is heavily fined to remove tannins and is colour-stripped by treatment with active carbon; this is last-resort winemaking producing a poor wine, with economics the sole motivation.

Choice of wines

Tavel in the southern Rhône Valley is arguably still the best-known specialist in rosé, but increasingly lives on the strength of its reputation rather than the quality of the wine in the bottle. Most Tavel is made by the pre-fermentation maceration technique, using uncrushed grapes, and produces a wine with a distinctive orange-onion-skin tint, high alcohol (a minimum of 11 degrees is required, but the wine often reaches 13), and signs of oxidation which rob the wine of freshness. The best winemakers are changing their methods to produce a wine with brighter colour, more aroma and fresher, crisper fruit – achieving this through better temperature control, better use of sulphur dioxide and careful handling of the wine between the

end of fermentation and bottling. The many enjoyable rosés of Provence are made more or less in the Tavel fashion.

In terms of volume sold Mateus and other Portuguese rosés have a far greater following than Tavel and Provence. They are bland, quite sweet, slightly carbonated at bottling to give them refreshing fizz and should be served fully chilled. They should not be subjected to critical sensory analysis – if they are the conclusions will not be flattering.

Ideally, any rosé should offer the flavour of fresh grapes in a clean wine with a refreshing cut of acidity or a little tannin. Not surprisingly the tastiest are made from the tastiest grapes: inevitably Cabernets and Pinot Noirs. Anjou on the Loire has a long tradition of making very pale (and often over-sweet) rosés from Cabernet Franc. The occasional Bordeaux rosé will be firmer and more robust (though not exactly seductive).

The rare French rosés from Pinot Noir can be precisely that. Marsannay in the Côte d'Or produces such a wine in tiny quantities. For a more plentiful (and much cheaper) source, Saint Pourçain-sur-Sioule in central France is the place to look.

New World rosés are made in a radically different mould. The typical Australian or California rosé will be a vivid, light, purple-red to bright pink colour, with not a hint of orange or onion-skin anywhere in its make-up. The bouquet will be extremely fresh and fruity. The best rosés made from early-picked Cabernet Sauvignon smell stridently of that grape, and counter the slightly green character of the fruit with just enough residual sugar to give balance. Ultra-protective winemaking techniques are used throughout, entirely excluding oxygen, using cold-fermentation in stainless steel and bottling at the earliest possible date.

Making Red Wine

CRUSHING

The old way was to tread the grapes: the modern way is to crush and then destem them with mechanical crusher-destemmers. The aim of crushing is to split the skins and release the juice, enabling yeast activity and fermentation to begin. Destemming is not always necessary and bunches may be crushed whole, but stems and stalks are usually removed if the winemaker wishes to avoid high tannin levels in the wine.

FIRST FERMENTATION AND MACERATION

Fermentation vats were traditionally made of oak. Many still are, but stainless steel has the advantages of being easier to cool and easier to clean. High uncontrolled fermentation temperatures burn out the fruit flavours in the wine but can also promote greater colour extraction from grape skins, so a good temperature balance is essential. The length of maceration, the period during which the juice is left in the vat in contact with the grape skins, depends on the depth of colour and tannin required in the wine. Not so long ago workers would get into the vat to break up and submerge the cap of skins.

Carbonic maceration
Carbonic maceration is an alternative fermentation process in which the fruit is allowed to ferment spontaneously under a protective layer of CO_2. The weight of the grapes is sufficient to crush the fruit and release the juice, known as free-run, without mechanical pressure. The resulting wines tend to be softer and less astringent than those fermented in the traditional way, so this method is well suited to grapes which normally give hard, acidic wines. Wines made by carbonic maceration are usually for drinking young (for example, Beaujolais Nouveau) and do not respond well to ageing.

PRESSING

Pressing the grape mass, or pomace, occurs after the free-run wine has been removed from the fermentation vat. This process is not as important for red wines as it is for white, and in fact is not always carried out at all. 'Press wine' is high in tannin and colouring pigments. At the discretion of the winemaker a percentage of it may be blended with the free-run wine to add tannins, character and longevity. Before being blended with the free-run wine, press wine must have been fully fermented and clarified.

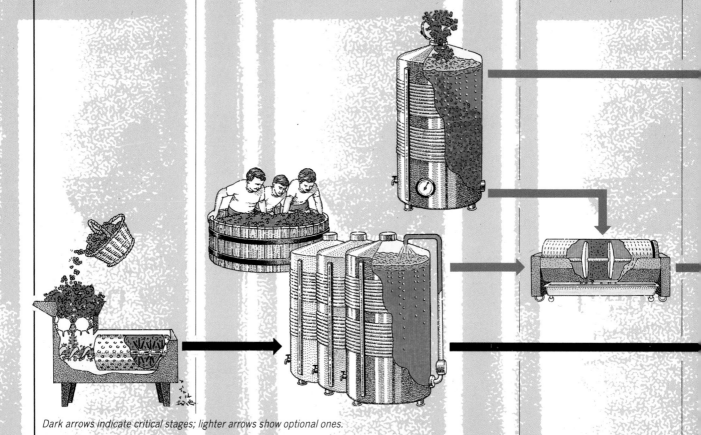

Dark arrows indicate critical stages; lighter arrows show optional ones.

MALOLACTIC FERMENTATION

This process is almost always encouraged in red winemaking. It is a secondary fermentation in which malic acid is converted into lactic acid and CO_2. It softens the acidity of the wine and, once complete, adds to its complexity and stability.

At this point the wines may be blended: they will certainly be analysed and checked before the maturation period begins.

MATURING

Maturation in oak
High-quality red wines today are almost always matured in oak. Oak contributes vanilla and wood tannin flavours. For how long the winemaker ages the wine in barrel is one of the crucial decisions, arrived at by regular tasting.

Racking
The wine is racked every few months by transferring it to a clean sterile barrel, gently aerating it and leaving any sediment in the bottom of the old barrel.

Fining
The object of fining is to clarify the wine. The fining agent (usually egg white or bentonite clay) is poured onto the surface. As it sinks through the wine it carries any solids to the bottom of the vat.

Filtration
The final option before bottling is whether or not to filter. Passing the wine through a fine filter guarantees (or should guarantee) its stability and 'brightness' even under fairly adverse conditions. But some winemakers believe it strips the wine of its character.

FINISHING

Before bottling the wine should be completely stable. It remains vulnerable to oxidation and contamination until the cork goes in. Mechanical bottling lines account for 95 percent of modern bottling. It is important to fill the bottles to exactly the right level to allow adequate room for the cork.

Right: *Chinon, on the river Vienne, one of Touraine's three red-wine villages (along with Bourgueil and St-Nicolas de Bourgueil), in a region dominated by whites. Cabernet Franc, the principal grape in the reds of the Loire, makes soft, fruity Bourgueil (below), which has echoes of both Bordeaux and Beaujolais.*

Reds from the Loire valley

St-Nicolas de Bourgueil is generally reckoned the fullest and sturdiest of a group of three appellations, followed by Bourgueil and then Chinon. The minimum statutory alcohol requirement of 9.5° gives the clue to the style of these Loire Valley wines, made at the western end of the Touraine region from Cabernet Franc (and up to 10 percent Cabernet Sauvignon). More than most wines, they prove that lightness of body does not mean lack of intensity. The very cool growing conditions have a number of implications: low alcohol, low tannins, intense aroma, crisp acidity, but (in quality terms) only a few vintages in which the grapes achieve their full potential ripeness. The vintage of 1961 was famously good; the drought year of 1976 made dark wines that held up for 15 years, and 1989 produced wines that may well prove to be in the same class.

Making Touraine reds

The wines are made by mainstream red-wine methods: the grapes are crushed and destemmed, with a standard fermentation but little maceration once the fermentation is over. The winemakers accept that robust tannins and dense colour are neither feasible nor indeed desirable. Ageing is in small- to medium-sized oak barrels and vats which are neither new nor ancient. A low percentage of the smaller barrels may be replaced each year. Barrel-ageing may extend for a surprisingly long time: up to three years, with regular racking over that period.

Beaujolais

Beaujolais at its best is the most gloriously fruity and aromatic of all red wines. Its freshness and exuberance (and the ever-increasing amount of wine made as Nouveau) mean it is not taken seriously, which is no bad thing, for it is a wine to be swallowed rather than sipped, enjoyed in high spirits rather than analysed and dissected. Some critics go even further, following in the footsteps of a legendary English author who gained his knowledge of the region by looking out of the window of his train carriage as it passed through. It deserves a closer look: while there is a great deal of Beaujolais which tastes the same even though the labels suggest it should not, there are some very good wines and (refreshingly) very few obviously faulty ones. If the wine list of a strange restaurant in a strange place looks depressing or unduly expensive, Beaujolais is often the safest haven.

Most books pass rather airily over the precise methods used to make Beaujolais, seemingly regarding it as insignificant. In fact, it is of fundamental importance in shaping the unique style of the wine, and is subject to a number of variations.

Carbonic maceration must have played a role in the making of the first wines consumed by our early ancestors, if the legends are true that grapes, stored in clay pots for winter, spontaneously fermented. It is thus curious that scientific knowledge of its chemistry is recent, and came about by chance. In 1934 a French research team set about developing methods designed to keep table grapes as fresh as possible between the time they were picked and the time they arrived on the table. One of the techniques tried was the storage of grapes at a temperature of 0°C under a cover of carbon dioxide. After two months it was found that they had become gassy and fizzy, with a strange but not unpleasant taste. Unfit for sale as table grapes, they were made into wine, which was likewise considered to be pleasant but unusual.

Research initiated by Professor Michel Flanzy (and continued since) shows what happens after a grape is harvested and placed in a container filled with carbon dioxide. The berry is alive, in the sense that it can (and does) initiate enzyme-triggered changes in its chemical composition. The first change is the consumption by the berry of its stored carbon dioxide, which it needs to stay alive. Enzymes then attack the sugar in the berry, turning it to alcohol and producing more life-sustaining carbon dioxide in the process.

If carbon dioxide is readily available from the surrounding atmosphere, the berry will also absorb it from this source. The fermentation which thus occurs within the individual cells bears no relationship to normal fermentation. It is neither triggered by nor proceeds with yeast. Over a one- to two-week period (shorter at higher temperatures, longer at lower temperatures) up to two degrees of alcohol accumulates inside the berry, at which point the alcohol effectively kills the berry, and the intracellular fermentation ceases.

During that fermentation period, though, glycerol, methanol, ethyl acetate and acetaldehyde will have been produced in significant quantities, along with a range of amino acids. It is these substances which give wines made using carbonic maceration their characteristic lifted, pear-drop bouquet. Indeed, immediately after the conclusion of the full fermentation (alcoholic as well as intracellular) the wine can have a quite unpleasantly pungent ethyl-acetate derived aroma reminiscent of the solvent-based aeroplane glue of one's childhood (or nail-polish remover for those who did not build model aeroplanes).

The key is carbonic maceration, employed in several different guises. The full-blown *macération carbonique* process sees the vat entirely filled with whole grape bunches. The bigger the vat, the greater the weight pressing on the bunches at the bottom, which will then split and exude juice. Either wild or cultured yeasts (the latter deliberately added) will cause this juice to start fermenting, giving off carbon dioxide which then fills the vat and protects the bunches higher up in the vat from oxidation and acetification, and which also progressively raises the temperature.

Thus two fermentations will be going on simultaneously but independently: the intracellular fermentation in the intact berries, and the alcoholic fermentation in the juice and split berries. As the alcoholic fermentation proceeds, the skins of the grapes in the bottom half of the vat will become softer (if the fermenting juice is pumped over the top of the vat, the change will be more widespread) and more and more bunches will collapse, so that the bottom third of the vat will be filled with fermenting wine.

At some point between three and seven days the fermenting wine will be run off, and the remaining must will be pressed. The free-run component will have little residual sugar (depending on how long it has been fermenting) but the must (with a high percentage of intact berries) will still be rich in sugar. The two parts will be combined and the fermentation will conclude fairly rapidly – extended perhaps for a few days by chaptalisation – but the essence of Beaujolais relies on a quick, relatively warm fermentation.

Carbonic maceration

In the vat the 'compôte' of unbroken grapes undergoes carbonic maceration – a spontaneous fermentation process during which the berries feed on their own store of sugar, releasing carbon dioxide.

Parallel ferments

An alternative method – also widely used in Burgundy – is to fill a third to a half of the vat with whole bunches, and then top up the vat with crushed grapes. Once again, the two different fermentations will proceed concurrently, and the subsequent winemaking does not differ greatly from the full *macération carbonique* method.

In both cases malolactic fermentation occurs naturally and quickly. A carbonic maceration wine has a higher-than-usual pH and more amino acids: both provide a favourable environment for malolactic fermentation – which is fortunate, given the speed with which Beaujolais Nouveau must be made and bottled.

Nouveau   Beaujolais Nouveau is made in much the same way as Beaujolais. The principal difference is that the must is pressed early (after only three days), resulting in fewer phenolic flavouring substances being extracted. It is also quite certain that (whatever the appellation) the best grapes are used for Beaujolais, the least good for Beaujolais Nouveau. Immediately Nouveau has finished its malolactic fermentation it will be racked, fined and filtered; within weeks if not days it will be on the market, in good years giving great pleasure, in poor years showing why critics deplore the fact that over half of all Beaujolais is made and marketed under this guise.

Beaujolais proper follows a slightly more leisurely path. In recent years there has been a tendency to embellish the richer *crus* (notably Moulin à Vent and Morgon) with new oak. While used by only a few quality-conscious winemakers, this is an alarming trend, for it confuses the issue (and the consumer). But oak apart, the emphasis remains on the exuberant fruit of the Gamay grape. Winemaking techniques are designed simply to stabilize and clarify the wine, not to embellish that which needs no embellishment, nor to give it complexity which will blur the clarion-call of the fruit.

Chianti

Chianti, together with its legitimate and illegitimate offspring, is such a moving target that categorizing it as light-bodied is as open to challenge as treating it as medium-bodied. It can in truth be either, although what it is clearly not is full-bodied. And of course there are differing weights and styles: Chianti, Chianti Classico, and Chianti Riserva. There are also highly skilled and dedicated producers; there are unskilled and unscrupulous winemakers; and there are great vintages and there are poor vintages. Then there are the challenges of the new wave *vini da tavola*, made in Tuscany – in Chianti indeed – but refusing to be bound by the dictates of the DOCG. The Italian view of things is fluid at the best of times, and there are significant implications for traditional Chianti emerging from the techniques used in making the new *vini da tavola*. The Chianti of yesterday was very different to that of today; it is a fair assumption that the Chianti of tomorrow will be quite different again. The underlying question is whether the wine will retain its distinctive character, or typicity.

Making Chianti   The basic formula for making Chianti was laid down by Baron Bettino Ricasoli in the middle of the 19th century. Even with the changes brought about by the DOCG status granted to Chianti in 1984, the formula has altered little. It is based on the Sangiovese grape, with a little Canaiolo to help colour, Malvasia to build fragrance and soften the palate, and (of recent years) perhaps a little Cabernet Sauvignon. Trebbiano is used as well, but for less laudable reasons (it was not used by Ricasoli) and in any event has assumed less significance since the DOCG regulations reduced the minimum contribution of white varieties to two percent.

The steps taken to vinify Chianti appear in the choices and consequences chart (*see* pages 146–147). There are three factors which help determine the taste, structure, and quality of Chianti. The first is geographic: is the wine from the core region of Chianti Classico, is it from Rufina (on a par with Classico), or is it from elsewhere, and is the region (there are seven) specified, or is it a blend? Second, is it

San Gimignano lies just outside the zone of Chianti Classico. The new Italian wine laws of 1992 are a determined attempt to preserve the integrity of regional traditions while allowing scope for ambitious winemakers with ideas of their own.

Chianti *simpliciter* (whether Classico or otherwise) or Chianti Riserva? Chianti Riserva must be aged for three years in oak or vat, Chianti for a minimum of only four or six months (depending on its region). Third, the combination of the options chosen in the winemaking process will have a dramatic effect.

Ancient v. modern

A modernist Chianti, for example, which has been made in a Vinomatic fermenting vat, has 10 percent Cabernet Sauvignon in its blend, has been given a lick of new French oak, is bottled as early as the regulations allow, and is sold immediately. It will bear no apparent relationship to a traditionally made Riserva, even where such wine has been made with great care and skill, and (on some Utopian judging scale) may be said to be of equal quality. But its typicity score will nonetheless be zero.

It may be realistic or it may be fatalistic to say that the market will ultimately determine the direction in which Chianti heads. At one level it is correct to say that the vast majority of wine drinkers are not in the least concerned with the issue of typicity; indeed they do not even know what the word means. They choose a label or a brand because of some broad-based expectation, and will make the decision to buy the wine again (or not) on the most simple criteria: did they like the taste, and was it fairly priced? However, over a long period of time it may be that Chianti will become indistinguishable from other red wines made elsewhere; once that happens the risk is that the word Chianti will no longer trigger the decision to buy in the first place. This decision will instead be determined by price or by the current fashion (probably inspired by advertising and promotion) for some other wine. In that circumstance Chianti will have paid the ultimate price.

The saviour of Tuscany?

This is why wiser heads are leading a move back to the core variety, Sangiovese (and to the Sangiovese Grosso clone locally called Sangiovete). The aim is to produce the highest-quality wine, recognizing it will be different from the Chianti of bygone times, but arguing that it will be recognizable nonetheless. The interaction of *terroir*, climate and variety unique to the region will mark the wine so that it cannot be duplicated elsewhere. Sangiovese, in this view, will prove to be the saviour of Tuscany.

Chianti

This choices and consequences chart illustrates those stages in the winemaking process in which the options chosen by the winemaker will fundamentally influence the taste and individuality of the final wine. Not every stage of the process is indicated: for that the reader is directed to the red-wine process chart on pages 140–141.

The making of Chianti, perhaps Italy's most famous red, and the mainstay of Tuscan viticulture for centuries, was in danger of becoming a complacent business. Tuscany has now become Italy's most innovative region in modernizing her wine industry, without obscuring the classic wines.

1
IN THE VINEYARD

Choice of grape variety
(a) *Sangiovesi 75%–90%*
(b) *Cananaiolo 5%–10%*
(c) *Trebbiano/Malvasia 2%–5%*
(d) *Other optional reds, including up to 10% Cabernet Sauvignon*
Varietal choice is one of the most hotly debated issues in Chianti today. One school of thought lays maximum emphasis on Sangiovesi and ignores the requirement of incorporation of other varieties, particularly white. It is strongly opposed to Cabernet

2
FERMENTING

Fermentation timing
(a) *Long – 2–3 weeks*
(b) *Medium – 7–10 days*
(c) *Short – 3 days Vinomatic*
Choice of fermentation technique is vitally important in determining wine style. Long maceration extracts all available tannins and accentuates the tendency of Sangiovesi to bitterness; it necessitates long cask maturation and (probably) the need for further maturation in bottle to allow the wine to soften. The mid-course produces wines with good balance, complexity and fruit, but perhaps not the same longevity.

Above: *The 'pomace' is what remains after pressing grapes – the residue of skins, pips and pulp.*

Right: *Fruity, fresh Chianti for local drinking may still be bottled in bulbous flasks (fiaschi), either covered in straw or plastic, but the more tannic, serious Chianti, intended for ageing, goes into Bordeaux-style bottles which can be stacked.*

Sauvignon which robs the wine of its typicity. The other school argues that the blends give the greatest complexity and that the marriage of Sangiovese and Cabernet Sauvignon is a synergistic one.

Left: *The American-owned Villa Banfi at Montalcino in Tuscany is one of the most technologically advanced operations in Europe. The pneumatic presses, like the entire winery, are computer-controlled.*

The recent move to short fermentation (usually associated with Vinomatic fermenters) produces a very fruity, very soft, brilliantly coloured *nouveau* style.

Governo
The use of the *governo* technique (adding must from 5–10% of grapes which have been left to dry and concentrate to vats of normally fermented wine in order to cause a refermentation) is subject to trend. While a handful of producers insist it should be used in *riserva* wines, most limit its use to Chianti made to be drunk young, where it freshens the wine with the touch of gas it creates and gives the illusion of a little sweetness through the glycerol it produces.

Malolactic fermentation
While most independent observers regard the softening effect of malolactic fermentation as highly desirable, some makers are still prepared to leave its occurrence to chance. Most, however, encourage it and seek to complete it quickly after the end of fermentation.

3

MATURING

Choice of oak
(a) *French* barriques – *old and new*
(b) *Tuscan chestnut – old and new*
(c) *Large old Slavonian oak*
(d) *No oak*
Next to the impact of Cabernet Sauvignon on Tuscany is the influence of new oak, so far used with discretion and sensitivity in the making of Chianti (but not so much so in the making of *barrique vini da tavola*). Oak choice is usually linked with fermentation choice; long fermentations with large old oak maturation; shorter fermentations with new small oak. Some winemakers reject oak in almost any form, preferring concrete or glass-lined tanks.

Maturation time
(a) *Very long – 3–9 years*
(b) *Medium – 1–2½ years*
(c) *Short – 3–6 months*
Once again, there is a link: long maturation in large, old neutral oak; the shortest in new *barriques*. This in turn links back to fermentation: a fresh, fruity wine low in tannin can be much improved by oak tannins.

Fining and filtration
The continuity continues: very long-vatted wines which have been racked many times are less likely to need fining (and are also less likely to be filtered because of the philosophy of the maker) than those which have spent a shorter time in oak.

Rioja

Bodegas Lopez de Heredia, one of the great bastions of Rioja tradition, ferment and age all their wines in oak – the minimum is three years.

Many of the issues confronting Chianti also confront Rioja. Specifically, should the wines be subjected to long cask ageing, which gives complexity, smoothness and softness but which also oxidizes and subjugates the fruit? And what role should oak play in shaping the taste of the wine? On the latter point, Rioja is moving in the opposite direction to Chianti; yet the new thinking in each region has a similar aim. Riojans have not (so far) burdened themselves with the complication of adding Cabernet Sauvignon or Syrah; the old Cabernet vineyard of the Marqués de Riscal is the one exception. All other Rioja reds are made from a blend of all or some of: Tempranillo (typically 75 percent), Garnacha (25 percent), Graciano (2.5 percent) and Mazuelo (2.5 percent). In the manner of Chianti, each grape contributes something special and different to the blend. Rioja has always indulged in winemaking on a grand scale. An indication is that a *bodega* must have a storage capacity of 7,500 hectolitres (equivalent to 83,000 cases) and at least 500 *barriques* before it can apply for permission to export its wines.

In the majority of *bodegas* the grapes are crushed and fermented in a wholly traditional fashion, with temperatures peaking at 30°C or more and finishing within three tumultuous days. The must is then allowed to macerate for seven days before being pressed. Thereafter the handling of the wine will depend on its grading or appellation, determined by the Rioja Consejo Regulador (set up in 1926). In each grade the wine may be either '*clarete*' (lighter-bodied and of lower alcoholic strength: between 10 and 11.5 degrees), or '*tinto*' (darker, fuller-bodied, higher in alcohol). *Tintos* are today far more frequently encountered than are *claretes*. During their long sojourn in barrel, the wines were traditionally repeatedly fined with egg whites and repeatedly racked, but a less rigorous regime is used with the current shorter oak-ageing. Cold-stabilization, pasteurization and filtration are all options open to winemakers before bottling; pasteurization is the most contentious, although it is not clear whether or how it affects the wine.

Ambivalence in oak

The oak used is almost exclusively American, a strange twist given the fact that most American wine producers prefer to import their oak from Europe. What is more, having selected this highly perfumed and flavoured oak, many Rioja winemakers go to extremes to tone down its flavour. New barrels are washed with hot water to reduce the flavouring compounds, then further seasoned with lesser wines. Once used for top-quality red wines, the lengthy maturation and consequent pick-up of oak aromas and flavour would be balanced by egg-white fining. Despite these apparent efforts, the oak does give the wines a marked vanilla-lemon perfume and flavour: a hallmark of the Rioja style. Another is the suppleness and smoothness of the texture: as a consequence of the fining and the very long cask and bottle-age given to the wines, the tannins are extremely soft. This unusual lightness of structure has historically made Riojas the first choice reds of Spain.

The small family firm of Bodegas Muga in the Rioja Alta claims to be the only producer in the region to use American oak exclusively for both fermentation and maturation.

The classification of Rioja

Wine	Maturation before sale
Rioja 3° año	Sold at least three years after harvest; must have spent at least one year in barrel.
Rioja 4° año	Sold at least four years after harvest; otherwise the same.
Reserva	Sold at least five years after harvest; at least two and a half years in barrel.
Gran Reserva	Sold at least seven years after harvest; at least four years in barrel.
	Note: Reservas and Gran Reservas can shorten the time in barrel, but must then be bottle-aged for an additional period twice as long as that by which the barrel-ageing was shortened.

Medium-Bodied Red Wines

Choices, consequences and techniques

No grape makes the choices open to a winemaker more critical than the Pinot Noir. Curiously, this was not always so. Traditional English texts on wine tend to stress the 'masculinity' of burgundy, when compared with the supposed 'femininity' of Bordeaux: the precise opposite to our present categorization of burgundy as medium-bodied, Bordeaux as full.

Burgundy, in truth, has changed through the years. In the 18th century the high fashion was for Volnay, so pale and light that it was called a *vin de primeur* – bottled in December and drunk before the next harvest. In 1728 Claude Arnoux wrote

> '(Volnay) *produces the finest, the liveliest and the most delicate wine in Burgundy ... its grapes are so delicate that they cannot abide the (fermenting) vat more than 12 to 16 or 18 hours, because if they are left in longer, (the wine) begins to taste of the stalks ... This wine is only a little stronger in colour than* oeil de perdrix.'

œil de perdrix

Later in the 18th century, and throughout the 19th, the fashion swung in favour of the *vins de garde* of the Côte de Nuits (above all Chambertin); wines which were deliberately made as strong as possible, with honey added (until Monsieur Chaptal introduced beet sugar) and vatted for long enough to make them fully red and relatively tannic.

vins de garde

These were the wines that gave burgundy its 'masculine' reputation, and which (in comparison with feather-weight Volnay) were easy to 'cut' with dark Rhône wines for export. It is only in the past 20 years that fashion has swung back in favour of pure, pale (if not *primeur*) burgundies. No small part of the reason is the insistence of the New World on 'varietal character'. Currently the feeling is that if you really want to taste Pinot Noir at its best you must handle it gently and be content with a pale, wonderfully aromatic but relatively light-bodied wine.

Pinot Noir in Burgundy

The temperamental Pinot Noir was born in Burgundy, selected and perfected by the Cistercian monks of Cîteaux in the Middle Ages. It reaches its apogee in the village of Vosne-Romanée, where the sea of vines laps right up to the walls of the growers' houses.

The colour of Pinot Noir

The Pinot Noir grape differs from all other important dark-skinned varieties of *Vitis vinifera*: it has fewer colouring pigments (anthocyanins) and is more prone to oxidation; it has fewer flavouring substances and fewer tannins, and is liable to lose a significant proportion of these during vinification. For these reasons, too, Pinot Noir is especially sensitive to climate and to its treatment in the vineyard – and in particular to over-cropping.

In the cellar

The choices – and the arguments – start the moment the grapes come into the winery: should they be crushed with the rollers on conventional spacing; should they simply be destemmed with the berries left intact (or as intact as possible); should whole bunches go into the fermenting vat; or should the entire fermentation start with nothing but whole bunches?

The decision on crushing will have an important influence on the final wine. Wine made from fully crushed grapes without their stalks tends to be simple in aroma and structure; that made from whole bunches is often very complex, with spicy or wild game nuances which emphasize any ethyl-acetate aroma. The drawbacks of using the whole bunches, stalks and all, may result in paler, less stable colour, higher pH and perceptible green tannins from the stalks. Many winemakers prefer to ferment whole berries (perhaps with a few stalks put back into the vat) or to use a mixture of whole bunches (say one-third) and whole berries.

At this point (immediately after the must has been put into the fermenting vat) the decision must be made whether or not to run off and dispose of part of the free-run juice (the French term for this is *saigner*). As yields have steadily increased, this practice has become very common: it is now not so much a question of whether juice should be run off, but how much. In years of good yields 20 percent is an accepted level; only in years of poor flowering or abnormally dry conditions will this figure be less. The very best winemakers concede it is basically an

The scarcely spectacular middle slopes of the Côte at Vosne-Romanée are Burgundy's most precious parcels of Pinot Noir. Here the Domaine de la Romanée-Conti conjures quite extraordinary intensity, complexity, depth and sheer beauty from its delicate grapes.

unsatisfactory choice, stemming from an excessive crop in the first place, and while it gives better colour and greater concentration of flavour, it also leads to an imbalance in the must. Relative to wines from optimum yields the resulting wine will be lower in acidity, less aromatic and fruity, higher in tannin and have a higher pH. In extreme cases, they can have an unnaturally 'thick' character. Nonetheless, if the crop has been excessive, it *is* the lesser of two evils, though 'bunch-thinning' (*see* page 154) is the best solution of all.

Extracting colour

Where traditional vats (open or closed) are used, conventional wisdom considers warm to hot fermentation temperatures (30–32°C) to be most effective in extracting colour from Pinot Noir. But there are those who believe that colour is best extracted in the absence of alcohol (ie before fermentation), that aroma and flavour come with fermentation, and that tannins come from the maceration afterwards. Either way winemakers of Pinot Noir in Burgundy and elsewhere are convinced that it is desirable for fermentation to reach a relatively high temperature.

The one exception lies with the use of the sidewise-revolving Vinomatic vats, which quickly and effectively extract maximum colour and flavour from all grape varieties, Pinot Noir included. Indeed, it is easy to over-extract material from the grapes this way – care must be taken to avoid doing so.

Chaptalisation

Chaptalisation is considered quite essential to the making of burgundy regardless of the naturally available sugar in the grapes. This view is challenged by a few iconoclasts such as Hubert de Montille in Pommard, but his is a voice in the wilderness. Its many proponents say quite simply that '*it is for the feel in the mouth*', an oblique reference to the fact that (particularly if it is added progressively in small amounts towards the end of the primary fermentation) it 'stresses' the fermentation and leads to an increase in glycerol.

Pinot Noir had no place in Spain until the house of Torres, already famous for magnificent Cabernet blends with traditional Catalan grapes, planted it in the highest vineyards of Penedès. The Torres barrel-cellars, sturdily traditional, give little idea of the innovative scope of the company.

Oak – a matter of taste   The conservative view is that new barrels are not only unnecessary for the production of fine burgundy, but may positively harm it. If the oak is of the wrong type, if it is clumsily handled, or if the wine is not sufficiently strong and rich, then oak may indeed detract from the wine's character (or fail to help it). But it is fundamental to the making of all of the wines of the Domaine de la Romanée-Conti, all of the Grand and Premier Cru wines of Méo-Camuzet and Domaine Dujac – and many other great winemakers – who use all new barrels every year. At the end of the day, it is a matter of taste.

The final bone of real contention is filtration: many of the top producers are implacably opposed to it, and no scientists or biochemists seeking to establish that it has no long-term adverse effects on colour or flavour will change their minds. Indeed, the anti-filtration camp often even avoids pumping Pinot Noir wherever possible, relying on gravity or gas-pressure movement. What is clear is that some unfiltered burgundies do not react well to being exported. Tranquil life in a cool Burgundy cellar is one thing; shipment in hot climates is another. Heat can trigger unwelcome bacterial activity, leading to 'off' odours, cloudiness and occasionally worse.

Filtration

At the risk of gross understatement, one can say that, for burgundy, the simpler (and more conventional) the winemaking process, and the less new oak involved, the simpler the wine. Commune and classification (Grand Cru, Premier Cru or commune) will then impose another layer of quality and character. But distinctions of *cru* are in a different category from those of winemaking technique: one must try to imagine a three-dimensional scale to understand the pattern. When one then looks at the performance of Pinot Noir in other parts of the world, even those sceptical about the meaning of *terroir* have to admit that there is something very special about Burgundy; a magical combination of *terroir*, climate and tradition.

In Europe Burgundy has no challengers. There are marketable Pinot Noirs from Italy's South Tirol; a serious attempt by the house of Torres in the high Penedès of Catalonia; a flood of anaemic Spätburgunders from Germany; and very frail Pinot Noirs from Sancerre, but none of these approaches the triumph of the Côte d'Or (and, to be fair, its neighbour, the Côte Chalonnaise). It has been left to the New World, and principally two countries – the United States and Australia – to throw out a so-far limited challenge to Burgundy. To date the quantity has been small, and the quality inconsistent. Most of the wine produced has been distinctly ordinary; only a few select regions and a few select winemakers within those regions have produced Pinot Noir of real style and merit. But what they have achieved in recent vintages holds great promise for the future.

New World Pinot Noir

New World methods of handling Pinot Noir vary even more widely than those of Burgundy, while paying due regard to what Burgundy is doing. The Californians and Oregonians have progressively moved away from whole-bunch fermentation (finding the tannins from the stalks too astringent) and compensated by using a longer period of maceration at the end of fermentation. Some are (justifiably) cautious about the amount of new oak they use, and if there is a criticism, it is a tendency to 'undermake' the wine rather than the reverse. The decision not to filter has become very fashionable – even if it means having to accept cloudy wine. Australasian methods are similar, the principal difference being greater use of whole-bunch fermentation, and intolerance of cloudy wine.

Over the last decade or more a belief has grown up in America that Oregon is the place for Pinot Noir and that the Napa Valley is not. But Mondavi's Reserve Pinot Noir dispels that myth: Carneros, south of Napa, and the Central Coast are making excellent Pinot Noirs. Australia's success has been concentrated in the areas surrounding Melbourne (Geelong, the Mornington Peninsula, Gippsland, Macedon and the Yarra Valley) which share a similar climate: cooler than Bordeaux, warmer than Dijon. And in New Zealand one area – variously called Wairarapa or Martinborough – is consistently producing strong and typical Pinot Noir. It is, though, a grape which remains a great enigma; the ultimate challenge. Confirmed Cabernet Sauvignon drinkers may never understand or appreciate it; something which causes Pinotphiles no concern at all. For better or worse, there simply isn't enough great Pinot Noir to satisfy existing demand: it would be a disaster if it suddenly acquired the popularity of either Chardonnay or Cabernet.

The Oregon climate, as uncertain as that of Burgundy, appears to be ideal for Pinot Noir. In a statement of faith Robert Drouhin, the leading Beaune grower/négociant, has planted 100 acres in the Dundee Hills. These rotary fermenters in his Oregon winery contrast with his oak fermentation vats in Beaune.

Pinot Noir

This choices and consequences chart illustrates those stages in the winemaking process in which the options chosen by the winemaker will fundamentally influence the taste and individuality of the final wine. Not every stage of the process is indicated: for that the reader is directed to the red-wine process chart on pages 140–141.

Pinot Noir is a difficult but alluring grape. No other *vinifera* displays such genetic variation, which creates problems for grower and maker alike. Clonal selection is vital in the battle against viral menace. Bunch thinning has proved beneficial in improving the quality of the fruit. Responding happily in cooler parts of Europe, especially in Burgundy which produces the finest Pinot Noir wines in the world, it sets a real challenge for quality winemakers in the New World. Despite plantings in Oregon, and cooler parts of California and Australia, there is no doubt that the grape is best suited to cooler, marginal climates.

1
IN THE VINEYARD

Bunch thinning
Removing a percentage of bunches from the vine in order to reduce the crop is becoming increasingly common. The quality of Pinot Noir is particularly compromised by excessive crops.

2
CRUSHING

Crushing options
(a) *Whole bunches*
(b) *Destem only*
(c) *Partial stem*
(d) *Total crush*
(e) *Stalk return*
Whole bunch fermentation takes additional time and space in the winery and demands open fermentation vats and *pigeage* (by foot or pneumatic ram) but results in complex, aromatic wines. Destemming without crushing is widely used;

3
FERMENTING

Choice of yeast
Choice lies between wild or cultured yeast; Burgundians overwhelmingly prefer the former, arguing that it gives greater complexity and subtlety.

Choice of fermentation vat
(a) *Open*
(b) *Closed*
(c) *Vinomatic*
Determined by the choice made at the crusher. Extraction of colour and flavour from the must is aided by pushing down the cap of *marc* into the fermenting juice by foot or by automatic plungers, or by pumping the must from the bottom of the vat up over the *marc*. The Vinomatic is an automatic vinifier which is

becoming increasingly common in Burgundy but must be used sensitively.

Temperature choice
Almost all producers believe Pinot Noir must reach 30° during fermentation but give different reasons – some say for colour, others for aroma and flavour.

4
MATURING

Choice of oak
(a) *Type of oak*
(b) *Percentage of new oak*
Well-chosen oak, handled in the right manner, is of fundamental importance for the greatest burgundies. Good burgundy (and Pinot Noir) can be made without new oak but lacks the complexity of the greatest wines.

Lees contact
Not an uncommon practice in Burgundy. Similar to lees contact with Chardonnay, except that stirring is not usually practised. As long as no off-characters develop, it can be very beneficial in adding weight and complexity to the wines.

Period in oak
Decision will depend on the percentage of new oak, the weight of the base wine and the style sought by the winemaker. It is easy to spoil Pinot Noir by leaving it in oak for too long.

Method of picking
(a) *By hand*
(b) *By machine*
Machine picking limits the options of the winemaker and in particular precludes whole bunch fermentation.

Left: *There is a high premium on undamaged grapes, since damaged ones begin to oxidize immediately. Time is of the essence in getting the picked grapes to the winery before they can spoil.*

fermentation is initiated faster and green tannins from the stems are avoided. A partial destem offers some of the advantages of both (a) and (b). Fully crushed and destemmed grapes give good colour but tend to produce simple wine. Many winemakers return a proportion of the stalks to strengthen the structure of the wine.

Juice run-off
Running off part of the juice before fermentation commences in order to concentrate it has become common practice in high-yield years. The end result is not as good as bunch thinning. The run-off portion is often made into wine to quench the thirst of grape-pickers during the following harvest.

Pre-fermentation maceration
Extracts colour and tannin from the pomace. Frequently takes place in Europe because the reliance on wild yeasts and the fairly high level of sulphur additions mean that fermentation takes 3–4 days to commence. Can be significantly extended by chilling the must and adding more sulphur dioxide.

Above: *Using a continuous press results in a 'cake' of solid matter. This can be used as cattle-feed or a vineyard fertilizer.*

Chaptalisation
Inevitable in Burgundy but forbidden in Australia. Undoubtedly it adds roundness and fatness to the texture of the wine.

Maceration choice
(a) *Post-fermentation maceration*
(b) *Partial barrel fermentation*
Conventional approach calls for 5–12 days post-fermentation maceration to extract soft tannins; a minority prefers to finish the fermentation in barrel, relying in part on the subtle oak tannins that are extracted.

Malolactic fermentation
(a) *Early (inoculated)*
(b) *Late (natural)*
More or less standard practice. Malolactic on lees gives an added dimension to Pinot Noir but may give off-flavours. Traditionalists argue that late, naturally occurring malolactic fermentation also gives added complexity.

Below: *The ultra-modern fermentation plant at Pacs del Penedès, owned by the house of Torres. Torres has invested in the latest wine technology as well as introducing some of the classic French varieties, Pinot Noir included.*

Fining
Gentle fining – usually with egg white – is often used, sometimes as an alternative to filtration, sometimes in addition. It removes excess tannins but must be used with discretion or it will detract from the character of the wine.

Filtration
Burgundian dislike of filtering is spreading to the New World. However, some unfiltered burgundies may react to heat during export which can trigger off cloudiness and off-odours.

Italian red wines

Italy produces such a profusion of red wines, made in diverse climates using ever-changing techniques, that all attempts neatly to classify and parcel them for overseas consumption have failed. The eternal Achilles heel of wine is that it is complicated, it intimidates. Italy achieves levels of complication and intimidation unparalleled in any other country, even Germany, partly through its own efforts but largely because of the accidents of its long history. The consequence is that its red wines are far less well known and appreciated than they should be. The selection here is but a small and inevitably arbitrary one. For those who wish to know more about the wines of Italy Burton Anderson's *Wine Atlas of Italy* (Mitchell Beazley, 1990) is the indispensable reference work.

Barrique-aged vini da tavola

Some might say it is typical of Italy that some of the greatest and most of the poorest wines share the same birth certificate which, if not quite alleging illegitimacy, certainly denies nobility. It is no less appropriate that it should have been the noble Marchese Mario Incisa della Rochetta who in 1948 started it all by planting Cabernet Sauvignon on the family estate at Bolgheri on the Tuscan coast. He called his wine Sassicaia, which from the start bore no comparison with any other in Italy. His nephew, Marchese Piero Antinori, recognized just what Sassicaia foretold, and took it – and its relatives – onto the world stage. The first Antinori creation was Tignanello, a blend of Sangiovese with a little Cabernet, which remains his best known of all. Pure Cabernet Sauvignons, Bordeaux blends, and pure Sangioveses followed in its wake in spurts and dribbles, it seemed, from the baroque fountains of every noble Tuscan *fattoria*; all failing to conform in one way or another with the DOC rules. It has been easy to deride the DOC system and its draftsmen but they were desperately unlucky: the system was promulgated in 1963, just a few years before the new wave of viticulture and oenology swept over the country. To all intents and purposes, the DOC regulations could have been written 100 or 200 years earlier and scarcely been more outmoded.

The significance of the new upmarket *vini da tavola* extends right across Italy, and has meant radical changes in both vineyard and winery. In the vineyard the changes are obvious enough: the planting of French varieties often at the expense of the traditional Italian grapes. In the long term the changes in the winery may prove even more significant, for they represent changes in attitude – of philosophy – which will alter the face of Italian wine forever.

Trends away from tradition

The methods used to make these wines are not unusual; it is the difference in approach which contrasts that of traditional Italian red winemaking. The traditional way was to take varieties naturally high in acid, tannin and potential alcohol, and ferment them in such a way as to extract every available particle of flavour and tannin. Having created a vinous monster, the winemaker would then seek to tame and soften it by prolonged ageing in large old Slavonian oak vats, with oxidation as a principal weapon in his armoury. The wines had a certain balance, and sometimes made a very memorable bottle, but did nothing to highlight the most desirable characteristics of the grape variety or region concerned.

The introduction of new oak in the form of Bordeaux-style *barriques* forced a complete change. Instead of three to five years in oak, the period was reduced to 12 to 18 months. This had a double-up effect: instead of tannins being reduced by the process of oxidation and ageing (and deposited in the barrel in the form of heavily stained tartrates), they were boosted by the tannins extracted from the oak. And new oak inevitably introduces another dimension of flavour and complexity (which traditionalists, of course, dislike). Taken together, these changes meant that the wine being taken from the vat had to be less tannic and more fruity if any semblance of balance was to be achieved by the time it was bottled.

Winemakers started to play down the vigour of their fermentation and macerate the wine for shorter periods afterwards. They also introduced grapes calculated to have a softening effect – most obviously Merlot and Cabernet Franc, but (surprisingly) even Cabernet Sauvignon. In such wineries fermentation (which may incorporate a percentage of whole bunches or berries) takes place in stainless steel vats with inbuilt temperature control, and typically lasts between a week and a maximum (including maceration) of two. Malolactic fermentation is artificially encouraged and finishes soon after the primary fermentation. Only then is the first sulphur dioxide added. Whether the wine is then matured entirely in new or near-new oak *barriques* or whether it will also spend some time in the traditional old oak vats (called *botte*), will depend on the winemaker. In all, it may spend between 15 months and two years in some kind of oak after fermentation.

While the *barrique*-aged *vini da tavola* originated in Tuscany, and while they are far more common there than elsewhere, they are gaining ground in a number of other regions. Piedmont is the other main centre of activity. But now Lombardy and Umbria are almost as *barrique*-conscious, and the word is spreading far and wide. New legislation (the 'Goria Law') in 1992 acknowledges that everything has changed.

The Tuscan wines fall most neatly into the medium-bodied category. They do so whether they are pure Cabernet Sauvignon, pure Sangiovese, blends in which Sangiovese is dominant, or blends where Cabernet Sauvignon takes the lead.

These wines are fragrant and supple; where Cabernet Sauvignon is dominant, it is gently herbaceous, but never tannic or astringent. While they will improve with bottle-age, they do not positively need it: five to seven years from vintage will see them reach their plateau of development, however long they may remain on that plateau thereafter. Rusticity or typicity have no place in these wines: sulphides, volatile acidity and oxidation are conspicuous by their absence; those aromas and flavours which are present are the result of very deliberate winemaking decisions.

This highlights the tension between tradition and opportunity: in some ways Italy provides an interface between the New World and the Old. Piero Antinori has no doubt that the advantages outweigh the disadvantages:

> '*I must say that while I admire French wines greatly, I consider myself privileged to be operating my business in Italy rather than France. It is so much more exciting to be in Italy, where so many things are changing, rather than to be in a rigidly established situation, even if it be at the highest level as it is in France. For many centuries Italy has been a producer of quantity rather than quality, for that is what the consumer wanted. Then it suddenly all changed, and in the last 20 years we have had this sort of revolution. Producers and customers have both discovered the enormous potential Italy has for quality wines of kinds we have never attempted before.*'

However, he does not see Chardonnay and Cabernet Sauvignon engulfing Italy:

> '*In the long term I see the future of Italian wine lying more in our own varieties, provided we are able to improve them through clonal selection, which I am sure we can. I believe in our varieties because we have such an ancient viticultural history and tradition. The world is being invaded by Chardonnay and Cabernet Sauvignon, but the consumer will want a wider choice, which Italy can provide with its traditional varieties. This does not mean there is no place for Chardonnay and Cabernet Sauvignon in Italy; clearly there is. There are regions where certain grape varieties have a real history and tradition, and these should be maintained and protected. There are other regions without a significant history, rather like California or Australia, and in these regions Chardonnay, Sauvignon Blanc and Cabernet Sauvignon should play an important role.*'

Whilst still producing its splendid Chianti Classicos, the Castello di Ama near Radda in the heart of the zone is as uninhibited as any Tuscan estate in its experiments with foreign grapes. Its vini da tavola *include Chardonnay, Merlot, Sauvignon Blanc and even Tuscany's most promising stab at Pinot Noir.*

The second Risorgimento?

The northern Rhône – Syrah

The wines of few regions fit less tidily into the categories of medium and full-bodied than those of the northern Rhône. The best wines of Hermitage, Côte Rôtie and Cornas are full-bodied: the wines of the best producers made in the great vintages emphatically so. Such wines explain why Hermitage and Côte Rôtie were rated as among the finest – if not the finest – in mid-19th century France; why Professor George Saintsbury wrote of an 1846 Hermitage as

'The manliest French wine'

> *'One of the three or four most remarkable juices of the grape, not merely that I ever possessed, but that I ever tasted . . . It was the manliest French wine I ever drank.'*

Moving down the appellation scale to Crozes Hermitage and St-Joseph, or taking the wines of less-exalted winemakers from lesser years in Hermitage, for example, the wines become medium-bodied. We look at the vinification techniques and options for all the wines of the northern Rhône (to avoid duplication) in this chapter but discuss the qualities of the full-bodied wines in the next.

Northern Rhône winemakers are as idiosyncratic and as definite in their views as any in France. The extreme example is Marcel Guigal who has broken with convention so far as to taint (as some still see it) his exquisite Côte Rôties with new oak. Such things may pass in Italy, where he could even (at the expense of his DOC) have added Cabernet, but the discipline of the French appellation system strongly discourages such outrage. Nobody, however, challenges Syrah's supremacy in the region. Even the varieties that are officially permitted to soften its ruggedness (Viognier in Côte Rôtie, Marsanne and Roussanne in Hermitage) are less used today as winemakers learn to handle the mighty Syrah on its own.

Yet because Syrah reigns unchallenged and because it is a variety which normally has intense colour and flavour, the winemaking choices become less vital than the differences in *terroir* and the vintage. The most important recent development after the use of new oak is the increased use of carbonic maceration, and here its effect is significantly less marked than it is in Burgundy and Beaujolais.

Right: *Terraced vineyards at Cornas in the northern Rhône. Cornas, sheltered from the Mistral, grows Syrah of a more consistent ripeness than anywhere else in the northern Rhône.*

Below: *La Chapelle, from the hilltop vineyard of the house of Jaboulet, overlooking the Rhône, is consistently one of the finest wines of Hermitage.*

The enormous production of the southern Rhône, the plethora of unfamiliar grape varieties, and the years of prostitution of the Châteauneuf-du-Pape label have all helped to obscure its superlative quality. As with the northern Rhône, there is also considerable diversity of style, nowhere more so than among the wines of Châteauneuf-du-Pape.

Only in Burgundy does one find such a bewildering array of options and sub-options for the winemakers as in Châteauneuf-du-Pape. Only in Burgundy can one find in a single appellation such a gulf between the great and the execrable; such diversity of style within a given level of quality. But Burgundy permits only one grape in the vat; Châteauneuf-du-Pape allows 13. Whether this is accumulated tradition or in fact a viticultural insurance policy is not clear. Grenache is always the dominant grape; Cinsaut, Syrah, Mourvèdre, the white Clairette and/or Picpoul are other essential varieties.

The greatest wines of the best years (and poor years are relatively rare in this hot, dry climate) are full-bodied by any standard, but they are made only by a small handful of conservative producers (headed by the Perrins of Beaucastel). Taken as a whole Châteauneuf-du-Pape can fairly be said to fall into the medium-bodied category. They can be incredibly rich on the mid-palate, but the tannins seldom have the astringent authority of the true full-bodied red wine. That richness comes from a number of factors: the warmth (aided and abetted by the stony *terroir* which traps the heat of the day and re-radiates it through the night), the generally low yields (the appellation allows only 35 hectolitres per hectare); and the resultant high alcohol of not less than 12.5 degrees, the legal minimum, but the best growers are happy with 14.5.

The possibilities are a mathematician's delight and a draftsman's nightmare. If one simply looks at the choice of fermentation methods, the permutations and combinations become obvious. A Châteauneuf-du-Pape may incorporate a percentage of all of the following fermentation methods: carbonic maceration, destemmed whole berries, destemmed crushed berries, whole bunches (without

The southern Rhône

Châteauneuf-du-Pape

Ancient bush-pruned Syrah vines baking in the sun of the southern Rhône appellation of Gigondas.

The rising status of Gigondas is confirmed by Marcel Guigal's stylish wines.

carbonic maceration), crushed but stemmed bunches, and crushed and destemmed fruit. But what is more, differing treatments may have been given to some or all of the grape varieties incorporated into the blend and, of course, those varieties may be up to 13 in number.

There are the usual choices – and arguments – about the subsequent maturation and handling of the wine. By far the greatest amount spends between 18 and 30 months in very large old oak vats (or *foudres*) or in waxed-cement or glass-lined steel vats. The effect of storage in such containers is minimal: there is obviously no flavour pick-up; oxidation will be at a minimum simply because of the size of the container; and precipitation of tartrates and other sediments will be slow – but nonetheless sufficient to allow most producers to indulge in their aversion to filtering their wine (and a lesser number to fining it). Neither new oak or used burgundian *barriques* show signs of making any real inroads here, nor should they. But in such a pervasive atmosphere of conservatism (for even the 'new' vinification methods are merely a collation of diverse techniques of long standing) there are always exceptions: Château de Beaucastel eschews filtration, uses traditional fermentation methods and ages its wine in old oak – but uses a sort of 'flash pasteurization' technique on the grapes as they leave the crusher as a means of extracting the maximum colour and flavour from the skins by rapidly heating them, then cooling the must before fermentation starts.

These are all wines driven by fruit and by their formidable alcohol (usually not less than 13 degrees). Since alcohol does not diminish, but fruit flavours do, the wines fall into two distinct camps: those which should be drunk at two to six years of age, and those which will live for 20 or 30 years.

Gigondas

The wines of Gigondas are as unpredictable as those of Châteauneuf. Almost every producer has a different idea about proportions of different grapes (although under the appellation regulations Grenache must account for at least 65 percent), and vinification methods vary likewise. Just to add a touch of spice, one of the best domaines, Les Gouberts, has taken to using new oak for its top *cuvée*, in the knowledge that the smell of oak is worth dollars.

Australian Shiraz (Syrah)

The only vineyards outside of the Rhône Valley to grow the Rhône varieties in large quantities have for a century been those of Australia.

Shiraz (Syrah) until 1965 was responsible for almost all of Australia's premium-quality red wine. Familiarity nonetheless bred undue contempt, and since that time Shiraz has been supplanted in popular esteem by Cabernet Sauvignon (and to a much lesser degree Pinot Noir). The reputation of Australia's greatest red wine – Penfolds' Grange Hermitage, from the Syrah grape – remains undimmed, however, and in terms of volume the variety remains extremely important. What is more, the establishment (or re-establishment) of cool-climate winegrowing in the southernmost parts of Australia has resulted in a resurgence of interest (and reputation).

Making Shiraz

An overwhelming proportion of Australia's red grapes – and Shiraz is no exception – are harvested free of rot or mould. Sulphur dioxide additions have always been low, but there is an increasing tendency to do without them entirely until the malolactic fermentation is complete. Since ample colour is normally not a problem, the loss of any extraction or 'binding' effects which the sulphur dioxide might promote is not significant. The only cases where protection with sulphur is fairly routine is when grapes harvested by machine (and therefore bruised and stalkless) are being trucked long distances for processing.

The grapes are almost invariably crushed and destemmed, and fermentation is started immediately with cultured yeast. Stainless steel fermentation vats are used: the most common are semi-enclosed, and either use devices called 'header-boards' to keep the cap of skins submerged, or autovinification (*see* page 179) in a Potter

Fermenter. Some smaller wineries use open vats and punch down the floating cap with rods; an alternative is to pump juice drawn from the bottom of the vat over the cap periodically to wet and partially submerge it, a traditional technique used all over the world. Fermentation temperatures are usually controlled between 18 and 25°C.

Penfolds, Wolf Blass, along with a slowly increasing number of smaller wineries, press all or part of their Shiraz musts before primary fermentation is complete (at 1 to 3 degrees Baumé), and move the still-fermenting wine to barrels, where the primary fermentation will finish, often in conjunction with the malolactic fermentation (initiated by inoculation while the primary fermentation is still going on). The alternative is the more traditional extended maceration at the end of fermentation (sometimes used for part of the wine, part being barrel-fermented). *Choices in ferment*

Almost all quality wine is matured in *barriques* or hogsheads; American oak has been the traditional choice and the sharply rising cost of French oak is likely to deter any decision otherwise. Fining is common, filtration almost universal: the great majority of Australian winemakers regard the suggestion that filtration has anything more than a transient effect on a robust red wine as unscientific, sentimental nonsense.

Regular-quality wines undergo malolactic fermentation in vats, and are filtered and moved to barrels as inert wine around July, about four months after the harvest. The barrels will be turned 'on the shive' (with the bungs submerged to a 'two o'clock' position to avoid oxidation) and the wine left to mature until July of the following year when it will be racked, blended, filtered once again and then bottled. *'On the shive'*

The better wines will have received far more attention and work. The malolactic fermentation will have taken place in the barrel; the barrels will be kept with their bungs at 12 o'clock and topped up weekly or fortnightly; and they may be racked three or four times. This handling is much more costly, but produces a more textured, supple wine. The minimum-handling techniques produce a strangely sterile, 'undermade' wine.

Just as in the northern Rhône, Shiraz responds to the differing effects of climate and *terroir* – although in the Australian view climate has a much greater role than *terroir*. The Hunter Valley (with the warmest climate, much hotter than that of the Rhône) produces a wine which is often quite tough, tarry and tannic in its youth but which softens over 20 years into a velvety, gently earthy wine of sometimes remarkable elegance.

The Barossa Valley is (nominally at least) home to Penfolds' Grange Hermitage. Grange is made from 60- to 80-year-old, dry-land, bush-pruned vines which yield a mere 20 to 25 hectolitres per hectare. The grapes are picked at 12 to 12.5 degrees Baumé; not an alarmingly high degree of sugar, representing between 11.5 and 12 percent potential alcohol (*see* page 229). To compensate for the fact that the wine is partially barrel-fermented, extra tannins are added in powdered form in the fermenter, and it spends 18 months in all-new American oak hogsheads. *Barossa: home to 'Hermitage'*

The result is a massively concentrated and flavoured wine which is not sold until it is five years old, seldom drinkable under ten, and which can be magnificent after 20 to 35 years. Even at that age the incredibly rich cassis/berry fruit flavours and sweet vanilla extracted from the oak sustain the wine.

A third style of Shiraz is the spicy, peppery, cherry-like wine of southern Victoria, tasting for all the world like an elegant vintage of the northern Rhône. Further north in Victoria, near Great Western, the Mount Langi Ghiran vineyards achieve the weight and flesh of a great Hermitage or even a top Châteauneuf-du-Pape.

Northern Rhône: Syrah

This choices and consequences chart illustrates those stages in the winemaking process in which the options chosen by the winemaker will fundamentally influence the taste and individuality of the final wine. Not every stage of the process is indicated: for that the reader is directed to the redwine process chart on pages 140–141.

The vineyards of the northern Rhône cover a 40-mile stretch running from Vienne to Valence, with the finest wines coming from well-exposed terraced vineyards overlooking the river. The granite-based soil allows the grapes to produce wines of an almost unrivalled intensity of bouquet and flavour.

Above: Water-cooled stainless steel fermenting tanks make the task of controlling temperature far simpler, but mean major investment on the part of the winemaker.

Right: Temperature of the fermenting grapes in an open vat is continuously monitored. If the temperature inside the vats gets too high or low there is a danger of the fermentation 'sticking'.

1
IN THE VINEYARD

Choice of grape variety
(a) *100% Syrah (Cornas and Crozes Hermitage)*
The differing weight and intensity of Cornas (intense and powerful) and Crozes Hermitage (much lighter) highlights the importance of site and *terroir*.
(b) *85% Syrah, 15% Viognier (Côte Rôtie)*
Viognier gives aroma to the bouquet and a little extra fruit to the palate but lightens the colour and structure. Its use is declining; those who do use it (including Jaboulet, Delas, Champet and Duclaux) do so at only 4–5%.

2
CRUSHING

Crushing options
(a) *Whole bunches*
Crushing the whole grape bunches with their stems by *pigeage* (foot-stamping) is used by a number of major makers including Chapoutier and Chave.
(b) *Partial crush*
Jaboulet prefers partial crush, partial whole bunch (60%) with pumping over.

3
FERMENTING

Carbonic maceration
This practice, where fermentation begins inside the grape itself, yields wine full in flavour and bouquet. It has become more popular over the last 20 years, but tends to produce wines 'semi-nouveau' in style that are best drunk young.

4
MATURING

Maturation
(a) *Old oak vats*
Traditionalists strongly argue for their use of old oak, believing that any interference with the flavour of Syrah bought about by the use of new oak is undesirable, reducing or obscuring the typicity of their wines.
(b) *Used burgundy* barriques
Ageing in 1–2 year-old burgundian casks is favoured by many of the better Rhône producers, sometimes in conjunction with old oak for part of the maturation period.

(c) *85% Syrah, 15% Marsanne and Roussanne (Hermitage)*
The use of Roussanne and Marsanne in Hermitage is less common these days. Their effect is similar to that of Viognier in Côte Rôtie, although they are less overtly fruity.
(d) *90% Syrah, 10% Marsanne and Roussanne (St Joseph)*
Once again, the white varieties are not much used in practice, although permitted up to 10%.

A mixture of some stalks and leaves with the grapes is hard to avoid with mechanical harvesting, and some of the fruit will be damaged. Fermentation has already begun in the truck transporting these grapes to the winery.

(c) *Total crush and destem*
Total crushing and destemming is used by lesser appellations and tends to produce wines lacking in complexity.

Below: Remontage, the system of pumping juice over the grapes during fermentation to extract the maximum colour and flavour from the solids.

Choice of fermentation vat
(a) *Stainless steel*
The cooler fermentation temperatures possible in stainless steel can enhance fruit flavour and freshness in Syrah. Not yet widely adopted.
(b) *Old oak/concrete*
In the alternatives to stainless steel – wooden or concrete vats – temperatures can rise above 35°C giving burnt jammy flavours. Control of high temperatures will be attempted with cooling coils or by pumping over.

Fermentation time
Long fermentation and maceration (3 weeks) used by most producers of Côte-Rôtie, Hermitage and Cornas are partly responsible for strength and depth of structure. Short fermentation (10 days) is used for lighter styles – including those given carbonic maceration.

(c) *New oak*
Some have successfully experimented with new oak – particularly Guigal with his prestige bottlings of Côte Rôtie. Others are following cautiously on a small scale.

Maturation period
(a) *Short (1 year)*
The prime exponent of relatively short oak maturation is Jaboulet with his Côte Rôtie and La Chapelle Hermitage which are matured in used burgundy *barriques*.
(b) *Long (3–3½ years)*
Guigal gives his top wines 3–3½ years in new oak *barriques* which adds a major dimension to their flavour and structure.
(c) *18–24 months*
Most winemakers adopt an 18–24 month mid-path.

Clarification
(a) *Fining*
Barrel maturation and racking eliminate the need for this process but those who choose to clarify use egg white.
(b) *Filtration*
Similarly, filtration is infrequently used; Delas is the principal proponent.

Full-Bodied Red Wines

Choices, consequences and techniques

The distinguishing feature of a full-bodied red wine is the authority it has on the finish. In its youth this authority is frequently astringent and aggressive, and even though the wine may be high in alcohol and have a strongly flavoured and constructed mid-palate, it will be the finish which dominates – and which must soften before the wine becomes a pleasure to drink. One of the key issues confronting the maker of such wines (and ultimately the consumer) is whether such youthful toughness should be encouraged, tolerated or discouraged. In the most simple terms – for it is but one indicator of a more complex issue – how much tannin is too much tannin?

Bordeaux and the Cabernet family

Few wine-lovers anywhere dispute the proposition that the greatest full-bodied red wines of all are those of Bordeaux, and above all of the Haut-Médoc. Rather more might wonder how the overall standard of the wines of the 1950s, 1960s (1961 excepted), 1970s and 1980s will look from a standpoint 50 or 100 years hence – but then, that same question is raised about every generation, children or wines.

Growing a mixture

Bordeaux's growers can certainly select one or more of the varieties in the vineyard at the expense of others, but they would hesitate to alter the proportions of Cabernet Sauvignon, Merlot and Cabernet Franc which time and custom have endowed them with. To some extent the varietal mix is the persona of the property: a château is what it grows. It needs a brave owner to tamper with his inheritance. But it is also true that if growers thought they could ripen Cabernet Sauvignon reliably every year, the role of the other varieties would diminish in importance. Merlot is grown in the Médoc and Graves partly as a form of insurance (it ripens earlier and is less susceptible to autumn rain), and dominates St-Emilion and Pomerol because the heavier clay soils of those regions will only ripen Cabernet Sauvignon in exceptional vintages. If these limitations did not exist, arguably the function of Merlot, Cabernet Franc, Petit Verdot and Malbec would be a support role to balance the structure of the Cabernet Sauvignon according to the dictates of the particular vintage. Not that anybody in Pomerol would agree, of course.

The influences of vineyard practice (in particular fertilizers and sprays) and of clonal selection have been examined in the first part of the book. In Bordeaux, as elsewhere, yields seem to rise inexorably. One of the principal responses of the winemaker to ever-increasing yield has been bunch-thinning in July or August, now often used in tandem with juice run-off (removing part of the juice from the vat immediately after the grapes have been crushed and before the start of fermentation).

In the cuvier

The changes in vinification in Bordeaux in the last 20 to 30 years have been far less dramatic than in many other parts of the world. The introduction of stainless steel fermentation vats to Châteaux Haut-Brion and Latour in the early 1960s was seen as revolutionary, but in truth it was not. Stainless steel is easier to clean (and keep clean) and modern vats all have in-built refrigeration plates (serviced by an external source of 'brine', a mixture of methylated spirits and water). However, cooling may be effected by pumping the must through must-chillers, and these can be used whatever the nature of the fermentation vat. Much more important is the size of the fermentation vessel. The smaller it is, the greater the degree of control.

Particularly following the abundant 1982 vintage, which fermented in ambient temperatures more like summer than autumn, cooling facilities of one kind or another have become far more common. In previous vintages the last resort had quite commonly been to throw large blocks of ice into the vat.

The standard procedure varies little: crush and destem with moderate sulphur dioxide additions; wait for the fermentation to start naturally after a lapse of two or three days; allow the temperature to build to 29 to 30°C without attempting to check it, but be concerned (and use controls) if it goes over this level; pump over (or plunge) the cap of skins three times a day; and, as the primary fermentation subsides after three or four days of activity, progressively chaptalise with the aim of extending fermentation to five or six days; and finally allow the must to macerate for anything from seven to 21 days thereafter.

The decision on maceration time is critical: in abundant years the winemaker may wish to extend it to 21 days or more (because of the probability that the tannins will be naturally low). The problem is that all the vats are needed for fermenting; where can the wine be left to macerate? But maceration is an essential part of winemaking in the cool Bordeaux climate: the skins are seldom high in pigments, and certainly never to excess.

The use of new oak *barriques* has become a key issue in determining the style (and the quality) of the wine (*see* page 168). While only the first-growths and 'super seconds' regularly use 100 percent new oak for each vintage – and arguably are the only châteaux with fruit intense enough in flavour to justify this expenditure – some new oak is essential if the château is to achieve its potential. As a rough rule of thumb one-third new oak each year is considered the least investment a château aspiring to make the best possible wine can afford. (It is true that in poorer years less oak is required: thin wines are quickly dried out by it; the yardstick is for good to great years.)

There is a progressive *assemblage* (or blending) of the individual barrels throughout the year following vintage, sometimes but not necessarily in conjunction with racking. Fining and filtration are not emotive issues; they are simply used or not, according to need.

While there is no doubt about the Cabernet Sauvignon-dominant wines of the Médoc and Graves belonging in the full-bodied category, there is scope for considerably more discussion when it comes to the Merlot-dominant wines of Pomerol and St-Emilion. The latter are softer, sappier, can be more fragrant, and tend to mature more quickly.

The central feature of the wines of Bordeaux is their structure. Just as the Burgundians consider the bouquet of prime importance, the Bordelais are principally concerned about the way the wine tastes and feels in the mouth. They see this as driving everything else: the bouquet, the finish and the aftertaste. This is built around the variety (most obviously Cabernet Sauvignon), the vinification (particularly post-fermentation maceration) and the use of new oak.

The reason why these wines are revered around the world is the extraordinary harmony and balance they achieve with age. The question 'when to drink' is an intensely subjective one. It is hard to imagine anyone (even the French who prefer to drink their red wines younger than do British or American consumers) suggesting a 1970 Bordeaux is anything other than superb at 20 years of age.

The first-growth Château Lafite epitomizes the difficulty of classifying red wines by their 'body'. Its wines are tannic and sinewy in structure, living as long as any great Médoc. yet usually relatively 'light' or delicate beside its rival Pauillac first-growths, Latour and Mouton-Rothschild.

The Cabernets of California are widely accepted as the finest in the world outside Bordeaux. In 1979 when Baron Philippe de Rothschild joined forces with Robert Mondavi to produce Opus One it seemed the ultimate compliment had been paid to the Napa Valley. Christian Moueix managed to reinforce it when he laid the foundation for Dominus in the early 1980s. Even the producers of the greatest red Bordeaux look with admiration (even awe) at the spectacle of 'their' Cabernet

*California
Cabernet
Sauvignon*

ripening so perfectly, seeming to offer year after year the opportunity to make the sort of great wine Bordeaux sees perhaps once in a decade.

Making California Cabernet

The Californian approach to Cabernet is closely modelled on that of Bordeaux. As with Chardonnay, avant-garde winemakers have sought to go beyond the simple expression of fruit and *terroir* to seek the subtlety and nuances which seem to flow so easily from the hands of Bordeaux's winemakers. Changes in philosophy – and with philosophy, technique – have closely paralleled those developed for Chardonnay, but in the case of Cabernet have tended to focus on the quantity and the quality of the tannins. While many Californians would disagree, most outside observers found the tannin levels of California Cabernets from the 1970s and early to mid-1980s unacceptably high and aggressive. Once again, we quote California's eloquent ambassadors for change. First, Tim Mondavi, for the Robert Mondavi Winery:

> 'I see a lot of changes with Cabernets, specifically in relation to the tannin levels. If you look back, much of the equipment we used was designed simply to get a job done: we used a pragmatic, engineering-type approach, and relied upon objective features such as sugar, acid and pH to tell us about grape and wine quality as opposed to an overall understanding of the fruit. So when you took those factors, along with brutal crusher-destemmers which did the job but without concern for the fruit, followed by a short, fast fermentation with brutal pumping over techniques, short skin contact time and then a hard pressing, it was not surprising we produced hard, bitter wines. I think all of that has passed; or at least for us it clearly has.'

Zelma Long expresses the thinking at Simi Winery:

> 'We are looking for a wine which has plenty of ripe tannins; and ripe tannins come initially from the way you grow your grapes and the way you time your harvest. But you must also control every aspect of vinification: how you crush the grapes, how you pump them over, when you press them. We are aiming to make a wine which has abundant soft tannins, has concentration and has complexity; we are also interested in achieving blackberry/cassis/dark cherry fruit flavours with some overlay of soft herbal qualities, rather than the green pepper/bell pepper/herbal components.'

There is no doubt that the face of California Cabernet Sauvignon is changing; that the wines are becoming more supple and harmonious in the mouth, and that the best are quite magnificent. But to say that the tannins are better balanced, softer and riper than they once were begs the question. The real issue is whether the starting point is valid: is the Bordeaux tradition of long maceration after the fermentation really the best winemaking method for grapes grown in the warm dry Napa Valley climate, often on low-yielding vines with minimal assistance from irrigation? It may very well be – as most Napa vignerons assert – that the tannins extracted later in the maceration are softer and more supple.

Australian Cabernet Sauvignon

Australia's and California's Cabernets are just as different as their Chardonnays. Australia has a wide range of climates and soils in which Cabernet Sauvignon is grown, but the wines emerge with a surprisingly broad homogeneity of style. With the exception of a few badly made, over-extracted wines (usually the produce of very small wineries), all Australia's Cabernet Sauvignons are far softer, far fruitier and far more accessible than their Californian equivalents. The winemakers might be accused of making wines which are simple and unsophisticated. The reality is that the wines taste almost directly of their fruit: the varietal flavours come through very clearly, and so does the influence of *terroir*.

Coonawarra Cabernet Sauvignon is recognized as Australia's finest, yet much of it is made in a fashion which suggests that, like its Californian counterpart, it could be better still – much better still. Most of it is machine-harvested from machine-pruned vines yielding 60 to 70 hectolitres per hectare. A significant percentage is then transported to the Barossa Valley, eight hours away. It is fermented in very large, temperature-controlled stainless steel vats at 18 to 22°C, and is pumped over two to three times a day. The winemakers of some of the most highly regarded, trophy- and gold-medal winning wines habitually 'bleed off' 20 percent or more of the juice after crushing. This pale liquid is then used for low-price red wines. Maceration time after fermentation varies enormously: from none to 40 days. Frequently there will be an ultimate *assemblage* of parcels of wine picked at varying times and vinified quite differently. Some such Cabernets are partly fermented in barrel; all the good ones are aged for a while in new oak. It is quite common to find barrel-fermentation in American oak followed by ageing in French oak (or vice versa). After 12 to 15 months' maturation, and several rackings, the wine will be sterile filtered and bottled.

More down-market Cabernet Sauvignon from less exalted regions will be fermented (in stainless steel) with oak chips for an instant touch of class, before being racked and then filtered 'star bright'. A certain amount will receive a perfunctory period of barrel ageing in four- or five year-old oak; tannin and acid will both be adjusted, and the wine bottled after the minimum of handling.

Top of the range Cabernet Sauvignons (and the Pinots and Syrahs) are hand-made in precisely the same way as at a top French château or Californian winery. This means hand-pruned vines, hand-picked grapes (with rigorous selection), careful crushing, fermentation in small vats, either maceration after the fermentation, or the fermentation finished in barrels, extensive use of new French oak, a deliberate choice between exposure to air or total protection from it, racking, the possible elimination of lesser barrels, and high-quality packaging.

Making Australian Cabernet

If the southern hemisphere has a 'first-growth' it is Penfolds' Grange Hermitage. But Penfolds, based at their Nuriootpa winery in the Barossa Valley, produce a range of red wines in which the qualities of South Australian Cabernet and Merlot as well as Shiraz find their fullest expression.

Cabernet Sauvignon and blends

This choices and consequences chart illustrates those stages in the winemaking process in which the options chosen by the winemaker will fundamentally influence the taste and individuality of the final wine. Not every stage of the process is indicated: for that the reader is directed to the red-wine process chart on pages 140–141.

Cabernet Sauvignon is considered by many to be the best grape variety in the world. It is the easiest to grow and harvest and adapts admirably to different environments, Old World and New. It is *the* grape of the Médoc, producing some of the finest red Bordeaux. A very high ratio of pip to pulp makes it extremely tannic. It is usually blended, especially with Merlot, to soften the tannins and needs ageing in oak and in bottle. Cabernet Sauvignon has a natural affinity with oak – top estates leave their wines in new oak *barriques* for over a year.

Above: *A fermentation vat being emptied of its vigorously frothing contents.* Right: *Winemakers go to great lengths to clarify their wines. Solid yeast particles left behind after fermentation need to be removed if the wine is to be clear and bright. 'Fining' is carried out in traditional wineries by using a natural coagulant – here, beaten egg white.*

1 IN THE VINEYARD

Choice of variety
Choice of grapes may be imposed by climate or *terroir* or may be that of the winemaker seeking to balance the structure of pure Cabernet Sauvignon, usually with Merlot, Cabernet Franc and Petit Verdot.

2 CRUSHING

Crushing options
(a) *Crush and destem*
(b) *Whole berries*
(c) *Stem return*
Crushing and destemming is the almost universal method practised in Bordeaux but with the use of modern crushers with adjustable rollers, a percentage of whole berries can be used in some ferments. In some cases a proportion of the stems will be returned to the must to increase the tannin levels.

3 FERMENTING

Choice of fermentation vat
(a) *Traditional oak/stainless steel*
The choice between traditional upright oak vats and stainless steel only has important implications if temperature regulation is required because only the stainless steel vats are temperature controlled.
(b) *Open plunging/closed pump over*
Open fermentation with hand plunging is perhaps old-fashioned but gives good colour and tannin extraction. Closed tanks are widely used, either with a

4 MATURING

Choice of oak
The choice between new or used oak and the type of oak is a key issue in determining taste and quality. Nevers or Allier are most widely used. The better the grapes the more oak the wine can sustain, in which case there will be a greater use of new oak.

Bunch thinning
A practice which is becoming increasingly common. Removing a percentage of grape bunches from the vines will produce a smaller crop which will make more intensely coloured and flavoured wine.

Method of picking
Machine picking is an option in almost any vineyard – size and terrain permitting – because Cabernet Sauvignon grapes are invariably crushed so it is not critical that they remain whole at harvest.

Juice run-off
Removing part of the juice from the fermenting vat immediately after crushing and before the commencement of fermentation is sometimes practised in order to decrease the juice to skin ratio and produce more intensely flavoured wine.

Pre-fermentation maceration
This stage frequently takes place in Europe (whether or not it is a matter of choice) because the reliance on wild yeasts and the sometimes high level of sulphur additions mean that fermentation takes 2–3 days to commence. This maceration extracts colour and tannin from the pomace.

Choice of yeast
The choice lies between slower-acting wild yeasts or more predictable cultured yeasts.

Above: *Colour is extracted from Cabernet Sauvignon grapes by spraying the fermenting must over the cap of skins.*

'floating cap' or with the cap held submerged by boards.
(c) *Vinomatic*
Vinomatics, large automatic vinifiers, are as yet rare in Bordeaux but will become more common and are more likely to be used in years with low colour.

Temperature
Most makers choose a 25–29℃ range in Bordeaux, slightly lower in the New World. With the strong structure of Cabernet Sauvignon, temperature control is not critical.

Chaptalisation
Almost invariably carried out in France; seldom in the New World. A process that is necessary if the sugar content of the grapes is too low owing to unfavourable weather during the vintage cycle.

Post-fermentation maceration
Standard practice in Bordeaux, California and Italy; common but not invariable in Australasia. The aim is to extract more tannins and to soften those tannins already present.

Malolactic fermentation
Invariably improves the quality of red wine by lowering the acid level and adding to the complexity of the flavour and so is systematically encouraged. The only choice lies between starting the process with cultured bacteria or relying on natural triggers.

Maturation period
Prolonged maturation of bygone years is now seldom practised; 12 to 18 months being most common period.

Racking frequency
Racking aids clarification and softens the wine. This might be carried out as frequently as every month for the first few months.

Fining
In Bordeaux fining takes place towards the end of the maturation period in order to clarify and stabilize the wine. Elsewhere it may only be used for excessively tannic or heavy wines.

Filtration
Filtration before bottling is generally practised in Bordeaux and universally in the New World.

Five generations of growers and winemakers at the Cantina Aldo Conterno in Monforte d'Alba have helped to establish the classic Piedmontese style of tannic Barolo, astringent Barbera and mouth-filling Dolcetto. But here too the style is changing, as new technology and new grapes move into this ultra-traditional region.

Piedmont – Barolo and Barbaresco

Nebbiolo in ferment

A variety of minor, and some major, revolutions are recorded in these pages, but perhaps the modernization that is sweeping through Piedmont in Italy amounts (for those who know its wines) to the most epoch-making of all.

Piedmont is the perfect place to examine the dilemma winemakers face in weighing up the relative values of tradition and new technology. There is no question that viewed by international standards – the perfect, universal palate-in-the-sky as judge – the new Barolos and Barbarescos are better wines. But are they better Barolos? Are they better Barbarescos? Perhaps the only real answer is that time will tell. The revolution has been so quick, so strong in its impact that the wines have not had a chance to speak for themselves. Will the new wines age with grace? No-one can yet point to wines supporting their case (whichever side they are on). Experience suggests, though, that a grape with so marked a character as the Nebbiolo, growing in soils and a climate as distinct as those of Piedmont, will eventually assert its traditional style.

Fault or character?

The Piedmont chart on pages 172–173 indicates the two fundamentally different approaches to the making of Barolo and Barbaresco. The modern approach, most famously espoused by Angelo Gaja with Barbarescos, and the Ceretto family with

Angelo Gaja has been the Gorbachev of the revolution that is sweeping through Piedmontese winemaking. He angered and amazed many of his countrymen by introducing classic French grapes and oak barrels to the region, but has maintained his reputation by insisting that the venerable reds of north-east Italy deserve more recognition as being among the world's great wines. He is the Yeltsin, too.

their Barolos, produces more internationally acceptable styles of wine. One does not have to be an aficionado of Nebbiolo or the wines of Piedmont to understand and enjoy them. The traditional approach tolerates a degree of toughness, a touch of volatility, some tarry, farmyard characteristics and slight oxidation: the underlying strength and durability of the wine can carry these blemishes when young, and allow them to meld with age into a matrix of such complexity that to identify or complain about the faults seems churlishly pedantic.

The avant-garde style emphasizes fruity freshness and urges that technical faults should not be condoned simply because they are 'typical'. It categorically denies that its wines will not age with grace, pointing to better chemical composition and the absence of any bacterial activity and spoilage. Traditionalists believe the aromas they are accustomed to are the essence of Nebbiolo in their soil; they do not distinguish between fault and character. Whereas wines such as these were once supported and judged by parochial regional markets, the judgment of today is increasingly international in perspective. If for no other reason, this guarantees that over time the modern approach will dominate, yet hopefully not to the degree that the essential character of these wines is compromised.

Piedmont

This choices and consequences chart illustrates those stages in the winemaking process in which the options chosen by the winemaker will fundamentally influence the taste and individuality of the final wine. The example is Piedmont, home to some of the best of Italy's native grape varieties. Not all the stages in the winemaking process are shown: for that the reader is directed to the red-wine process chart on pages 140–141.

Piedmontese traditions are strong, adhering to the old viticultural concepts. Typically, the vineyards occupy hills, not plains, and yields have been sensibly restrained. Despite this strong wish to preserve the heritage (the native Barbera and especially Nebbiolo grapes have long occupied the best vineyards, even with the introduction of foreign varieties), the application of modern technology and growing acceptance of external influences, such as the use of French *barriques*, have meant that new styles of wine are emerging – a direct reflection of choices made in the winery.

Hygiene standards and control of temperature during fermentation have been revolutionized by the introduction of stainless steel vats, even in such redoubts of tradition as Piedmont. Wine matures more slowly in steel than in wood barrels.

1
IN THE VINEYARD

Grape variety
The Nebbiolo grape produces Piedmont's classic wines, Barolo and Barbaresco, and is probably the region's most prestigious variety – the optimum choice for many growers, and usually allocated the best south-facing vineyard sites.

2
FERMENTING

Choice of fermentation vat
(a) *Stainless steel*
Fruit aroma and flavour can be retained by keeping must temperatures low during fermentation. Stainless steel vats allow such control, usually maintaining temperatures at 23–29°C. This is an option now widely favoured by modernists and traditionalists alike.

(b) *Old oak vats*
Now less likely to be used for Piedmont wines because of the lack of temperature control. This can lead to considerable loss of the fruit flavour which many see as vital for counter-balancing the Nebbiolo's inherent acidity. Aside from the initial expense in investing in stainless steel, oak does retain a slight advantage in that it can contribute to the wine's complexity.

3
MATURING AND FINISHING

Maturation time
(a) *Long maturation (up to 4 years)*
Traditional makers favour long maturation for their wines, relying on time to mellow high tannin levels – especially those caused by lengthy maceration and oak fermentation.

(b) *Short maturation (Barbaresco: 1 year; Barolo: 2 years)*
Other winemakers give freshness and fruit flavour priority, these being better achieved by maturing for shorter periods.

Other varieties making full-bodied Piedmont reds include the widely planted Barbera, also used for 100% varietal wines, and chosen for its acidity and its high-yielding reliability.

Harvesting

(a) *Early*
Piedmont's wine-growers currently favour higher acidity, more pronounced grape flavours and less tannin than formerly; achieved by harvesting grapes at optimum balance in terms of ripeness and of flavour. Essentially, this means picking earlier.

(b) *Late*
More traditional Piedmont growers might seek to obtain high alcohol and high tannin levels so harvest as late as possible (October to November) to allow the build-up of sugar and anthocyanins.

Below: Contrasting starkly with the shining steel vats, oak botti (the large ones) and barriques (the French term is current) for maturing wine. French oak casks are increasingly being used to age Italian wine, giving new dimensions to the classics and opening new vistas for winemakers.

Post-fermentation maceration

(a) *Prolonged (up to one month)*
(b) *Short (10–12 days)*
From the winemaker's viewpoint, the shortening of the maceration time must be as significant as controlling the fermentation temperature. Not only is the amount of tannin diminished but the near-certainty of oxidation over the longer period is also reduced. The resultant wines are more supple and balanced though still retaining strong tannins when compared to other wine styles. It is quite possible they will not have the same longevity, however.

Degree of malolactic fermentation

(a) *Immediate and total*
Control of malolactic fermentation is best achieved by using temperature-controlled stainless steel fermentation vats. These enable wines to be held at warm temperatures (20°C) after their first fermentation to ensure a quicker onset, control and completion of the malolactic process. Once finished, the winemaker can apply protective sulphur dioxide, to achieve a cleaner, fresher and more stable wine.

(b) *Delayed or incomplete*
Complexity and softness in a wine is often achieved by slow malolactic fermentation, but if left to run its course naturally (as would happen in oak vats in Piedmont) there is a risk that it will draw to a halt before all the acid has been transformed. In such cases, malic acid remaining in the wine may cause unwanted sour flavours.

Maturation vessel

(a) *Old Slovenian oak/chestnut*
Choice of maturation vessel is swayed by the tannin content desired. The addition of as few wood tannins as possible to the already abundant grape tannins present in Piedmont reds is ensured by using large oak vats for maturation. These are the traditional choice.

(b) *New barriques (for part or all of maturation)*
Some winemakers take the view that oak tannins are complementary to grape tannins,

so promote ageing in new barrels. Similarly, wines undergoing shorter post-fermentation maceration may also be seen to benefit from contact with new oak.

Blending and bottling

(a) *Wines from many sites (house style)*
Blending wines from different sites, thus creating the optimum combination for each vintage, is the traditional approach for making Piedmont wines. This produces wines of distinctively differing house styles.

(b) *Individual cru bottlings (from a specific site)*
Single vineyard bottlings have yet to establish a track record. It takes the status of producers like Gaja to give these *cru* or vineyard

labels the cachet necessary to convince buyers that the distinction is valid and worth paying for.

Hermitage and Côte Rôtie

The grapes of Hermitage: Syrah from the steep slopes of the northern Rhône achieves a concentration and structure that puts it among the world's most individual red wine – maturing in time to a character not unlike that of the finest red Bordeaux.

In deference to tradition and Professor Saintsbury, a chapter on full-bodied red wines should also include Côte Rôtie and Hermitage from the Rhône Valley. The world heavy-weight class contains other champions: Vega Sicilia from Castile, Brunello di Montalcino from Sienna, even that sublimated black-strap Priorato from Catalonia. But for a model of body, strength and complexity, delicacy even, outside the world of Mouton and Latour, one must turn to the great wines of the northern Rhône. Because new oak has not traditionally been used in fashioning them, it is possible to see their layers of fruit-driven flavours and equally to see the changes which occur as the wines evolve in bottle. *Terroir* is all-important: whether one is comparing Hermitage with Côte Rôtie, or the two rival Côte Rôtie vineyards, La Landonne and La Mouline, the differences are consistently observable. But this is no rustic backwater simply relying on typicity and historical reputation: the influence of the winemaker is no less observable.

Marcel Guigal in Côte Rôtie has emphatically demonstrated that Côte Rôtie and new oak can make a spectacular impact. Not many winemakers will wish to follow precisely in his footsteps, but it seems probable that there will be increasing (though hopefully judicious) use of some new oak in the years ahead. As in other parts of Europe (and the New World) this may indirectly lead to more winemakers following the example of the house of Jaboulet and shortening the time the wine spends in oak (be it new or old) before it is bottled.

The very nature of the vineyards – the steep terrain, the schist-rock soil – and the climate, have protected the integrity of the grapes to an uncommon degree. What has changed most of all is the celebrity of these wines. First the English, then the American market has 'discovered' the stature of wines that have been in their midst, remarkably consistent, marked on every map, indeed situated alongside what might be described as France's main highway, for centuries. Those who have drunk and loved them for years must wince at what fashion has done to their prices. The compensation is that if they are profitable they will improve. It was always thus. Fine wines can only be – have only ever been – made for discriminating markets.

Fortified Wines

Choices, consequences and techniques

There is no catch-all definition of fortified wine except that at some stage in its making its alcoholic strength is increased by the addition of spirit, usually brandy. Fortified wine did not come into existence until the 17th century, when distillation was commercialized (first by the Dutch). Port, which most regard as the best example, took its present form around 1775 (as did champagne). As late as 1754 the British merchants in Oporto complained about '*the habit of checking the fermentation of the wines too soon, by putting brandy into them while still fermenting; a practice which must be considered diabolical, for after this the wines will not remain quiet, but are continually tending to ferment and become ropey and acid.*'

'Fortified wine' means a wine containing alcohol which has been added and which is not simply the end-result of the alcoholic fermentation. The amount added varies substantially, as does the stage at which it is added:

Fortification

(i)   Before fermentation. Some wines are fortified before fermentation starts, and thus never ferment at all. A few table wines (called *vins de liqueur* in France) are made this way: they lack structural complexity and develop very slowly in bottle. Slightly more common are wines which are subsequently barrel-aged for many years. The most noteworthy are certain – though not all – muscats and tokays from northeast Victoria, Australia. These demand the addition of the greatest volume of fortifying spirit, as the final alcohol strength (18 degrees or more in the case of tokays and muscats, much less in the case of Sauternes-style wines) is almost entirely derived from addition.

(ii)   During fermentation. All vintage and tawny ports and many muscats are fortified during fermentation. Fortification in fact arrests fermentation. The timing of the addition, and the calculation of the amount of spirit required, are crucial in determining the final style of the wine. The misleadingly named *vins doux naturels* of southern France (most famously Muscat de Beaumes de Venise) are also fortified for the purpose of ending fermentation.

(iii)   After fermentation. The best example of fortification after the end of fermentation is sherry. The degree of fortification is significantly less than for port, both because the natural alcohol level is higher and because the finished wine is generally lower in total alcohol.

The sterilizing and stabilizing effect of adding several degrees of alcohol to dry table wine has long been used to protect wines shipped in barrel. This caused great dispute in the late 19th century as Australian table wines started to make substantial inroads into the English market: arguments raged as to whether or not the wines were lightly fortified or achieved their very high alcohol levels naturally. The question was important because of a duty differential: although the Australian winemakers were adamant that they were able to achieve 16 degrees of alcohol with ease in areas such as northeast Victoria, the English authorities thought otherwise. The debate ended inconclusively, but a bottle of 1880s 'Hearty Burgundy' from the famous firm of B P Burgoyne tasted in 1990 left no doubt that at least some of these wines were indeed fortified, even if only lightly.

Making Sherry

CRUSHING AND PRESSING

Drying
Grapes destined for the fuller-bodied *olorosos* or for sweet wines, are left to dry in the sun to increase their sugar content. The bunches are laid out in the open in long lines on *esparto* grass mats, protected at night by plastic sheets.

The modern practice is for the dried grapes to be lightly crushed and destemmed before pressing. In the past they would have been taken straight for pressing.

Pressing
Only in the last few decades has treading grapes in nail-studded boots in troughs (*lagares*) been gradually abandoned in favour of mechanical presses. Of these, the best quality is the batch-type – either the horizontal or inflatable bag press. The alternative, the continuous press, incorporates long sloping screws which produce must of different qualities by varying the pressure. The rules of the Consejo Regulador allow only 70% of the potential juice to be squeezed from the grapes to make sherry.

The must is left for about 24 hours for solid matter to settle out before being pumped into the fermentation vats.

FERMENTATION

Traditional fermentation vessels are oak butts and the huge Ali-Baba-type concrete or earthenware vats. Most *bodegas* now favour stainless steel or other modern materials, although barrels are still used.

The first stage, in which most of the sugar is transformed into alcohol, lasts for 3 days to a week and is quite violent. With the onset of the much slower, secondary fermentation, a range of organic compounds evolves.

Ideally the temperature of the fermenting must should be kept below 25°C for *fino* and below 30°C for *oloroso* style wines. At the end of fermentation (in late December or in January) the must 'falls bright' as suspended matter falls to the bottom of the tanks.

CLASSIFICATION

After fermentation is complete sherries will be classified into three broad categories: *fino*, *oloroso* and (inferior) *rayas*. The *fino* wines are lighter and will develop into 'Fino' and 'Amontillado' styles, the *olorosos* are heavier, most of them destined to be blended with sweetening wines as 'Cream' sherry (although old dry *oloroso* can be superb).

As a result of this initial classification the *fino* wines are fortified to 15.5°, which is the optimum degree for the growth of *flor*, and the *olorosos* are fortified to 18°. *Flor*, the yeast which forms like a skin on the surface of the wine, is indigenous to the Jerez region and imparts the distinctive aroma and flavour which is characteristic of *fino*.

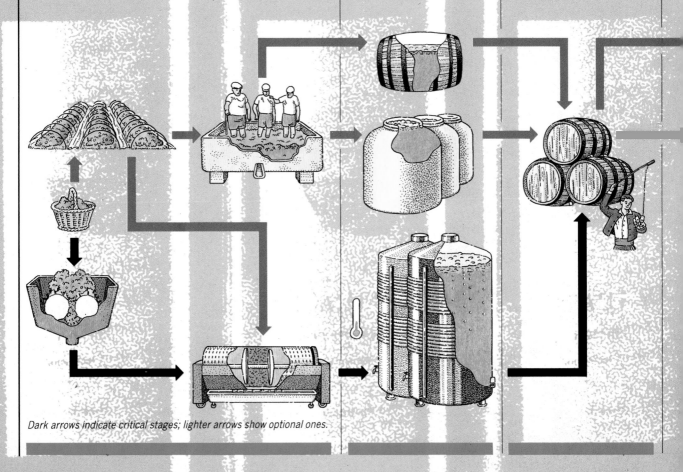

Dark arrows indicate critical stages; lighter arrows show optional ones.

SOLERA SYSTEM

At this stage the sherry may be put in a *criadera* or young wine reserve before it is taken on to the *solera*.

The *solera* system ensures a consistency of style and quality by blending young wines with older wines over a period of 3 or 4 years. The *solera* consists of butts of wines of varying ages. The oldest, always at floor level, is the *solera* proper, and stacked on top are the second, third and fourth scales.

As the older wines are drawn off for blending or bottling, so the butts are replenished from the next in age and so on to the end of the series. The result is that younger wine refreshes each barrel on the way down and just enough nutrients pass down to the older wines to keep their *flor* alive (at least in the case of *finos*). No more than a quarter to a third of the wine will be drawn off at a time. The youngest butts are topped up with young wine of the same type, from a *criadera*.

The success of the system depends on the fact that the younger wines rapidly take on the character of the older wines to which they are added.

FORTIFICATION

The alcoholic degree of *fino* is reduced during its period in the *solera*. Having been fortified to 15.5°, it is likely to be down to around 14.7° by the time it is ready for bottling perhaps 4 years later. The practice is to refortify *finos* up to 15.5 to 17°.

Oloroso sherries actually increase in alcoholic degree whilst they are in the *solera*. Without the covering of *flor* they are exposed to air and very slowly evaporate, bringing them up to 18 to 20°.

BLENDING AND CLARIFYING

All sherries are dry at this stage. Sweet sherries are made by adding sweetening wine. For dark cream sherries this is usually 'PX', the sweet, dark, concentrated, fortified juice of the Pedro Ximenez grape. *Mistela*, the fortified, raisined juice from Palomino grapes is sometimes used for sweetening medium sherries.

Sherry is slightly cloudy when it is drawn from the *solera* so it requires clarifying. Traditionally it was fined with egg white. The albumen attracted to itself suspended particles which were then carried down to the bottom of the butt by adding 'Spanish earth'. This process is still used in smaller *bodegas*. In the larger, mechanized *bodegas* the wine is clarified by filtration.

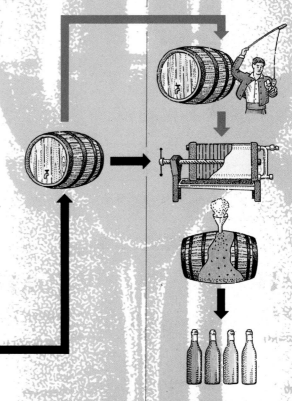

Port

If wine is fermented dry, and then fortified, it undergoes no risk at all; if it is fortified before the end of fermentation, the risks increase as unfermented sugar may well re-ferment; it was precisely this fact which caused the English merchants so much anxiety in 1754. However, adding one or two degrees of alcohol to wine which had completed its fermentation incurred no such risk, and it was thus that the wines of the Douro started their life. Fortification of the ferment started sporadically in the early 1700s, reached the current 'formula' by 1775, but did not become uniform practice until around 1850.

All the grapes for port are harvested by hand. While Portugal does not have the vast agrarian labour pool it once enjoyed, the wild vineyards of the Douro – awe-inspiring with their size and palpable sense of history – are suited neither physically nor emotionally to mechanization. It may come, one day, but the fact that foot-treading in the *lagares* has survived (against all expectations) suggests that change will be slow.

Fermentation takes place either in the small *quintas* or farmhouses of the independent grape growers, or in the very much larger wineries of the port houses. Wines made 'up-country' in the *quintas* are often still foot-stamped in the traditional manner. The *lagares* are like over-sized granite spa-baths, filled with grapes to a little over knee-height, which are then foot-trodden by teams of swaying workers who (especially in tourist-frequented *quintas*) are entertained during the monotonous hours by a band playing assorted drums, pipes, accordions and tambourines. This may seem like a cross between a cabaret and sheer primitivism, but it is a very effective way of producing high-quality wine; above all

Below: The best Quinta De Vargellas grapes are used for Taylor's Vintage Port. Mechanization of these vineyards high in the Douro valley seems unlikely: steep rocky terraces and the traditional labour-intensive ethos of the 'up-country' quintas have so far precluded any major technological advance.

Right: The Viking-style barcos rabelos *are mere museums today. Once these beautiful vessels, laden with barrels, were used for the journey down the Douro from the* quintas *to the shippers' lodges. When the river was dammed for hydro-electric power the journey became impossible.*

of extracting colour and tannin from the grape skins. The high quality of the wines produced in this way is also helping to preserve them from extinction.

Autovinification

The vast majority of port, however, is not trodden. The fermenting vessels that replace the labour of stamping are therefore designed to the same end: to extract all the pigments they can. The vats used by most of the major houses are called Ducellier Autovinifiers; these work with a complicated system of pressure build-up and release, driven by the carbon dioxide created during the fermentation. The violent agitation of the must promotes maximum extraction of colour and flavour compounds over a short period of time. However, less aggressive fermentation methods are increasingly sought: submerged caps (held below the surface by 'header boards'), allied with pumping over; Potter Fermenters (of Australian design), and simple floating caps, also regularly pumped over, are among the methods gaining favour.

The fermentation is interrupted when about one-third of the sugar content has been converted to alcohol, the fermentation reaching approximately 9 degrees Baumé; the must is then pressed, and the wine is fortified to around 18 degrees. From this point on the wine can go in radically different directions, depending in part on the quality of the vintage, in part on the quality of the wine.

The fortifying spirit

Many port-drinkers very reasonably assume that much of the character and quality of the wine derives from the fortifying spirit used. Nothing could be further from the truth. The Junta Nacional de Aguardiente until recently held a monopoly on the supply of spirit to the port houses. What it supplies is distilled from cast-off wines from Portugal's southern vineyards, or (less frequently) from the Douro. It is

not called *aguardiente* (burning water) for nothing: it is raw and it is fiery. The sole aim of the houses, in making their choice from the small range of samples available, is to select the most neutral spirit. The limited effect of the Portuguese spirit was graphically demonstrated in 1904: little or no spirit was available from the Government agency in that vintage, the only alternatives were German spirit distilled from potatoes and grain, and small quantities of *aguardiente* imported from the Azores. The vintage ports of that year, however, are still revered for their quality and style.

The fortification formula

The calculation of the amount of fortifying spirit to be used is unexpectedly complex and depends on many factors: the starting sugar-content of the must, how much remains at the point of fortification, how much sugar is to be left and what degree of alcohol is required. It has to be remembered that the volume of spirit added is quite substantial, and will dilute the sugar in the wine. Winemakers either use a complicated set of tables or a chart to gauge exactly how much to use.

Types of Port

Port is unique in offering such a diversity of styles – ranging from ruby to tawny to vintage wines – from a more or less common starting point. 'More or less', because while the vinification method up to the point at which the future of the wine is decided will have been the same, certain vineyard sites and certain varieties will almost inevitably go in the same direction every year. The destiny of each lot of wine is decided on the basis of intensive and repeated tastings over its first 18 months. The best wines of the best years will be destined for bottling at 18 months as Vintage Port. Thereafter nothing but time and the dark bottle itself witness its transformation. Tawny Ports, by contrast, are actively worked on in the shippers' lodge for years on end.

The maturation and blending of old Tawny Ports

During the first few years of its life, a Tawny Port will spend time in a variety of containers: stainless steel vats, concrete vats, large old wooden vats and smaller (650-litre) casks. Once its career as a Tawny Port is determined, it will be transferred to the elongated casks called pipes (each with a capacity of 523 litres). For the first ten years or so the wines will be racked once a year: the ostensible reason is to remove the deposits which collect at the bottom of the pipe (and hence by degrees to clarify the wine and make it more brilliant), but the racking also accelerates the process of oxidation which takes place almost imperceptibly in the pipe. During the early years the deposits will be a mixture of dead yeast cells, tartrates and various particulate matter of organic or bacterial origin. As the wine ages, the deposits lessen in volume and the racking takes place once every 18 months rather than once a year. The nature of the deposit also changes: it becomes almost entirely composed of polymerized anthocyanins (colouring compounds) which gradually precipitate, reflecting the progressive change from red to reddish brown to light brown to the final almost golden and luminescent hue of a very old Tawny Port.

The colour changes – and the chemical changes which they indicate – are inextricably bound up with the process of oxidation and the production of the aldehydes which give these wines their all-important '*rancio*' character. At no point, however, should the flavour of oak play any part: port winemakers go to considerable lengths to ensure that the barrels are 'seasoned' before they are put into use, and prefer older oak.

Apart from the deliberately oxidative methods used during racking, the ageing wine may have additional spirit added. Normally, though not invariably, in the warmth of a port-lodge the alcohol will evaporate more quickly than the water, leading to a reduction in the alcoholic strength. It may also be 'freshened' by the addition of a percentage of young wine: it is quite possible for old wood-aged wines to become stale, and it is preferable to freshen them in the cask rather than simply rely on the blending process.

Blending takes place shortly before the wine is bottled; port sees none of the

Traditional terraced vineyards above Pinhão, pinned to the steep valley sides by banking up the rocky schist between the rows of vines to prevent the soil from being washed down-slope.

gradual 'fractional' blending of a sherry *solera*. Its mathematics are by no means simple. If a ten-year-old Tawny Port is to be blended, it will have a weighted average age of not less than ten years, but it will by no means be half 15-year-old and half five-year-old wine. Rather it will be predominantly ten-year-old material, with a small quantity of much older wine and a little more five- or six-year-old wine: both the very old and the very young wine will have a disproportionate (if varying) influence on the blend.

Portuguese Tawny Ports compared with their equivalent from other countries are above all elegant: the spirit is much more evident than in those of other countries, not because it is stronger per se, but because the fruit is more delicate and fine. As in all of the great fortified wines, while the taste on the palate and tongue is sweet, the finish is dry. The sweetness should never cloy thanks to the complexity, which is summed up in the term '*rancio*'.

New World ports

South Africa, the United States and Australia are the chief winemakers of port-type wines outside Portugal. No one from other countries has managed to come up with a name for these wines which does not unashamedly steal from the original yet gives some idea of the style. So 'Vintage' and 'Tawny Port' is what they are called.

South Africa

The Cape has had a reputation for fortified winemaking since the great days of its dessert muscat Constantia in the 18th and 19th centuries. The original Constantia disappeared a century ago (although it is being revived today). Tawny Port has – to a limited degree – taken its place. The climate of Paarl is very warm to hot, and extremely rich, full-bodied and at times heavily sweet Tawny Ports are made there. These are even further away in style from those of Portugal than the Australian versions; they are mouth-filling, rich wines which rely on power rather than persuasion.

USA

More Vintage than Tawny Port is made, but until very recently both types were extraordinarily bad, given the range of available climates and the very high level of technological skill, not to mention the vast quantities of fortified wine made over the years. The United States wine industry was for decades based on fortified wine production. The Vintage Ports seem to suffer from extremely aromatic but rather unpleasant fortifying spirit, which obscured whatever quality or style the base wine may have had (which usually was not much, with Thompson Seedless or Sultana as the principal grape variety). There are one or two specialist winemakers today who are doing much better.

Australia

In 1960 70 percent of all Australian wine was fortified, much of it of sherry style, but also large amounts of port of every imaginable style and hue. In the 1990s fortified wine is no longer a major sales category: small amounts of very high quality Tawny and even smaller quantities of very good if idiosyncratic Vintage Port are made, but most of the fortified wine sold these days is cheap Cream Sherry. One notable exception is B. Seppelt & Sons, which has some 100-year-old liqueur ports that achieve extraordinary concentration: one, from 1887, with a potential alcohol (unfermented sugar expressed as degrees Baumé with actual alcohol) of 40 degrees. This level of concentration has occurred through prolonged evaporation during the 100 years of barrel ageing.

The top Australian vintage ports – made by The Hardy Wine Co. and Château Reynella – are made from Shiraz (Syrah) grown in the McLaren Vale and fortified with high-quality young wood-aged brandy. The combination of fruit and spirit gives the wines an extremely high-toned, flowery, aromatic bouquet and palate; they need 15 years to start reaching their peak, longer still to become easily drinkable. These wines also differ from their Portuguese counterparts by having 3.5 to 6 degrees Baumé sugar in contrast with 3 to 4 degrees Baumé of true Vintage Port. Other than this difference, the vinification and maturation methods are basically the same as those used in Portugal.

Port

This choices and consequences chart illustrates the principal stages in the portmaking process in which the decisions taken by the maker will fundamentally influence the taste and individuality of the final wine. Port is one of the most strictly controlled of all wines – every stage of its making is overseen by a body of statutory authorities.

Port is one of the great 'processed' wines. The industry for which Portugal's Douro region is justly famous is based on long-established, unchanging blends on which the major houses have built their names. Despite increasing mechanization of some of the stages, there is no substitute for the skill of the winemaker in timing the fortification and in the assessment and blending of the port wine.

Quinta do Noval, perhaps the most famous of the quintas *on the Douro, perched high above Pinhão. Old Noval vintages were among the most magnificent of all ports.*

1 IN THE VINEYARD

Choice of grape varieties
Nine varieties are permitted to be planted but only six are commonly used in the best Vintage Ports. While the selection of varieties is becoming more important, much more attention is paid to the location of the vineyard from which the grapes for Vintage Port come.

2 CRUSHING

Crushing
(a) *By foot*
Foot stamping in open *lagares* is still used for a percentage of the finest wine from the best of the small *quintas* selling to or owned by the major houses.
(b) *By mechanical crusher*
Mechanical crushing is the alternative, and this is by way of a vertical crusher peculiar to the Douro; stalks are not removed in

3 FERMENTING AND PRESSING

Choice of fermentation vat
(a) *Lagar*
The traditional fermentation vat is the same granite or slate *lagar* in which the grapes are crushed. The must is broken up by men using wooden implements.
(b) *Autovinifier*
The port autovinifier is a closed system whereby the must is forced up and over the cap due to the pressure created by carbon dioxide build-up during fermentation.

4 BLENDING AND MATURING

Assessment, blending and classification
The process of tasting commences in the Douro immediately fermentation is finished, and continues in Vila Nova de Gaia after the wines arrive there the following March. At this point the general style of the wine will be shaped, although its precise destiny may take years to determine.

Method of picking
Almost all the grapes are picked by hand; at the smaller, up-country *quintas* into square, woven cane baskets which are then transported to the winery by all manner of locomotion, and at larger *quintas* into rectangular steel 'skips' to be taken by truck to the larger wineries.

a hot year but most of them are in a cool year when more grape acidity is retained, and green, bitter stalk tannins would over-balance softer fruit.

Left: *Treading grapes to the sound of a local band takes place in the cool of the night at the more traditional* quintas.

Below: *Vintage Port is like champagne in being virtually 'made' in its bottle.*

(c) *Open tank with pump-over system*
Gentler and more widespread (as electricity becomes available in the Upper Douro), the open-vat alternative is a system where the must is sprayed over the cap by pump.

Fermentation temperature
Fermentation temperatures range between 26° and 29°. The large surface area of the *lagares* and the frequency of the convulsions of the Autovinifiers allow circulation of cooler air. With the open tank system the larger volumes of must needs to be cooled.

Fortification
Grape spirit (*aguardiente*) is added before fermentation has finished so that some of the natural sugars remain in the wine. The timing of this fortification is critical and involves the use of either a complicated mathematical table or the winemaker's intuition, developed over decades of experience, to ensure the correct level of sweetness remains.

Pressing
Either continuous presses or Vaslin type plate and chain presses are used. Because of the colour and tannin remaining in the partly fermented skins, pressing is always thorough – designed to extract every drop of juice. The pressings are always used in the finished wine because they add balance and complexity.

Wood-ageing and bottling
Vintage or vintage style port will be bottled young – between 18 months and 6 years, then left to mature in bottle. Otherwise the wine will be wood-aged to produce a kaleidoscopic range of port styles.

Stabilization
Cold stabilization of young wines destined for any of the bottle-aged categories is extremely important as it removes the excess tartrate crystals which would otherwise form during maturation. The wine is cooled to −10°C.

Clarification
Wood-aged ports may be lightly fined before being bottled and gelatine is the most commonly used fining agent. Wines like Old Tawny may not need fining having been racked many times during barrel-maturation.

Madeira, a volcanic island off the coast of Africa, rises steeply out of the sea. Fire destroyed much of the original forest cover but the layer of ash deposited on the already rich (but sparse) volcanic soil proved beneficial to farmers. Vines, like the island's other crops, are planted in precarious places on narrow terraces created out of the rocky slopes.

Madeira

The madeira effect: ordeal by heat

The evolution of Madeira into the only fortified dessert wine that can challenge the greatest port is an epic of serendipity. First the discovery of the island, then its importance to transatlantic shipping, the long tropical voyages of its modest wines to the Indies (West and East) and their arrival there as something far better than when they left are the happy chances that led to a unique way of making wine.

Madeira, though, is not one kind of wine, but half a dozen. What they have in common is their island origin, and the fact that, like the favourite wines of ancient Rome, they are baked in ovens as part of their 'elaboration'. The great bulk of Madeira today has no greater destiny than a sauce in a French kitchen. It is made of various grapes, but mainly Tinta Negra Mole, picked as early as August, fermented almost dry in concrete vats, then sweetened and fortified with unfermented must stopped by adding alcohol (known as *vinho surdo*), before being given three months in a 50,000 litre vat heated to 50°C by a heating coil.

This is the most summary way of producing the madeira effect. Fine madeiras are made by variations on this method – the most important of which are selection, care and time. Four styles of madeira are sold under the names of the grapes from which, in theory at least, they are made: in ascending order of richness, concentration and strength Sercial, Verdelho, Bual and Malmsey (or Malvasia). In practice the supply of these premium grapes has been short ever since first oidium, then phylloxera, devastated the island's vines. It is normal for a certain amount of Tinta to enter into all except the very finest lots of wine.

Sercial and Verdelho are made as white wines, fermented after pressing, without their skins. Some Sercial vines are grown as high as 700 metres above sea level; their grapes may not ripen until late October with only enough sugar for a mere eight percent alcohol. The wines are fermented to dryness, then fortified and sweetened (Sercial more fortified, Verdelho more sweetened) with *vinho surdo*.

Bual and Malmsey are crushed (they were formerly trodden like port), then fermented as red wines, skins and all, until the Bual has consumed at least half of its sugar, the Malmsey perhaps a third – when, again like port, their fermentation is stopped by adding spirit. Originally this was cane spirit (Madeira grows excellent

Space being at such premium on Madeira, vines are trained up pergolas, leaving the ground beneath their leafy canopy free for growing a second crop of fruits or vegetables. Pergolas also allow air circulation around the grapes, important in a warm and humid climate.

sugarcane); today it is grape spirit from mainland Portugal.

The procedure for a high-quality wine is then the same, whether a dry Sercial or a very rich Malmsey. At a total strength of 17 percent it is run into 650-litre casks of American oak (known as scantling pipes) which are then stacked in a hot store, or *estufa*. The store is heated by hot-water radiators to a maximum temperature of 50°C for between three and six months (six months at 40°C is a preferential treatment for a potentially top-quality wine). The effect is partly to caramelize the sugar in the wine while achieving the *rancio* effect by thorough oxidation. The wine is then allowed to cool very gradually and left to rest for a year or more while its further destiny is considered. During this time it is racked by pouring from a height to give it a thorough exposure to oxygen.

The rancio effect: ordeal by oxygen

Very exceptional wines are kept apart, under observation for as long as 30 years before being offered as vintage madeiras. The majority join an island variant of the solera system of fractional blending, deriving a good deal of their style from the well-aged oak butts that have held their predecessors for generations.

The late Noel Cossart's *Madeira, the Island Vineyard* (Christie's, 1984), is the standard work on the subject. He tells a curious story of how as a young shipper he had tried the experiment of blending Sercial, Bual and Malmsey together, having been told that by tradition the wines would not mix. He was happy with the result until the hogshead arrived at its final destination, Newcastle-on-Tyne, where it was found to have completely fallen apart. '*One could draw off the Sercial from the top, the Bual from the middle and the Malmsey from the bottom.*'

In other respects madeira, after its ordeal by heat, is the most stable of all wines. It carries what appears to be a perilous load of volatile acetic acid and more than its share of aldehydes. But air cannot harm it. The greatest madeiras have spent many years in cask, and often in wide glass carboys, in warm climates where they feed on oxygen – only becoming more concentrated and complex in the process. An old word for their penetrating quality was 'eager'. Michael Broadbent has used the word 'swingeing' for the degree of acidity that keeps these relics of ancient Rome immortally fresh.

Madeira

This choices and consequences chart illustrates those stages in the winemaking process in which the options chosen by the winemaker will fundamentally influence the taste and individuality of the final wine. There are four principal styles of Madeira (ranging from dry to sweet) but differences in blending and ageing creates further diversity, as the classification indicates.

The original grape varieties for making Madeira – Sercial, Verdelho, Bual and Malmsey – have been joined by another: Tinta Negra Mole. This grape produces varying styles of wine, reflecting the site on which it is grown, and consequently emulating to different degrees the characteristics of the original four. (Sercial, Verdelho, Bual and Malmsey are styles of Madeira as well as grape varieties.)

Classification of madeira wines

Sercial A pale light-bodied wine with a nutty bouquet; darkens with age and softens. Sugar levels at 0.5–1.5° Baumé and the driest of the wines, but particularly smooth.

Verdelho Golden when young, darkening with age until it reaches a deep green-brown. Medium bodied and of medium sweetness. Full and quite dry with age. 1.5–2.5° Baumé.

Bual Rapidly darkens and never less than medium dark. Fragrant fruit with an almost smoky complexity which mellows with age. Fully sweet with 2.5–3.5° Baumé.

Malmsey Dark in colour, almost black with age, tinged with olive green. Enormously fruity, honeyed and luscious. Baumé at 3.5–6.5°.

Finest, Choice, Selected (3 years) Will typically be made from Tinta Negra Mole, the most widely grown grape. The basic madeira with simply an indication of whether it is dry, medium, sweet etc. No grape variety is specified.

Rainwater (3 years) A 3-year-old wine made from Verdelho. It takes its name from an 18th-century blend which accidentally included rainwater. Soft, easy drinking style, usually medium sweet.

Reserve (5 years or older) A blended wine of a number of vintages, the youngest of which must be at least 5 years old (after *estufagem*). The grape variety may be specified; if it is, it must contain 85% of that variety.

Special Reserve, Old Reserve (10 years or older) The same requirements as for Reserve, except that the youngest component will be 10 years old. Much richer in style and more complex.

Extra Reserve (15 years or older) As before, but with a minimum of 15 years.

Vintage Must be made from the noble varieties, have spent 20 years in cask after *estufagem*, and an additional 2 years in bottle. Must be 100% of the specified variety.

Solera A dying art, though once very famous. Only 10% can be drawn off and bottled at any one time and must be replaced by wine of similar quality. The date is that on which the solera was established and is not a true indication of the average age.

---

1 CRUSHING AND PRESSING

Crushing

(a) *Foot crushing in lagares*
Still believed by the traditionalists to produce the finest wine but in fact it is now uncommon.

(b) *Mechanical crushing/destemming*
Widely adopted in the larger wineries, though for madeira, the

2 FERMENTATION AND FORTIFICATION

Fermentation vessel
Large concrete vats are normally used for fermentation, but some argue that better wines benefit from the 'seasoning' effects of new oak pipes. By the time the wine has been heated, blended and bottled, though, much of the new oak flavour will have disappeared. Autovinification has also been introduced at some lodges, allowing constant pumping over, which enables increased extraction of colour and flavour from the grapes.

3 CONTROLLING THE TEMPERATURE

Heating (Estufagem)
Estufagem is the slow heating process by which madeira's sugars are caramelized, resulting in its unique flavour.

(a) *By shipping (Vinho da Roda)*
The origin of the practice of maturing Madeira by shipping it around the world as ballast is lost in the mists of time, but the benefits of such prolonged heating were well noted by the mid-18th century, and this method was actually practised until World War I.

4 FINISHING

Fortification

(a) *Initial fortification*
All madeiras are ultimately fortified to 17° alcohol. The amount of fortification for Sercial and Verdelho will be small (3–4°), but this may be the first time these wines have received any spirit.

(b) *Further fortification*
Conversely, for fine Bual and

choice whether or not to crush or to destem is not believed to greatly influence the final product.

Pressing

(a) *Pressing before fermentation*
For Sercial and Verdelho wines the grapes are usually pressed and the juice separated before fermentation begins – these are drier madeiras, which benefit less from prolonged skin contact.

(b) *Pressing after fermentation*
Grapes for Bual and Malmsey wines are pressed after they have been fermented, their natural sweetness being complemented by grape skin flavours.

Fermentation and fortification

(a) *Fermentation until dry*
In order to retain the grapes' drier characteristics Sercial and Verdelho undergo total fermentation and are not fortified at this stage.

(b) *Fermentation arrested by fortification*
Bual will be fermented until approximately half the sugar has been converted to alcohol. Malmsey, the sweetest of the Madeira styles, will be fermented for only a few hours and retains virtually all its natural sugar.

Racking
The first grading of Madeira occurs after the wine has been racked off its fermentation lees. Each style is then classified according to its quality.

Fortification

(a) *Fine wines*
The addition of alcohol reduces the wine's vulnerability – winemakers consequently choose to carry out most of the fortification of their highest-quality wines at this stage, raising alcohol levels to 17%. The sweeter base wines, not having undergone full fermentation, will require higher alcohol additions to reach this percentage.

(b) *Lesser wines*
Lesser quality wines are not fortified at this stage as they are

more prone to alcohol loss during the heating process which follows. The least alcoholic musts – Bual and Malmsey – do need some fortification, however, to increase their stability.

(b) *Storage under natural heat (Canteiro)*
The modern equivalent is storage in south-facing lofts of winery lodges, resulting in the wine being heated to 45°C each summer day, cooling overnight. The wine (in pipes) can be stored for up to 30 years (rare).

(c) *Pipe storage in heated sheds (Estufas)*
The most common method for medium to good quality wines is storage in *armazen de calor* – special buildings heated by hot water ducts – the best wines

being kept for 6–12 months, at 40°C and over, in high pipes which rise to ceiling height.

(d) *Heated vats*
Basic generic Madeira is heated in large ceramic-lined concrete tanks with built-in heating coils – held at 50°C for 3–4 months. After this period, the wine is fortified, having lost much of its alcoholic strength during its rigorous heating.

Cooling
Gradual cooling is critical for all wines, but particularly for lesser-quality Sercials and Verdelhos which at this stage will be most vulnerable, having not been fortified at all. Both oxidation and acetification are real risks.

Below: *Vintage madeira, much rarer than vintage port, spends at least 20 years in cask in the wine lodges in Funchal, the island's capital. Malmsey, the original of the four principal grapes, makes the richest wine.*

Malmsey this may be the third stage of fortification: initially in the fermentation, adjusted after racking to 17° and now again to compensate for the loss during heating. Old wines may need yet further fortification at blending and bottling.

Filtration and fining
The wine is either fined with gelatine or bentonite, or filtered, and then allowed to rest for 12 to 18 months before classification.

Racking and final classification
After the rest period, the wine is filtered and given a vigorous aerated racking; its fate is then determined and it will be stored according to its final destiny. It may spend as little as 18 more months in cask, or over 50 years.

Sherry   The original purpose of fortifying port with spirits was simply to stabilize a very rich wine which travelled badly. The taste for a high degree of residual sugar evolved later, until stopping the fermentation at an early stage became standard practice. (*See* the sherry-making process on pages 176–177.)

Added to a finished wine, one whose fermentation is complete, with no residual sugar, spirits have no such dramatic effect: they merely strengthen the brew and protect it from bacterial accidents. Dry sherries are the classic example of fortification for this purpose.

The inherent instability of sherry, at least of the finest natural dry sherries, determines the way these delicate and exquisite wines are made. Delicate may seem a strange word to use about a wine with 16 percent alcohol, but in hardly any wine is freshness so important as in true *fino*. Kept too long in bottle, or in cask under anything but perfect conditions, its extraordinary fragrance and vitality disappears and will not recover. An over-aged *fino* may find a second life as an *amontillado* – but that is a different style of wine.

The fragility of sherry starts in the vineyard, with grapes of little flavour, low acidity and high pH. The sherry grape, the Palomino, makes poor flabby table wines; only its performance under the special conditions of Jerez, in the stark, white limey clay known as *albariza*, saves its reputation.

It is picked very ripe, because high natural alcohol is essential to its performance. Grapes intended for making the heavier styles of sherry are then left to shrivel slightly in the sun – which further lowers their already low acidity. Those for *fino* are pressed as rapidly as possible, but not until they have been dosed ('plastered' is the old term) with gypsum. *Yeso* or gypsum is an additive which has been used since Roman times. Today one kilogram is added to each 700 kilos of grapes – whose must will fill one butt. *Yeso* is pure calcium sulphate (naturally present in the Jerez soil, but now prepared industrially). It reacts with potassium bitartrate in the wine to produce (insoluble) calcium tartrate, (soluble) potassium sulphate, and valuable tartaric acid. The precise reactions which make *yeso* an essential ingredient of sherry are still being studied, but their effects include a more moderate rate of fermentation, increased acidity and the production of aromatic esters and ethyl tartrate. *Yeso* also encourages the growth of the vital yeast, flor.

The formation of flor   The all-important *flor* is caused by the growth of yeast cells on the surface of the wine within a few weeks of the end of fermentation. The same yeast – or one of the same yeasts – which triggers the primary fermentation (*Saccaromyces beticus*) is responsible for the growth of the *flor*. Initially specks, then islands of *flor* appear; these coalesce into a thin, continuous film which thickens and becomes wrinkled, changing in colour from white to light grey and ultimately to brown. At this point, portions break away and sink to the bottom of the cask, and are promptly replaced by new, thin film. The 'flowering' of the yeast normally occurs in spring and autumn, dropping in summer and winter – basically in response to changing temperature.

The effect of flor   Modern methods of analysis have identified more than 100 volatile compounds affecting the flavour of *flor* sherry. The main compounds are acetaldehydes, an integral part of the *rancio* character, and compounds called acetals. Under the action of *flor*, glycerol decreases, thinning the texture of the wine to the gloriously crisp, dry flavour of fresh *fino*. A further effect comes from the autolysis of the dead yeast cells which fall to the bottom of the butt. Only one other wine gains so much character from its interaction with yeast: champagne.

In the hot Jerez autumn, run-away tumultuous fermentation has always been a problem, leading to loss of both wine (spurting from the bung-holes of casks) and a degree or more of alcohol. There is also likely to be a loss of valuable but volatile aromas. Although Jerez now has giant temperature-controlled vats in its bigger *bodegas*, new oak casks are its traditional fermenting vessels, still very much in use.

It is the best way of maturing the casks and preparing them for later use in the *criadera*, the young wine nursery, and the *solera*, where the physical properties of oak are as essential as its flavour is unwelcome.

Much has been written of the classification of new sherries into styles, butt by butt as it develops in the *bodega*. In practice it would be strange if a wine intended to be a *fino*, picked at the right ripeness in a vineyard known for *finos*, turned out to be an *oloroso*. *Olorosos*, stronger, broader and more pungent wines without the delicacy of *finos*, are fashioned just as deliberately. What is in doubt, and demands patient tasting and retasting, is the real quality of a given butt: whether it deserves to join a top-quality *solera*, or should be kept for lowlier blending purposes.

Oloroso wines are fortified, using grape spirit, to about 18 percent alcohol before joining a *solera*; *finos*, from their lower natural fermented strength of about 12 percent, to 15 percent. More alcohol would not permit the growth of the *flor* which is the essential distinction of a *fino*. Any *flor* growing on an *oloroso* is thus killed by its fortification.

Under a vigorously growing protective layer of this unique yeast the delicate wine is protected from oxygen and the attack of acetic acid. Without it it would soon be vinegar. To keep *flor* flourishing, frequent refreshment with young wine is needed. A *fino solera* therefore is a relative hive of activity, with wines regularly being drawn off and the butts replenished, while an *oloroso solera*, its wines without *flor* protected by their fortification, needs very much more time to achieve maturity.

A *solera* is not the end of the blending process. Indeed it might be described as the beginning. It is rare for straight *solera* wines to be sold without at least some further blending, because all *solera* wines are fully dry. Most commercial sherries are well-tried blends from more than one *solera*, adjusted to customers' tastes by a little sweetening with sweet wine (*dulce*) made either by stopped fermentation or added sugar.

The chief exceptions to this further blending are top-quality *finos* and sherries now marketed as *almacenistas*, which are straight *solera* wines from individual growers' stocks. These unsweetened wines of wholly distinctive character are the ultimate expression of the region, and must be counted among the finest white wines in the world.

A *solera* is an aggregation of butts divided into equally sized stages, each stage containing sherry of different (steadily increasing) average age. For wines such as *manzanilla finos* that depend on freshness there may be as many as ten stages; for old, slow-moving *amontillados* or *olorosos* there may be only five or six.

Taking a five-stage *solera* as an example, the youngest wine will be in Stage V (in the mists of time when the *solera* was in the course of establishment that wine will have all been young and of a single vintage year). The oldest wine will be in Stage I. Sherry will be taken from Stage I twice a year; on each occasion a little over 20 percent of the actual contents of each butt will be removed for bottling or blending. Expressed as a total of the wine in the *solera* this represents 5 percent of the total on each occasion, or 10 percent a year.

The wine removed from Stage I is replaced by an identical quantity of wine from Stage II and so on up the chain. Stage V, the youngest, is in turn refreshed from a 'nursery' or *criadera*, which could be described as a tributary flowing into the mainstream of the *solera*. The *criadera* is in turn run on the *solera* system so that its oldest wine is only slightly younger than the wine in the solera Stage V. Only the youngest stage in the *criadera* is refreshed with *añada*, or new wines.

'Running the scales' of a *solera* is not simply a question of taking around 95 litres from each butt in the higher stage and putting it in a butt in the next (lower) stage. If the wine is being removed (say) from Stage IV and going into Stage V, the wine drawn from each single butt in Stage IV will be divided equally among all the butts

The bodega of Antonio Barbadillo is the biggest in Sanlúcar de Barrameda, the original sherry-shipping harbour at the mouth of the river Guadalquivir. The district produces the freshest, most delicate fino sherries that take on the character known as manzanilla in the ancient bodegas of the town. The sea air gives manzanilla a slightly salty tang.

The solera system

in Stage V, an immensely tedious process but essential for guaranteeing the uniformity of the blend. In smaller *bodegas*, or with *soleras* of extreme quality, the process will be carried out using pitchers into which the wine is siphoned by gravity, and which are used to pour the wine through a perforated copper tube into the next stage: the perforations ensure the gentle passage of the incoming wine so as not to disturb either the *flor* on the surface or the lees on the bottom of the cask. In larger *bodegas* the process will be done by gentle pumping, with the wine withdrawn being mixed in a vat and then pumped back to the next stage.

Choice of sherry style

Fino

Anyone who has visited Jerez and drunk *fino* at 11am in the sun-dappled, leafy courtyard of one of the *bodegas*, drawn direct from a butt chilled in a cool room overnight, will know just what a glorious wine *fino* is. The word is drunk, not sipped: the mid-morning *tapas* (appetizers) simply add fuel to the fire. It underlines another unique feature of *fino*: it is best drunk straight from the butt; next best when consumed within days of being bottled; will not suffer unduly from a few months in bottle; but loses freshness progressively (and significantly) over the months thereafter. It is no more than an unfortunate recognition of commercial reality that the shippers decline to put legible bottling dates on their *finos*.

The wine is fundamentally shaped by the *flor*, and to a much lesser degree by its fortification: it has that 'cut' to both its bouquet and taste which adds to its crispness, intensifies its dryness. It should be drunk slightly chilled in summer, and should be regarded as a first-class alternative to, let us say, a Chardonnay: after all, its alcohol is not so very much higher. It is also exceptional value for money.

Amontillado

The extra age in butt, the significantly higher levels of aldehydes, and the somewhat higher alcohol content (in the sherry *bodegas*, water loss through evaporation comfortably exceeds alcohol loss) all act to give *amontillados* a nutty warmth on the mid-palate, a rounder softer feeling, before the cleansing dryness of the finish. If *fino* is the wine for spring or summer, *amontillado* is the wine for

Far left: A solera *system in a Jerez* bodega. *In a* solera, *which could be described as a fractional blending system, wine is drawn from the oldest of a series of butts, which is then topped up from the next oldest, and so on. Each addition rapidly takes on the character of the older wine to which it is added. But the ageing wine must be carefully chosen to match the old.*

Left: *Australia's most successful answers to the fortified wines of Europe are its creamy, long-matured sweet muscats. The Brown Brothers' vineyards, in the hills of northeast Victoria, provide grapes for their most luscious liqueur muscat.*

autumn (or a rainy summer's day). It should not be chilled, but otherwise treated in much the same way as *fino*.

Take out the *flor* influence, but add an extra dimension of *rancio*, and the many-layered complexity of *oloroso* takes shape. These are wonderfully intense and concentrated wines; if sherry aficionados are divided in their views as to which of the three styles they prefer it is a question of personal choice rather than quality. If *fino* is the wine of summer, *oloroso* is the wine of winter.

Oloroso

If any New World fortified wines deserve a place alongside the classics in this chapter it is the limited production of Liqueur Muscats and Tokays from northeast Victoria – particularly from the district of Rutherglen.

The very hot, highly continental climate of northeast Victoria allows the grapes to reach exceptionally high sugar levels in years when late vintage rains do not interfere: readings of over 20 degrees Baumé are achieved in the greatest vintages, though normally 15 to 16 degrees Baumé is considered adequate. Sweetness comes through simple dehydration and raisining: botrytis is not welcome, although it, along with even less welcome moulds, sometimes makes its mark.

The grapes are crushed and destemmed (no easy task if they are fully raisined at very high Baumé levels) and fermentation initiated with cultured yeasts. Depending on the starting Baumé, the quality of the grapes (or must) and the desired style, fermentation may be arrested almost immediately it has started or left until the must has 8 to 10 degrees Baumé unfermented sugar. The earlier the fermentation is arrested, the greater the spirit addition required to produce the required balance – and the higher the cost of the finished wine.

The real magic comes with prolonged wood-ageing, often accentuated – as in madeira – by storage at the top of corrugated iron sheds to intensify the heat. Just as with Tawny Port, the final wines are typically a blend of wines of different ages, centred around a core of wine roughly of the age of the finished wine.

Australian Tokay and Muscat

Making the wines

Oak and Wine

Choices, consequences and techniques

The bond between wine and oak was forged by the Romans. No doubt all sorts of woods were tried over the centuries, and some – notably cherry, chestnut and walnut – remain in limited use in some European countries today. Oak has many features which make it perfect for use in the winery, some which parallel its suitability for ship building: high tensile strength, light weight, malleability, and impermeability to water (or wine). The large barrels and vats fashioned from Roman times onwards look primitive and clumsy by modern standards but they did the only job that was expected of them: to act as vessels for storage or transport.

The role of the container

At some point fairly early in the history of the use of oak, winemakers came to appreciate and understand the softening and 'complexing' effect of the slow and gentle process of oxidation brought about by the entry of oxygen through the working apertures of the barrel or cask and through the oak itself. In cellars of relatively low humidity there will also be considerable evaporation of the wine, which in economic terms the winemaker may wish to prevent, but which in all except extreme cases will hasten the barrel-ageing process and almost certainly improve the wine by slightly concentrating it.

In old oak vats (which the French call *foudres* or *demi-muids*, the Germans *Füders* or *Stücks*) tartrate crystals will gradually accumulate and completely coat the inside of the vat. Apart from preventing any possibility of the pick-up of oak flavour, and adding to the impermeability of the oak, the crystal lining helps precipitate the tartrate present in the new wine most recently placed in the barrel. In cold European cellars, winter partially cold-stabilizes the wine, something which New World winemakers achieve through refrigerated cooling to 0°C (or below) in stainless steel vats (and, it must be said, achieve more completely).

Old barrels which have been used many times impart no oak flavour to the wine.

The larger the container, the slower will be the process of softening and oxidation; and over the centuries some countries and regions moved to smaller barrels – perhaps originally for transport, then for maturation, although initially not for fermentation. The distinction between fermentation and maturation is important: large oak vats (which have various configurations) can be used for both tasks, whereas the small barrels (*barriques*, hogsheads and puncheons) are only used for the fermentation of white, not red, wines (sometimes also for the final stages of fermentation of some red wines after they have been pressed).

It has only been in the last 30 years that much attention has been paid to the other characteristic of oak: its ability, when new, to impart an extra dimension of flavour to wine. This characteristic has always been known of course; the Italians, the Portuguese, the Spanish (in Jerez) and the Champenois went to considerable lengths to avoid it. When new pipes are introduced into the port lodges, mediocre-quality table wine is made in them for two or three years before they are first used for vintage port. But in Bordeaux and Burgundy the attitude was (and is) very different, with the flavour being prized; now the interest in the differing flavour characteristics of different oak types has become a matter of intense study.

The principal types of oak used are *Quercus alba* (from eastern North America), and *Quercus robur* and *sessilis* (from Europe). Within Europe oak is harvested in and sold from a number of countries: French, German, Balkan and Portuguese oaks are the most common. French is by far the most significant, with the all-important differences between its forests being the focus of attention in the New World. Sometimes it is suggested that oak finds its way from Baltic countries to be 're-badged' as French. With the freeing-up of East–West trade, Baltic oak may well rise in importance, and act to stabilize escalating prices of French oak.

Limousin excepted (briefly in vogue for use with Chardonnay in parts of the New World, notably America) French oaks are more subtle than American, German or Portuguese. But any winemaker using a significant amount of new oak knows there is disconcerting variation in flavour (and quality) between two barrels, even when the oak, the 'toast' and the cooper are the same. With oak from different coopers, the variation can be even more marked. The reasons for the variation are many and varied. The growth rate of the tree is influenced by the climate and soil variations of the area, the density of the tree stands within the forest, and the age of the tree. The slower the rate of growth, the tighter the grain and the better the flavour of oak in the wine. Chemical analysis shows that more desirable phenols are extracted from slower-growing oak. Another source of variation derives from the seasoning of the oak after it has been milled into green wood staves. (Staves can be machine-sawed or hand-split, the quality of the latter being significantly better.) The variables are: seasoning for three years in stacks in the forest; for three years in the cooper's yard which allows for periodic water spraying of the stack; and for seasoning for 18 months to two years, followed by adjustment to bring the moisture content to the desired level of 17 to 18 percent. Kiln-drying is a quick-fix method, but one not used by the best cooperages.

The build up of tartrate crystals in a much used cask needs to be checked – or the volume available for wine is reduced.

Making the barrels

Then there is the manner in which the casks are made. The characteristic oval or egg shape of the barrel means the staves are bent by being heated. The wood may be heated by steam, by being immersed in boiling water or by being grilled over an open fire. French coopers have largely preferred to use the open fire technique (one or two immerse the staves in water first), and it was from this that the realization came that the level of browning (or 'toast') of the surface of the oak has a very significant effect on the flavour in the wine.

The effect of toasting

Tasting and chemical analysis have both increased our understanding of the effect of toasting. Seven principal aldehydes, 18 phenols and seven other aromatic compounds (principally lactones) have been identified as contributing to the oak aroma and flavour in wine. If the oak is slowly toasted over a small fire (rather than charred quickly over a hotter, larger fire) the aromatic aldehydes and flavour compounds are increased by a factor of many times. There are, of course, some winemakers (and some kinds of wine) for which more is not better, and not all barrels are made with medium or high toast levels.

New and used barrels

So far as the winemaker is concerned there is a very significant difference between a new barrel and one used for a second, third or fourth time. It is generally agreed that the useful life of a barrel in making quality table wine in which oak aroma and flavour is important is between four and six years. Since the cost of a new barrel is very high (around 2,500 francs for a *barrique* ex the French cooperage in 1992) and its functional life as a container is 60 years or more, a number of lateral approaches have been tried. One of the obvious solutions is to disassemble the barrel, shave the staves, reassemble and re-fire it. The results have been satisfactory, but have their limitations. If the barrel is three or four years old, shaving will markedly improve it but it will not emulate the performance of a new barrel. Another approach has been to use chips or finely ground shavings: if the quality of the oak is good, and if the chips are skilfully used (eg during primary fermentation) the result can be disconcertingly good. But one cannot eliminate barrels: the other effects of barrel-maturation are still essential to give the wine the appropriate texture. At some point, though, they will be passed on like clothes from an older sibling, serving in making lesser quality table wine and ultimately in making fortified wine (quite possibly very good fortified wine).

Oak

The ability of wood to influence the smell and taste of wine was recognized only recently. Originally oak barrels served primarily as vessels for convenient transport or storage using a material readily available. This choices and consequences chart illustrates some of the options available to those winemakers who introduce the effect of oak into the winemaking process and the way the wood adds to the flavour and aroma of the final wine.

The source of the oak and the tightness of the wood grain are critical to its quality, and vary according to the climate, the soil and the nature of the forest in which the wood was grown. The way in which the barrels are prepared by the cooper, the number of times the barrels are used, and their size, are as important as the very fact of using oak to add complexity to the taste of the wine.

1
IN THE FOREST

Choice of oak type
(a) *French*
   Tronçais
   Nevers
   Allier
   Vosges
   Limousin
(b) *Other*
   Baltic
   Balkan
   Portuguese
   German
   American

Choice of oak type is of primary importance; see page 193 for the varying uses and implications of the choice. It should be realized, however, that the quality can and does vary greatly from cooper to cooper and even from barrel to barrel.

2
IN THE COOPERAGE

Right: *New French oak barrels await filling in the cellars of Wolf Blass in Australia.*

Far right: *The staves of a barrel are cut (or, better, riven) straight, then curved by being heated on a fire.*

Choice of grain
(a) *Tight grain*
(b) *Loose grain*
Given a choice, most makers would unhesitatingly choose the slow-grown tight-grained oak in preference to the loose-grained oak, which gives a less subtle and fine flavour.

Left: *The state-owned Tronçais forest in the Allier in central France produces the most-prized barrel oak on a 160-year rotation.*

Seasoning of oak
(a) *Time*
(b) *Air dried*
(c) *Kiln dried*
Once again, given an effective choice, it would be for air-dried oak seasoned for 3–4 years. In practice, the choice may not be available, or if it is, becomes very expensive. Some winemakers accordingly buy and season their own oak, which they then send to the cooperage to be made up into barrels.

Method of making
(a) *Machine sawn or hand split staves*
(b) *Steam bent or wood fired*
Barrels made from hand split staves are better in every way than those which use machine-sawn staves, but are more expensive. Similarly, barrels made over a fire are generally preferred to those made using steamed staves. In each case the heat is necessary to allow the staves to be bent into shape.

Level of toast
(a) *High*
(b) *Medium*
(c) *Low*
If the barrel has been wood-fired, it is possible (indeed common) to elect the level of toast or char. The choice is very much a subjective one, determined by the style of the wine the winemaker wishes to make. High-toast barrels give a distinctive spicy/smoky tang admired by some and not others.

3
IN THE WINERY

Choice of barrel size
(a) *Barrique 224 litres*
(b) *Hogshead 315 litres*
(c) *Puncheon 450 litres*
(d) *Others up to 450 litres*
As a general rule, the smaller the barrel, the greater the extraction of oak flavour and the more rapid development of the wine. For some winemakers this is desirable, for others it is not. Cost also enters the equation: the larger the barrel, the more economic it is.

New or old oak?
(a) *100% new*
(b) *Mixture of new and old*
(c) *100% old*
Once again, the choice is primarily determined by the philosophy of the winemaker (and the desired taste of the wine) and secondarily by considerations of cost. The strength of flavour of the raw wine, the period over which it is intended to age, and conventional expectations of the final taste of the wine are all factors determining choice.

Storage conditions
(a) *Controlled*
(b) *Ambient*
The need to control temperature and humidity will vary from country to country but the end result of cool, humid storage is not in doubt: better wine, all other things being equal. Cost is a limiting factor.

IN THE BOTTLE

The Chemistry and Methods of Analysis of Wine

The analysis of grape juice or wine enables the winemaker to determine what chemical adjustments should be made (normally the addition of acid, sulphur dioxide or sugar) and what treatments are necessary (filtration and cold stabilization being two examples). The decision will be made using chemical indices, the four most commonly cited ones for dry table wine being: alcohol, acid, pH and volatile acidity.

Alcohol

Alcohol is produced by the fermentation of grape sugar, which usually accounts for 15 to 24 percent by weight of the must before the onset of fermentation. Approximately half the sugar will be respired as carbon dioxide during fermentation, the other half producing the alcohol in the wine. As a rule of thumb, one degree Baumé of sugar will produce one degree of alcohol, although some yeasts can actually increase the alcohol by up to five percent: ie 10 degrees Baumé grapes may produce wine with an alcohol content of 10.5 degrees.

The effect of alcohol on flavour

The alcohol produced does not have any flavour in the narrow sense, but does have an important impact on the taste and balance of the wine. It adds a sweetness and a roundness which can be felt as much as it can be tasted; characteristics which come into clear relief at the extremes. Thus a high alcohol Chardonnay (14 degrees or thereabouts) will often seem to have unfermented sugar, so obvious is the sweetness. High alcohol may also give a slight burning sensation to the finish. At the other end, low alcohol wines are characteristically thin. An even more dramatic illustration is the effect on high-quality wines of standard alcohol content which have part of that alcohol reduced by techniques such as reverse osmosis (*see* pages 228–229). The wine so treated tastes extremely acid (and thin), yet the acid content has in fact remained constant. The removal of the sweetening influence of the alcohol simply throws the wine out of balance – German makers of *Kabinett trocken* wines take note.

Opposite: *Patriarche Père et Fils in Beaune claims to have the biggest cellars in Burgundy with a history dating back to 1780.*

Methods of alcohol adjustment

Chaptalisation

The alcohol content of table wines is commonly increased (and rarely decreased). The principal method of increase is the addition of one of a number of forms of sugar to the fermenting wine: it may be refined beet sugar or cane sugar, or added as concentrated grape juice (grape sugar). The process is usually called chaptalisation, taking its name from Jean-Antoine Chaptal, Napoleon's minister of agriculture who formally sanctioned its use in 1801.

To raise the level of alcohol by one degree requires the addition of 17 to 19 grams per litre of sugar, which may not sound a great deal, but in reality quickly adds up: 40 kilograms of sugar for a very small (three-tonne) vat. Wines are sweetened during fermentation; with some winemakers deliberately (although technically illegally) adding the sugar in repeated small quantities towards the end, with the dual aim of extending the period of fermentation and of 'stressing' it to assist the formation of glycerols.

In Europe, the EC has issued regionally based regulations which govern the use of chaptalisation: these lay down the minimum potential alcohol of the wine before chaptalisation; the maximum sugar addition; and the maximum alcohol content after chaptalisation. In the coldest, most northern regions chaptalisation is permitted in every year; in the central, moderate zones it is authorized in poor years; in the warm southern zones it is not permitted at all. In no case, however, may sugar and acid be legally added to the same wine – a rule which is as honoured in the breach as it is in the observance.

Effect on flavour

There are numerous misconceptions about the effect of chaptalisation, the most common being that it makes the wine sweet – that one can actually taste the sugar. Since it is entirely fermented, this is manifestly not so. But as we have seen, alcohol does give an impression of sweetness in the tactile sense; it is for precisely this reason that if one asks a Burgundian why he chaptalises in the years in which sufficiently high natural levels of alcohol can be achieved without chaptalisation, he will answer 'for the feel', meaning the feel of the wine in the mouth. And like any winemaking technique, if used with discipline and sensitivity, it can very significantly improve wine quality; if used lazily or unintelligently, it can be positively harmful.

Concentrated grape juice

German wines designated as Qualitätswein mit Prädikat may not be chaptalised, but may have their potential alcohol increased by süssreserve, provided it is made from grapes of the same quality and potential alcohol as the must being sweetened. In Australia a similar situation exists: the use of sugar is prohibited (other than in sparkling wine) but the use of concentrated grape juice is permitted. The drawback of such concentrates – particularly for red wines – is the diluting effect on both flavour and colour and from this perspective sugar additions remain the best method of adjustment.

Freeze concentration

This method of increasing alcohol simply commercializes (or industrializes) the principles underlying the production of German Eiswein: in any given solution, the water content will freeze first, leaving the other constituents in a concentrated form. When applied to full-scale wine production a coil or hollow plate through which chilled brine is continuously pumped is placed into the vat holding the grape juice; a large ice-block gradually forms which is then lifted out of the vat – or the concentrated juice pumped out, leaving the ice to melt in place. This is a technique most suited to sweet white table wines but has also been used to advantage with dry white wines.

Osmosis and reverse osmosis

These are techniques developed principally for concentrating fruit juices, milk products and the like, but have very promising potential for wine. The research station in Beaujolais has been experimenting with osmosis as a means of by-passing the need for chaptalisation, while an Australian group associated with the Coonawarra winery Katnook has secured worldwide patents for a reverse osmosis technique (see pages 228–229).

Portugal has progressed from an almost medieval wine-culture two decades ago to some very modern facilities indeed. João Pirès, at Pinhal Novo, just south of Lisbon, took the radical step of employing an Australian winemaker. Wine is not made in the laboratory, but accurate analysis is an enormous help.

Acid

Several different kinds of acid may be present in wine; tartaric, malic, lactic and citric acids are the most common. Tartaric and malic are the principal grape acids and lactic acid is formed in the wine by the conversion of malic in the course of malolactic fermentation. If the wine does not undergo this fermentation (some white wines do not, almost all red wines do) lactic acid will not be present. Naturally occurring citric acid is present only in tiny quantities.

The effect on wine flavour

Wines which are deficient in acid taste characteristically flat and flabby; up to a certain point acid both intensifies the taste and (with white wines) can even make the fruit flavour seem sweeter. Malic is the 'sourest' acid, followed by tartaric, citric and malic.

Adjusting acidity

In countries in which it is permitted, adjustment (up or down) is a simple matter. The real questions for the winemaker are how much to add, when to carry out the adjustment, and which acid to use? For the consumer, the questions (and the commonly held misconceptions) are similar to those relating to chaptalisation.

As a rule of thumb, acid correction is permitted in Europe when chaptalisation has not been used, and is generally permitted in the New World countries. If nature – and appropriate viticultural techniques – permitted it, no winemaker would wish to adjust acid (or any other component of wine). But in the warmer regions of the New World acid adjustment is as essential and as widely practised as is chaptalisation in the cooler parts of Europe. It is quite remarkable that as one crosses the equator or the Atlantic, sugar and acid undergo some mysterious alchemy which makes one perfectly acceptable in one country and frowned on, if not actually despised, in the other.

Major corrections – the addition of one, two or three grams per litre of acid – are best made while the wine is fermenting. Opinions are sharply divided as to whether acid corrected at this time can ultimately be detected in the finished wine, but all would agree that the best results (in terms of taste) are obtained where the acid is added earlier rather than later. Those who say they can identify a wine which has had acid added claim the finish is harder (at an identical acid level) than a wine with only natural acid. In countries such as Australia the argument is a suspicious one,

Before the days of laboratory analysis the winemaker's eyes, nose and palate were the only tools available. A Burgundian used a silver tastevin *as his sole equipment. There are some who still rely entirely on their senses and experience and who still make incomparable wine.*

because virtually every wine will have had acid added to it, and the claim of 'recognition' of the fact can almost never be wrong.

The acid added at this point will almost invariably be tartaric; subsequent 'fine-tuning' additions (typically at the conclusion of the malolactic fermentation and just prior to bottling) may be of any one or more of tartaric, malic or citric acid – the latter being widely used in Spain. The addition of as little as a quarter of a gram per litre before bottling can have a considerably beneficial effect on the taste – and in particular the balance – of the wine.

De-acidification, on the other hand, occurs quite naturally as the wine undergoes malolactic fermentation. Where fine adjustment is necessary natural tartaric acid is precipitated out of the wine using potassium bicarbonate or calcium carbonate to make it insoluble. Once precipitated, the acid is removed by filtration. This process will eventually start up the natural de-acidification chain that leads to malolactic fermentation and is sometimes used specifically for this purpose.

pH   pH is another measure of acidity: it measures active acidity, where 'titratable acidity' takes account of both free and bound acidity. pH simply measures the number of hydrogen ions and thus tells us the real or active acidity of grape juice or wine. It is this 'real' acidity which determines how resistant wine is likely to be to bacterial attack, and is also a very good indicator of how well a dry table wine will age.

What is low pH and what is high pH in wine are questions which have to be placed in a broader perspective. pH has a range from zero (that of extremely strong acids such as sulphuric or hydrochloric) and 14 (an alkali such as sodium hydroxide). Neutral liquids such as blood or milk have a pH of around six to seven. Moreover, the scale of pH is logarithmic, which means that a solution with a pH of three has ten times as much as real acid as one with a pH of four, which is in turn ten times more acid than a pH of five.

Champagne and sparkling wine have a pH of three or less; most white table wine is between three and 3.5; red wines usually range between 3.4 and 3.8; while fortified wines may have a pH as high as four.

Effect on colour and flavour

The effect of pH levels on the colour of white wine is less marked than in the case of red wines where the pH has a major influence: young wines with a high pH will have a distinctive, slightly dull, blackish-purple hue which will rapidly turn brown with only a few years of bottle-age.

Partly because pH does not directly correspond to titratable acidity, some chemists allege that the pH of a wine cannot be determined by taste, but experienced wine tasters strongly disagree. At the one extreme they would point to the soapy, stewed taste of red wines with high pH, and at the other extreme to the hard, almost metallic edge of wines with excessively low pH. And while there is no precise mathematical equation which will convert pH to acidity or vice versa, it is certainly true that the lower the pH, the higher the acidity (and vice versa).

Even the most experienced winemaker cannot tell you in abstract what the titratable acidity and pH of a wine *should* be. He or she can only give that answer on a case by case basis, as so much will depend on the other flavour constituents: alcohol, sugar (if any) and total extract (including most notably tannins).

Adjustment of pH

Cold stabilization (chilling the wine to below 0°C) is the only wholly natural method of pH adjustment, and may not have any effect in some circumstances. Adding tartaric acid is the principal legal method in countries which permit it; a technique called ion exchange (banned by the EC) is another; while the addition of sulphuric acid (almost universally banned) is technically the most effective of all.

The longer term answer is to improve viticultural techniques so as to provide grapes which will have the appropriate chemical balance and bypass the need for adjustment.

Volatile acidity

Volatile acid is initially formed during fermentation through the action of acetic acid bacteria which convert alcohol to acetic acid and ethyl acetate. Contrary to commonly held belief, all commercial table wines have a certain amount of volatile acidity: it is simply that below a certain level, volatile acidity is not perceptible. In most countries there are upper limits of volatile acidity imposed by regulation, ranging between 1.2 and 1.5 grams per litre (expressed as acetic acid).

Tasting 'VA'

The threshold at which a taster can detect volatile acidity will vary according to the volume of other aromatic and flavouring compounds in a wine: it will be easiest to detect (at around 0.4 grams per litre) in a light-bodied dry white wine, hardest to detect (with a threshold of around 0.6 grams per litre) in a full-bodied red wine or in intensely sweet table wines (which usually have very high levels of volatile acidity – above one gram per litre – and need those high levels to prevent the wine from cloying by giving it a certain degree of 'cut').

The effect of volatile acidity is to 'lift' both the aroma and flavour of wine; at low levels it is beneficial, at high levels destructive. Once it has formed, there is little that can be done to reduce it: any chemical reduction will also reduce the fixed acids in the wine.

The Changes of Age

From the moment a technically sound still table wine, white or red, is corked up in its bottle two things will happen: it will progressively lose primary fruit and secondary fermentation flavours and oak aromas and tastes, and (up to a certain point) its aromas and flavours will become more 'complex'. Complexity comes through the formation of tertiary compounds brought about by the largely unseen chemical changes which take place as the wine ages.

Bottle age is not a mystery

These chemical changes are technically known as 'reductive'. This is because most of the changes rely to a lesser or greater degree on the small storehouse of dissolved oxygen which is present in any wine at the time it is bottled. Many of the ensuing chemical changes use up this oxygen, progressively reducing the potential for further change (or further change of that particular kind).

The primary process of change is the interaction of oxygen with the tannins and the colouring matter (principally anthocyanins) and with the various acids present in all wines. Anthocyanins are essentially a coloured form of tannin; both anthocyanins and tannins are phenols which are principally extracted from the stalks, skins and pips of the grapes; tannins are also extracted from the barrel during maturation – the newer the oak, the higher the rate and amount of extraction.

In red wines

The tannins and anthocyanins interact with the stored oxygen (a process which can also take place in the absence of oxygen, albeit much more slowly) leading to the colour change of a red wine from the vivid purple-red of youth to the dark red of full maturity, thence to the brick red or tawny red of old age. This is brought about by the progressive aggregation into ever-larger molecular structures of the anthocyanins and tannins, which gradually form a fine sediment and ultimately a heavy crust or deposit which falls to the bottom of the bottle. Obviously enough, the greater the starting level of such phenols, the greater is the potential for change, reaching its highest expression with Vintage Port, its lowest with a carefully made Riesling or fine champagne. A concurrent but less visible change is the softening of the flavour of the tannins, which become much less astringent as they, too, polymerize.

The second most important change is that of esterification, which is unseen because it has no effect on the colour of the wine. It too involves the interaction of oxygen, this time with acids and alcohol to form esters and aldehydes. Opinion is divided about the impact of esterification on the bouquet of a mature wine: most commentators have taken the view that the esters are of importance in shaping that bouquet, but Professor Emile Peynaud doubts that this is so, observing that, when isolated, these compounds have very little smell.

The process of esterification similarly has only a minimal effect on the acidity, pH and alcohol of the wine. Contrary to widely held belief, acid does not diminish; certainly it initially appears to soften, but this is principally due to changes in the other components of the wine (which gain in complexity) and only to a minor degree due to chemical change per se. Indeed, at the very end of the life of a wine, the acidity tends to become more obvious as the other flavour components degrade.

Because white wines have almost no anthocyanins, and are very much lower than red wines in phenols (including tannins), the opportunity for change is much more limited, and much less well understood. Indeed, the whole subject of colour in white wine is something of a mystery. While it is relatively easy to account for the full yellow colour of a Chardonnay which has been given extended skin-contact (24 to 36 hours) before pressing, and has then been barrel-fermented, it is much less easy to explain why a dry Riesling, made in a fashion which reduces the phenolic content to an absolute minimum, has any colour at all. *In white wines*

The explanation, such as it is, is the presence of a yellow pigment found in the skin of a white grape: a form of glycoside called 'flavone'. The difficulty is that flavones are present only in trace quantities in the juice and in the finished wine. There is no dispute, though, about the inhibiting effect on colour development of high concentrations of carbon dioxide (usually short-lived) and of sulphur dioxide (the higher the starting level, the longer-lasting the effect). Both will cause the wine to retain its pale, green-gold or yellow-green colour of youth for far longer than wines with smaller concentrations. As they develop in bottle, wines which started with low phenolic levels will gradually become more golden-hued, exceptionally fine wines often shot with green and seeming to glow from within. Those with higher phenolic levels (particularly wines made with skin-contact) will rapidly assume a deep yellow colour, moving towards an almost orange yellow (like a dark egg yolk) at four or five years of age. In both instances white wines are intriguingly different from their red counterparts: the latter become progressively lighter with age, the former progressively darker. *Changes in colour*

A third possible development is the browning which occurs in wines which are oxidized or maderized, often due to insufficient sulphur dioxide. A substance called 'catechin' is the major component of flavones in white wines and is highly susceptible to oxidative browning. It hardly needs saying that colour development of this kind is not desirable, and is always associated with a loss of flavour intensity.

Variety and type will also play a role: Gewürztraminers and Muscats often have a faintly pink or bronze tinge, while wines affected by botrytis are also deeper in colour at all stages of their development.

Both white and red wines undergo progressive changes from the time the grapes are crushed. Smelling unfermented grape juice may or may not be a rewarding task: some juices (for example Muscat à Petits Grains, Gewürztraminer and Sauvignon Blanc) proclaim their variety, others (notably Chardonnay) do not. Chardonnay juice gives off little more than a smell vaguely reminiscent of hay. *Changes in aroma*

The next stage is the secondary aroma evolved during fermentation. This is usually extraordinarily intense (once one clears the masking effect of the volumes of carbon dioxide continuously liberated from fermenting wine) but is frequently strongly influenced by the yeast. Cold-fermenting Chardonnay using an inoculated yeast, such as *Prise de Mousse*, is a wonderfully exotic cocktail of grapefruit and sundry other tropical fruits, the taste (with four or five degrees of unfermented sugar, enlivened by as much gas as one will ever find in champagne) no less seductive. In Beaujolais they have a word for this indulgence; the drinking of sweet and fizzy half-fermented wine. They call it '*Paradis*'.

How quickly a white wine loses these fermentation aromas depends to a large degree on what the winemaker does next. A Riesling which is kept under a protective blanket of carbon dioxide after a long, slow fermentation and bottled early will often have a closed, almost sweaty aroma which can only be described as 'armpit'. It is a New World characteristic much disliked by German Reisling-makers who aver such wines should be deliberately slightly oxidized to eliminate this character. Such wines will also have a touch of *pétillance* from the ample supplies of dissolved carbon dioxide.

Chardonnay kept on yeast lees and subjected to regular stirring or *battonage* will also retain fermentation-yeast aromas unless and until the reductive (oxygen-absorbing) effect of the lees is terminated by racking. So indeed will Muscadet bottled *sur lie*, in other words bottled direct off its lees, with the concomitant generous dose of carbon dioxide.

'Bottle-shock'   If a wine is bottled with these characteristics it will retain them for some years, and quite possibly never entirely lose the better components of them. If on the other hand it is either deliberately or accidentally partially oxidized before it is bottled (or very often as it is bottled) these complex secondary aromas will be severely diminished. Certainly the fermentation and yeast aromas will disappear, and the underlying fruit aroma will be much diminished. The latter may partially return with age: 'bottle-shock' is a well-known phenomenon which occurs no matter how skilfully a wine is bottled. But it is a fact of life that more white wines are spoiled at bottling than at any other stage of their making, simply through inadvertent oxidation.

The other variable is sulphur dioxide. This is only perceptible as such in its free form – and gives that distinctive prickle or sharp sting in the nose and throat – when present in excessive amounts. It gradually diminishes with age as it becomes chemically bound; it is largely responsible for the hint of cabbage in many white burgundies, or for the flinty, gravelly aroma of Chablis. A small degree of sulphur can and often does merge into the wine as part of the complexity of its flavour; as a positive addition to its character. All too often, though, it dominates the wine, severely detracting from the fruit aromas which one almost can see struggling to escape. Only age can cure the defect, and then no more than partially, for a stale, slightly sickly aftertaste is always there as a giveaway.

Bouquet   Ignoring the special effects of sulphur dioxide (and for that matter heavy new-oak influence), bottle-age brings the development of tertiary aroma or bouquet. In fact, the basic distinction used throughout this book is between the primary and secondary aromas (often lumped together under the simple classification of primary) on the one hand, and bouquet on the other. This second stage is often referred to as 'vinous', in contrast to 'fruity'; it reflects the chemical changes which occur in maturing wine discussed earlier.

In broad terms, the aroma softens and gradually becomes either more honeyed, nutty, smoky or toasty according to the variety. Riesling may or may not develop a kerosene character; sometimes it simply becomes toasty. Sémillon may take on a strong honeyed/nutty bouquet which gives all the appearance of being derived from oak, even though the wine has never been in oak of any description. Chardonnay gains in complexity on a scale more or less reflecting its quality; it can become intensely honeyed while still retaining some of its primary fruit, which may have been anywhere in the grapefruit, fig, melon, peach spectrum.

Changes in taste   Changes in flavour echo and reflect those of the bouquet, but are as much tactile as they are simply to do with taste. From the exuberant, lively, crisp, tingling acidity of youth, the wine takes on a progressively more languorous cast, becoming more honeyed (in feel and flavour) and soft, before commencing the downhill slide as the fruit sweetness starts to break up and the wine slowly dries out.

These changes reflect underlying polymerization and esterification. If there is any weakness in the cork, the intermediate stage is often referred to as maderization, reflecting the gradual seepage of oxygen into the bottle as the space between cork and wine (known as the ullage) increases. Sometimes a partial vacuum forms, sometimes maderization (or oxidation) simply doesn't occur: it is one of the lotteries of opening an old, partially ullaged bottle. It may be great; it may be quite undrinkable.

How quickly white wines age in bottle depends upon a host of variables: pH, sulphur dioxide levels, storage conditions, quality of cork, grape-variety and winemaking methods. The effect of higher or lower yield is by no means to be ruled out either. One of the great misconceptions is that white wines do not repay cellaring. Some do not, but many are just as long-lived as red wines. The German Rieslings of earlier centuries (when yields were much lower) were the longest-lived of all wines; good 1959s, 1964s and 1971s (the latter conspicuously) are latter-day examples of fine wines still at their peak. The Chenin Blanc wines of the Loire Valley (particularly the sweet and *liquoreux*) have taken over the mantle from Germany, comfortably living for 50 years. Australian Sémillon is frequently majestic at 20 years of age, many Rhine Rieslings likewise. Quite simply, white wines can age superbly. Many, just like closed-in mature reds, need decanting to allow them to catch their breath.

There is an immense range of colour in young red wine. The grape variety is decisive, but pH and winemaking practices (not least sulphur dioxide additions) also significantly affect both the new wine colour and its subsequent changes.

The spectrum of reds

Pinot Noir has the lightest and most unstable colour of the great varieties, while Cabernet Sauvignon and Nebbiolo are among the strongest-coloured. Some cross-bred *Vitis vinifera* varieties such as Ruby Cabernet and Alicante Bouschet have particularly striking colours, either in hue or in density. In between there are over 20 recognized shades of red. But it is not simply a question of colour as one finds it on an artist's or house-painter's colour sheet: clarity (or brilliance) and density are equally important, and tell you almost as much about the wine as does hue.

Wines low in pH have a much more brilliant aspect than do high pH wines, which become progressively duller as the pH rises. This dullness has nothing at all to do with sediment or suspended particulate matter. Nor does it reflect the fact that low pH wines require less sulphur dioxide to preserve them from bacterial attack: sulphur dioxide can strip or reduce colour in young wine (usually temporarily) but it does not affect the clarity or brilliance of a wine.

Unlike white wine, a red lightens with age. This immature red Bordeaux is still a rich, dark colour.

Red wine colour derives not from the pulp of the grape (the rare exceptions are so-called *teinturiers*) but from the skins, and the effectiveness of the winemaker in leaching the colour from the skins will determine (primarily) the density and (secondarily) the hue. There is much debate about the best method of extracting colour: should it be sought before the start of fermentation, during fermentation, or after? There are proponents of all three. Should it be extracted by fermentation temperatures under 20°C, between 20 and 28°C, or between 28 and 32°C? Once again, there are three schools of thought. Is sulphur dioxide the friend or the foe of colour? It can be both.

Many drinkers, particularly Americans, believe that the colour should be dense and deep, purple-red. Any wine that is light in colour, and in particular which has brick or tawny tints, is considered either inferior or 'over-the-hill'. It is the Achilles heel of Pinot Noir, and no doubt the genesis of the pointed comment by the late André Noblet (of the Domaine de la Romanée-Conti) about the irrelevance of its colour.

It is a simplistic view; one with a sufficient grain of truth to make it plausible, but no more than that. What is important is that the colour should be brilliant, that it should have neither black nor blue tinges, that the development of brick or tawny tints should be consistent with the age of the wine, and the depth consistent with the grape variety and source. For it is perfectly possible to over-extract colour and flavour, producing a coarse, unbalanced and bitter wine which age will not cure: by the time the wine softens, the fruit has dried out, leaving a mere shell.

This mature red Bordeaux has turned a lighter, brick-red colour.

There is a progressive shift from purple to brown, from dark to light, during the lifetime of any red wine; again the changes are caused by the polymerization of the anthocyanins and coloured tannins into progressively larger agglomerates, which finally fall out of solution as a deposit. Anthocyanins have very little flavour; it is the tannins (both in coloured and non-coloured forms) which primarily affect

Changes in colour

flavour. Nonetheless, the progressive change in hue and lightening of colour are a strong indication of the likely changes in aroma and flavour, and it is here that a knowledge of the comparative performance of the same or similar wine is all-important. If there are two bottles of the same old wine, and one is much paler in colour than the other, it is highly probable it will be of much lesser quality – even if the ullage (or fill-level) is the same or better than the deeper coloured wine.

Changes in aroma   It is truly remarkable that so much of each year's production of Bordeaux should pass through six or seven rapid-fire sales steps and reach the consumer as 'future' or '*primeur*' offerings a little over six months after the grapes were harvested, and a full year before the wine is finally fined, filtered and bottled. Or that the reputation (and price) of each year's burgundy is so much influenced by the annual auction at the Hospices de Beaune, held on the third Sunday of November, less than two months after the end of harvest.

The Bordeaux reds when they are first tasted and traded are very probably finishing their malolactic fermentation, with all the off-aromas and flavours this brings in its wake. The burgundies will have barely finished their primary fermentation, and will probably have just initiated the malolactic. If one is a very experienced taster, one can form a good idea of the overall quality and style of the vintage, and make a pretty shrewd guess about the future of each individual wine. But a final decision on the part of the consumer to buy, based upon hearsay opinion formed thousands of miles away? It is not simply remarkable, it is madness. It has flourished over the past decade simply because there has been a bull market since the great wine crash of 1974–1975; mistakes have been easy to forgive or (better still) sell at a handsome profit, all because the market has moved steadily upwards. The day of reckoning is at hand.

This digression is prompted by the fact that the aroma of a very young red wine is profoundly influenced by its malolactic fermentation, and seldom pleasantly so – the opposite of a young white wine. Not until the wine nears the end of its allotted period in oak does its raw power start to soften, allowing the taster to form a reliable and accurate view of its future. It is different for the winemaker and the very experienced professional consultant or wholesale wine buyer: they can draw not only on their knowledge of what they are smelling and tasting that day, but what they have tasted in the same château over the previous 20 or more years, and how those earlier wines (and even older wines) have evolved in bottle. The buyer of a yearling racehorse pays as much attention, if not more, to each horse in the family tree as he does to the youngster nervously skittering about the ring. So it is with a young red wine.

The aroma may show the effects of one or more of hydrogen sulphide, ethyl acetate and aldehyde, surrounded by the sheer raw power of the young wine. If new oak has been used, it will often be 'splintery' and unintegrated. While raw tannins do not have an odour of their own, experienced tasters can accurately guess how tannic or astringent the wine is simply by smelling it. All this adds up to a harsh and angular smell (more so for Cabernet Sauvignon, Nebbiolo and Syrah-based wines, less so for Pinot Noir) which still exhibits a mixture of primary and secondary aromas.

The formation of the bouquet is in part triggered by the quite rapid dissipation of the carbon dioxide dissolved in new wine in its barrel. This happens both during racking (quickly) and through maturation in oak (slowly). The other triggers leading to the bouquet are the chemical changes of polymerization and esterification (principally in bottle) and of the associated gentle oxidation (in cask and to a lesser degree in bottle). What was once harsh and angular becomes progressively rounder, softer and more harmonious. After the wine is bottled (and assuming the cork is sound) it is limited to the small amount of oxygen stored in solution, which it gradually depletes in the reductive process of ageing.

The bouquet of a young wine will be powerful, still dominated by the smell of its fruit. It reacts positively to air, and hence to decanting. Normally its bouquet will increase in the decanter for three to four hours in a short burst of polymerization and esterification. An older wine, fully mature and at the height of its power, will have developed an intense bouquet which is a balanced amalgam of fruit and that wonderfully complex matrix of cedary, spirity, earthy esters which proclaim a great wine. Exposure to air for some hours in a decanter may improve it, but it may not. In the absence of recent knowledge of the particular wine, it may be prudent to pull the cork, carefully clean all mould and debris from round the mouth, and sniff the wine in bottle before decanting it. If the smell is sweet, leave well alone and decant it shortly before serving. If the smell is musty, decant it in the hope (and expectation) that the 'bottle-stink' will dissipate over the next few hours.

'Bottle-stink'

A very old wine is necessarily extremely fragile, and reacts rapidly to exposure to air: here the rule is that you can wait for the wine, but it will not wait for you. In other words, decant and serve it immediately; if there is bottle-stink, wait the ten or 15 minutes it usually takes for it to diminish, and then capture the wine in the short time-window during which its ethereal fragrance will be at its greatest. Remember that its storehouse of aroma and flavour-inducing polyphenols will have been all but exhausted during its long life in bottle.

The eternal fascination of wine lies in its infinite capacity to surprise, in the fact that no two bottles of mature wine will ever be precisely the same. This is the basis of the old French saying '*There are no great wines; only great bottles of wine.*' A few very old wines will be extraordinarily robust; one château proprietor in Bordeaux insisted on opening a particular century-old pre-phylloxera vintage 24 hours before serving it. The dregs in century-old bottles, and even the glasses they were drunk in, have been known to smell sweeter the following morning than in the evening when they were drunk.

Changes in taste

Given the correlation between bouquet and taste, it is not surprising that the same chemical changes are responsible for the development (and eventual decline) of taste as for bouquet. The more expert the taster, the more attention he or she will pay to the bouquet in assessing a wine. Some Australian wine judges (who regularly judge 200 wines a day in Australia's hard-fought state and national competitions) say that 90 percent of their total knowledge of 90 percent of the wines they judge

The taster 'looking at' a young wine during its time in barrel is now only searching for clues as to its likely future development. The maitre de chai *must judge exactly when it has achieved the maximum benefit from barrel-ageing and is ready for bottling. Once in bottle, its development takes a completely different course.*

Bottles of great Bordeaux wines stored in their own château's cellars can not only survive but continue to improve for up to a century, and then only very gradually fade away. The ideal cellar for indefinite storage (here at Château Margaux in the Médoc) has very high humidity (which soon destroys labels).

will come from the bouquet: only for one in ten wines will the taste do more than 'top-up' the knowledge gained through smelling the wine (without decrying the importance of that last 10 percent). For the one in ten wine, the palate will reveal entirely unsuspected qualities, good or bad; in that circumstance the judge, on reexamining the bouquet, may well find the same character there after all.

American wine journalists frequently use the expression 'tannin to lose' in discussing California Cabernet Sauvignons. The same expression could be applied to 1975 Bordeaux and 1976 burgundies; the question with such wines is whether the tannins will soften before the fruit fades; will the process of polymerization take out more fruit than tannin? A young red wine may be raw and aggressive; the components may be unintegrated and taste as though they are in separate compartments; but it must be fundamentally in balance at the outset if it is ever to be completely satisfying.

If it is, the mouth-puckering, tannic astringency of youth, balanced by the intensity of the primary berry fruit flavours, will slowly soften. A series of flavours which have an affinity with oak (cedary, cigar box, briary, tobacco) will start to emerge as the exuberant sweet fruit subsides. In fact these flavours derive just as much, if not more, from the grape as from the oak. At the same time the finish and aftertaste will become finer yet more intense.

Ultimately these drier flavours will entirely dominate the wine as it starts to decline; all the balancing sweetness will disappear, and the acid (as it did at the very start of the wine's life) will become sharp and aggressive, perhaps 'lifted' by the insidious accumulation of acetic acid, especially if the bottle has ullaged. In such a case chances are that the wine will have begun to oxidize, too. While a sound cork is an effective barrier against oxygen, as it loses its elasticity (after 20–25 years in the case of a high quality cork), the passage of air (and indeed wine) past and through the cork becomes a reality, the destruction of the wine only a matter of time.

The technique of recorking

Château recorking is an option open to extremely few. Unless there is a relatively large quantity of wine of a great vintage, none except the first-growth châteaux wishes to have anything to do with bottles of ullaged or semi-ullaged wine. So self-help is the only solution, and the recorking procedure is as follows.

The bottles to be topped up and recorked should be stood vertically for at least a week. The capsule should be cut and the neck of the bottle and the top of the cork carefully cleaned, using a fine blade to scrape away hard debris, a damp cloth for less obstinate refuse. One bottle, which is to provide the topping-up wine, should be opened, and a pipette full (approximately five millilitres) withdrawn (but without moving the bottle from the vertical) and tasted. If it is sound, the airspace should be filled with nitrogen from a small cylinder and tube.

One by one the remaining bottles should be carefully uncorked; have a bone marrow spoon or similar device to retrieve any cork fragments which break off into the bottles about to be recorked. If the wine is more than 20 years old, add ten parts per million of sulphur dioxide (with another pipette), fill the air space with nitrogen, fill the bottle via a pipette, and then immediately recork it before moving on to the next wine. Leave all the recorked bottles standing up for at least 24 hours to allow the cork to fully expand, and thereby prevent weeping along the tiny creases which all hand-operated corkers make in the sides of the cork. The key to the procedure has been the minimal movement of any of the bottles during the process, thereby reducing the amount of oxidation. It follows it should be carried out in a cool place free from draughts – most probably the cellar itself.

The rationale for recorking

The aim of recorking is to minimize the oxygen that comes in contact with the wine. As fresh oxygen becomes available, the normal chemical ageing processes are unduly accelerated, and other far less desirable ones may be triggered. These include the build up of acetic acid, and simple oxidation. What is more, off-flavours (typically mushroom and mould accented) from the cork itself and from the cellar (particularly if it is moist and harbours mould growth) are likely to taint the wine.

Anyone who has assembled even the most modest collection of wine will have had to grapple with the question of establishing a cellar. It is an acute problem in modern houses in temperate climates, although much less difficult in colder countries with old houses (or better still, castles). One of the most celebrated collections of pre-phylloxera claret was auctioned by Christie's of London in 1971. The wine had been stored undisturbed in the cellars of Glamis Castle in Scotland since its acquisition 100 or so years earlier. The temperature hovered around 8°C through most of the year, the humidity near-perfect at around 75 percent. The vast collection of magnums and bottles of Château Lafite and Château Mouton Rothschild were in extraordinary condition, yet there was no suggestion that they had ever been recorked. Their development had simply been retarded, their condition more like that of a 40- or 50-year-old wine cellared under normal (good) conditions.

Most of us, of course, wish to drink the wine we buy within our lifetimes, and conditions leading to a state of suspended animation are no more desirable than practicable. The ideal cellar will have a year-round temperature of 15°C and a humidity around 75 to 80 percent; the two really critical features being the constancy of temperature and the humidity. In other words a cellar which fluctuates in temperature from 10 to 18°C will not be as good as one with a constant 18°C; if the temperature fluctuation is diurnal it will indeed be extremely destructive, but even a seasonal variation of this magnitude is highly undesirable.

The reason why temperature fluctuation is so harmful is the expansion and contraction of the fluid contents. While the cork is young and retains full elasticity, it will stoutly resist the build up of pressure caused by increased temperature. If it is of poor quality, or has a flaw, it will be an ineffective seal from the outset. But even the best of corks gradually lose their resilience and elasticity, finally shrinking to the point where they barely maintain contact with the bottle neck.

Long before the cork has reached this stage, minute quantities of wine will have

External influences on ageing

made their way alongside the cork and (usually) evaporated without trace. In extreme cases a sticky deposit will exude, sometimes corroding the capsule, sometimes being trapped within it. It does not always follow that oxygen will immediately enter the bottle to replace the lost wine: modern bottling machines usually bottle wine under vacuum, withdrawing all the oxygen from the space between the bottom of the cork and the top of the wine. This vacuum may be maintained for some considerable time, and even be enhanced with age. It is where the vacuum is at least partially maintained that old wines with significant ullage (as the air space is called) can show no ill effects; where fresh air has entirely filled the space (the amount of ullage being the same) it is highly probable there will have been some deterioration. A second complicating factor is the period of time over which the ullage develops: the quicker it deepens, the less the chances for the wine. Hence Christie's of London publish a cautionary diagram at the front of each of their wine auction catalogues, showing what they regard as 'normal' ullage for a wine of a given age.

It is to prevent undue ullage occurring that many Bordeaux châteaux proprietors recork their cellar reserves every 25 to 30 years; and that Château Lafite occasionally sends senior cellar staff on odysseys around the world recorking old Lafites with branded corks. If the wine has been recorked regularly by skilled tradesmen and if it has been topped up with identical wine, recorking should guarantee a wine in excellent condition. But what if abnormal ullage had developed before the wine was topped up? It might already be acetic or oxidized, and topping and recorking it will achieve nothing.

What, on the other hand, if the bottle used to top up is itself out of condition? Or, as is rumoured to happen, what if a much younger wine is used to top up with? This practice is known as 'refreshing', and is said to have once been common in Burgundy. It may indeed improve the old wine. Whether it is acceptable depends on whether authenticity is your first priority.

Above: *However good the quality of corks, their useful life is probably over after 20–25 years. To avoid the risk of air getting in and spoiling the wine, recorking is necessary, done by hand to keep disturbance of the wine to an absolute minimum.*

Opposite: *In the cool tranquillity of the cellars of Château Lafite the 'library' of old vintages reaches back to 1796, a wine described by the owner as 'like a very frail but elegant old lady'.*

Wine Faults

Wine fascinates us simply because it is so complex and ever-changing. The interaction between more than 500 hundred substances affecting the flavour and structure of wine makes it very difficult to assess the importance of any of them taken in isolation. The champagne blender knows the magic he can create by blending 40 or 50 different base wines, and will never presume to predict the result of the inclusion or rejection of even one of those wines. Nor will he exclude from consideration a wine which, on its own, may appear to have shortcomings or a minor fault. He knows from long experience that it may blend symbiotically with the other wines and add something unique and desirable. Consider, then, the underlying web of differing chemical and biochemical influences at work in each of the individual wines in the blend, and one has a science of such complexity that it can only be of practical use if it is treated as an art.

There are a considerable number of wine faults. Here, many of the more obscure faults described in textbooks are ignored, as they are (mercifully) seldom found in the mainstream of today's commercial wines. Visit an Italian or French farmhouse where the patron makes a little wine for his family and friends, and soon or later you will find the full array of faults; most probably sooner.

Varietal character or fault?

One of the siren-songs of wine is the appeal of the new taste, the new aroma. There is something strangely powerful and exciting about a wine from a region or a grape variety encountered by an experienced taster for the first time. Cabernet Sauvignon in Tuscany; machine-pruned and machine-harvested grapes from Coonawarra; the blending of Cabernet Sauvignon and Shiraz in the Midi; Greco di Tufo or Taurasi of Mastroberardino in Campania; Viognier in the northern Rhône Valley – the list goes on and on, some ancient, some new, but all different.

Strangely, so it is with at least some wine faults. For a variety of reasons, some easier to understand than others, Australian red winemakers have long had to contend with hydrogen sulphide formation in their wines which, if left untreated, often forms mercaptans. These give rise to a range of flavours ranging from rotten eggs to burnt rubber, none in the least attractive. The occurrence of sulphur dioxide is common in the Hunter Valley's red wines and the winemakers (and the consumers) have, in the past, gradually come to accept it as no more or less than part of Hunter Valley style, a hallmark of its typicity. It gives rise to descriptions of Hunter reds such as 'sweaty-saddle' (or the smell of a horse saddle after a hard day's ride), earthy, tarry, farmyardy – none intended to be so much as pejorative as simply descriptive.

Little wonder, then, that English and American professional tasters tend uncritically to accept the unusual smell and taste of a young Hunter red as simply a strange and exciting manifestation of regional and (if the wine was made from Syrah, known locally as Hermitage) varietal character.

Volatile acidity

No better example can be given of the fine and ever-shifting line between fault and virtue, hate and love, than volatile acidity (or volatility). It is present in all wine to a lesser or greater degree; the threshold of its sensory identification varies greatly from inexperienced to experienced tasters; and its interpretation, or evaluation, by tasters of similar experience varies no less. At the crudest, give two wines to the man or woman in the street, wines which are identical except for the fact that one has a normal level of volatility (accepting for the moment that there is such a level), the other a slightly elevated level. It is quite certain the latter wine will be preferred, even though the highly trained taster would (first) recognize the volatility and (secondly) probably reject or criticize it. Professor Peynaud in his masterly work *The Taste of Wine* (Macdonald & Co, 1987), unequivocally takes the latter approach.

> *'Some people would have it that a slightly high level of volatile acidity is necessary, that it accentuates the bouquet of some wines or even takes its place. Such people are bad tasters who are talking nonsense. Either they lack sensitivity or they do not know how to tell good from bad.'*

Causes of volatility

Volatility (or the presence of acetic acid and ethyl acetate) is caused in three different ways at different times and to different degrees. The initial level (present in all commercial wines) stems from their inevitable formation as by-products of yeast activity during the primary fermentation. The next cause is the malolactic fermentation, and the last – and most destructive – cause is bacterial activity: either lactic bacteria (which operate anaerobically) or acetic bacteria, which, in the presence of air, readily oxidize alcohol to acetic acid and ethyl acetate. The action of these bacteria can easily lift acetic acid levels to the legal limits of 0.92 to 0.98 grams per litre prescribed by the EC.

The aroma and taste of volatility

Acetic acid and ethyl acetate are usually produced concurrently; the legal limits are expressed in terms of acetic acid because it is much easier to measure. Simply because ethyl acetate is much more volatile (and thus more easily smelt), it is often only transiently present, sometimes grossly disfiguring a fermenting wine but disappearing shortly after fermentation comes to an end.

The level at which volatility becomes apparent varies with the wine (0.4 grams per litre in a light-bodied wine to 0.8 grams per litre in a full-bodied red) and of course with the taster. At low levels it manifests itself as an ever-so-slight piquancy. As the level increases, the piquancy becomes sharpness, the slight prickle in the bouquet intensifies and starts to muffle the other aromas; finally, the wine has a vinegary, fiery, sourly acidic finish to the palate, and a solvent-like aroma, which many will readily identify as aeroplane glue or nail polish remover.

Professor Peynaud is in no doubt that if volatility can be detected, it is by definition at an unacceptable level. One suspects that in putting the proposition so trenchantly he is wearing his school-teacher's hat, endeavouring to instil certain basic rules and disciplines into raw acolytes, and that his message to an honours class of post-graduate students might be a little softer.

Max Schubert's name will live in Australian wine history as surely as that of Dom Pérignon in France. He followed his instincts to create Penfolds Grange Hermitage, Australia's greatest red wine.

Max Schubert, the celebrated maker (indeed creator) of Australia's greatest red wine, Penfolds Grange Hermitage, deliberately induced higher levels of volatility in Grange Hermitage by leaving the bungs loose in the casks in the first year of the life of the wine. He argued that the very high levels of extract, the strength of the fruit flavour from the low-yielding vines, the strong new American oak influence and the high tannin levels needed to be 'cut' by a certain degree of volatility to prevent the flavour from cloying. One of his three most celebrated vintages, the 1971 (the others being 1955 and 1966) trembled on the brink: its level was right at the legal limit, and – according to the taster and the occasion – it either lifted the wine to the very heights or plunged it into an abyss.

Again, except in old wines, volatility seldom plagues the reds of Bordeaux, but is often seen as a problem in Burgundy. In analytical terms the levels are likely to be similar: it is just that the background structure in Bordeaux is so much more substantial. In Piedmont traditionally made wines manage to carry off high levels with style; so do such idiosyncratic wines as Château Musar from the Lebanon or

Vega Sicilia from Castile. At the end of the day two questions have to be asked: first, can you detect volatility? Second, does it detract from the balance of (and your enjoyment of) the wine? If both answers are yes, the wine is faulty.

The prevention and cure of volatility

There is in fact no cure for volatility; prevention is the only effective medicine. Maintenance of adequate levels of sulphur dioxide, the exclusion of oxygen, cool to cold storage in cask, and an appropriate pH level will help prevent the development of unwanted levels of volatility. Once a wine is bottled, prevention of undue ullage (allied with storage under stable, cool conditions) will protect it.

Oxidation

Louis Pasteur was the first scientist to demonstrate the harmful effects of oxygen on table wine, to characterize it as public enemy number one. It is accordingly a fault which most wine lovers have heard of and most probably think they understand. But there is one confusion which traps the unwary: there is a world of difference between the oxidation of juice or must (before fermentation) and of wine (after fermentation). Here we are only concerned with oxidation after fermentation (and to a minor degree with certain specialized forms of oxidation which occur during fermentation).

The causes of oxidation

There are two principal types of oxidation: chemical and microbiological. Chemical oxidation is a two-stage process: first, oxygen is taken into and dissolved in the wine. Depending on a number of factors, it will then slowly or quickly react with phenols in the wine, causing chemical changes principally seen as a loss in aroma and flavour, colour change and degradation.

Microbiological oxidation is caused by bacteria also being present during the process of chemical oxidation, and results in additional chemical or biochemical changes. One example is the action of acetic bacteria oxidizing ethyl alcohol to acetic acid and ethyl acetate; another is the conversion of ethyl alcohol to acetaldehyde, which in the case of sherry (*see* pages 188–191) is an altogether desirable reaction: the *flor* yeast film responsible for the change is but a special form of mycoderma, a surface growth known to almost all red winemakers which, if unchecked, causes a distinctive stale taste in red wine. (Happily, it is easily controlled, and only prolonged neglect will lead to permanent damage.)

Oxygen can be absorbed by wine in almost any circumstance in which it is brought into contact with it, but under certain conditions the rate (and amount) of absorption is increased. Any handling which involves movement or agitation will have this effect: racking, filtration (if misused) and transport are three examples. Any regular visitor to the cellars of France who tastes wine from barrel will have steeled themselves to the apology from the *maitre de chai*: 'This wine needs racking' or 'This wine has just been racked.'

Oxidases

Finally, there are specialized forms of oxidation which are triggered by specialized forms of enzymes known as oxidases, and which are found in the grapes. The first is tyrosinase, common in all kinds of fruits and invariably present in grapes to a lesser or great degree. Commonly called polyphenoloxidase, it is responsible (for example) for the browning of a freshly cut apple, and no less for the rapid browning of grape juice which has not been protected by sulphur dioxide. It is relatively easily controlled, and only creates significant problems with certain varieties: indeed, as we have seen, most Italian and some Californian winemakers allow it to carry out its work on white juice musts (in California particularly with Chardonnay). One rarely hears of it in red winemaking, even though its largely unseen occurrence is quite widespread. Polyphenoloxidase acts only on grape juice; it ceases to exist by the time the wine has finished its fermentation.

The other group of oxidases is laccase, which derives from *Botrytis cinerea* and which is altogether more serious. It is difficult to control, and leads to dramatic and irreversible changes in red wine colour, the most obvious being premature fading and browning. Some burgundies from the troubled 1983 vintage are prime examples, although traditional winemakers know what to do in such years: close up the vats at the end of fermentation and go hunting for a month. Chemists now understand why this apparent neglect was precisely the right response. Laccase survives fermentation, but slowly loses its potency in the presence of alcohol (and sulphur dioxide). It needs oxygen to do its harmful work, and a wine at the end of fermentation is saturated with carbon dioxide. If the wine is not moved, pumped or handled, it will remain largely immune to the action of laccase, which, and over a period of four weeks or so, will gradually be denatured and disappear.

Oxidation is usually more serious for white than red wine, simply because its consequences are less easily reversible and because the effect (while lasting) may initially be less obvious. If a white wine is highly protected by sulphur dioxide and ascorbic acid while it is still unfermented juice, but is subsequently oxidized as wine, its colour will darken dramatically; even if it is protected as wine, its colour will deepen in the course of maturation. If on the other hand the juice was either deliberately oxidized or incompletely protected, its subsequent colour development (given equal exposure to oxygen to a wine made from protected juice) will be much less. What interpretation or value one places on these colour changes is another matter. New Zealand Chardonnays, many of which are made with reasonably long skin contact and almost always have a degree of botrytis present, are typically deep yellow at two years of age. New Zealand winemakers are by and large perfectly happy with this, regarding it as normal. A Californian or a French winemaker would be horrified at such rapid colour development, and perhaps with some justification.

The aroma and flavour of a white wine will be 'stripped', modified or hardened by oxidation. Oxidation of the juice before fermentation will reduce the range and intensity of flavour in the finished wine; in some cases this effect may be wholly intentional and desirable. Oxidation after fermentation is in a different category: if not reversed (by the use of ascorbic acid and sulphur dioxide) it will lead to a dull, hard, stale character in the wine. It may happen at any stage up to and including

The consequences of oxidation

The aims of modern bottling equipment is to fill the bottles rapidly while avoiding any exposure of the wine to the oxygen in the atmosphere. Carbon dioxide or an inert gas (e.g. nitrogen) is often used to displace the oxygen in the bottle before filling.

bottling; if it does, the consequence will be largely irreversible, although obviously the degree of oxygen absorption (and of consequent chemical change) will be critical in determining the end result. All wines suffer a degree of bottle-shock when bottled, even where state-of-the-art bottling procedures give them maximum (perhaps even total) protection from oxidation. A white wine which is oxidized at bottling (through inadequate sulphur dioxide protection) may recover if the oxygen only marginally reduces its flavour. Properly bottled wines do recover in due course, producing the bouquet and flavour one is entitled to expect.

Red wines (other than those affected by laccase) are much more resistant, if only due to their much higher phenol levels. Nonetheless, careless winemaking can entirely destroy a potentially fine wine through this one fault. Oxidation will manifest itself in a browning or dulling of the colour, the development of an aroma of aldehyde, and a progressive dulling of the fruit flavour. Aldehydes in dry table wines are far removed (from the taster's viewpoint) from those in wood-aged fortified wines such as sherry and tawny port. Once recognized, the smell of aldehyde in a red wine is never forgotten: it is a stale, bitter aroma, sometimes likened to stale oil.

The prevention and cure of oxidation

Sulphur dioxide both inhibits and can (in certain circumstances) partially cure oxidation. If its use in white wine is supplemented by the use of ascorbic acid, it becomes even more effective. Restoration of sulphur dioxide levels in red wines which have been chemically or microbiologically oxidized, and have developed aldehyde aromas in cask, usually promotes recovery once the source of oxygen has been removed.

Red wine can in fact be positively improved by deliberate exposure to oxygen, an approach most obviously taken during racking. If a wine has become stale in cask, and in particular if it has developed sulphides or other off-aromas, the typical French reaction is to splash the wine through the air into a vat or other holding vessel before returning it to cask. If successful, this technique will not only rid the wine of the offending odour, but initially mute the aroma and dull the flavour; in the longer term (if it is not over-done) it will add to the complexity and subtly round the texture.

The effect comes into sharp relief when compared with reductively (or protectively) handled New World red wines. The less exalted of these may spend the first six months in a stainless steel vat, during which time they undergo their malolactic fermentation, and are then racked, fined and filtered star-bright. They are then put into barrels for six or nine months, with the bungs turned to two o'clock (so they are under the level of the wine) and are left until they are returned to vat for final adjustments: cold-stabilization, another filtration and bottling. These wines are extremely pure in flavour and aroma, but have an unmade, callow, and rather hard edge to their character which bottle-age may or may not cure.

The point with both white and red wines is that the die is cast once the wine is in bottle; much can be done to prevent or cure oxidation (and its consequences) up to this stage, but the potential for recovery in bottle is extremely limited. An oxidized wine may partially, briefly recover, but its ultimate demise will be significantly hastened, and it will never approach its true potential. It is certainly one of the least-forgivable faults in red wines, simply because (laccase excepted) it is so easily prevented.

Sulphides and mercaptans

One of the prime sources of hydrogen sulphide (and the more complex sulphur compounds which follow in its wake) is elemental sulphur. In many parts of the world elemental sulphur is used extensively in vineyards to control powdery mildew or oidium. Sulphur, lime and copper, the three traditional sprays of France, are sanctioned by organic growers, and are once again increasingly widely used throughout the New World as grape-growers seek to pull back from the systemic

Spraying with sulphur against fungal disease is routine in most vineyards. The higher the humidity and temperature the greater the risk. At Roxburgh (left) in the Hunter Valley, New South Wales, where vineyards are planted with mechanization in mind, growers will apply 'Bordeaux mixture' a bright blue blend of copper sulphate and slaked lime fatal to fungus. On a smaller scale (above), spraying is done by hand in English vineyards.

and more sophisticated chemical and biochemical sprays whose long-term side effects are uncertain. In the New World winemakers will normally cease using sulphur at least one month before harvest, but there is no withholding period prescribed by regulation, and less well-informed growers do not always follow prudent practice.

Another source of elemental sulphur is the use of sulphur matches, wicks or discs which are ignited and suspended in casks to disinfect them and prevent the multiplication of acetic acid bacteria. These devices are still commonly used in Europe and to a lesser degree in the New World; they lead to minute fragments of sulphur exploding off the side of the wick or disc and dropping (unburnt or partially burnt) to the bottom of the cask, vat or barrel.

Hydrogen sulphide is produced to a degree in almost every fermentation. Even if no elemental sulphur is present the yeast breaks down certain amino acids and in the course of doing so triggers the formation of hydrogen sulphide.

The cause of hydrogen sulphide and mercaptans

Any sulphur present is similarly reduced to hydrogen sulphide by the yeasts during fermentation, although any practising winemaker will tell you that not only does the amount of hydrogen sulphide vary greatly according to the type of yeast used (or the range of wild yeasts naturally present), but that the amount produced by a given yeast or yeasts is unpredictable, and finally that even during the course of fermentation hydrogen sulphide may appear and disappear with equal rapidity. If left untreated, though, it readily reacts with other chemicals in the wine to form more complex sulphur compounds usually called mercaptans, some of which are extremely difficult to remove.

The aroma and taste of mercaptans

The aroma of hydrogen sulphide needs no comment: every child's nose has wrinkled at the smell of rotten-egg gas, however or wherever produced. Mercaptans are far more varied, but can be smelt in even tinier concentrations: they are some of the most potent substances known to man, and may be detected in the most minute concentrations. They assume an ungodly range of totally unpleasant personalities: burnt rubber, tar, rotten game, fowl manure, rancid garlic, leather and gravel are some of the aromas, while the taste always has a bitter, astringent finish to add to whatever particular flavour it may have.

Of the three deadly wine sins, mercaptan is the least forgivable fault. A little volatility or a little oxidation may make a positive contribution to the flavour and complexity of wine. But despite the famous dictum 'Great burgundy smells of shit', most believe that mercaptan at any level of perception detracts from a wine. It toughens and obscures the taste; in a recently bottled red wine it may be confused with tannin (particularly on the finish of the taste) and in certain parts of the world (notably California) it frequently is. Californian winemakers by and large seem blind to the fault. By no means all their wines have it, of course, and they expect a certain degree of toughness and astringency in a young Cabernet Sauvignon: it is a badge of honour. If it is just tannin, and there is the fruit to balance it, all will be well: if there is mercaptan, the wine will simply become progressively more bitter and astringent as it ages.

Cure or prevention of hydrogen sulphide and mercaptans

It is remarkable how little discussion there is about mercaptans, either in popular or technical books dealing with European wines. And in truth – although accidents have been known – the occurrence is not great. The likely reason would appear to be the fact that the most effective prophylactic (and cure) for hydrogen sulphide is copper. The most commonly used spray to control both mildew and oidium is Bordeaux mixture, composed of copper sulphate and lime. It is applied with such enthusiasm that some vineyards actually turn blue towards the end of summer, and of course it provides ample copper to combat the sulphur which is also used. A second and possibly equally important source of copper is the widespread use of brass fittings in taps, pumps and machinery; one of the unsuspected consequences of the gradual replacement of brass by stainless steel fittings may well prove to be an increase in sulphides and mercaptans.

Hydrogen sulphide is also quite readily oxidized by contact with air; if the wine is a robust red, an aerated racking may quickly dispose of the problem. If it persists, the addition of a carefully controlled quantity of copper is the answer. This is usually added as copper sulphate which combines with the hydrogen sulphide to produce copper sulphide as a solid precipitate, which is then removed by racking.

Once the hydrogen sulphide has become fixed as a mercaptan its removal is much more difficult: silver nitrate works, but it is not a permitted additive in winemaking in many countries. All heavy metals are toxic, and trace residues have to be avoided.

Other faults The Achilles heel of the cork and of new oak casks is Trichloroanisole (TCA), which imparts a musty, mouldy aroma and flavour. The great problem with TCA is that its level of contamination can and does vary greatly. Even a raw amateur can recognize a grossly corked bottle of wine, but as the level of contamination reduces, so does the effect. Winemakers around the world are resigned to the fact that a significant number of their wines will be found wanting by consumers who do not realize that the faint bitterness they taste in the wine is in fact a cork mould. If it is a cask mould, the winemakers only have themselves to blame, for the contamination should have been recognized long before the wine went into bottle, and the wine disposed of – down the drain, if need be, for there is no way of removing the TCA taint once it has taken hold.

Cork and cask moulds

There is a range of microbiological spoilage of wine which is of interest chiefly to qualified winemakers and research chemists. But one spoilage has become somewhat more common – fashionable almost – as winemakers have tended to seek to delay and to reduce sulphur dioxide additions to wine. In consequence, it is not uncommon to hear smart amateur or non-winemaker professionals (media and buyers) on both sides of the Atlantic talking about Brett. Brett is not a mischievous winemaker, but a type of yeast called *brettanomyces*, which reacts with lysine (an amino acid) to create a taste which is exceedingly difficult to describe, but which in American technical literature is described as producing odours suggesting ammonia, mouse droppings, burnt beans and the pungent scent of barnyard animals.

Mousiness and 'Brett'

An alternative taint is mousiness formed by certain types of lactic acid bacteria, which may work symbiotically with *brettanomyces*, and which produce a nearly identical mousy (or mice-like) smell. The preventative is proper levels of sulphur dioxide; once a wine has been infected, the taste cannot readily be removed.

The story about the diner rejecting his wine because it is corked, pointing to a fragment of cork in his glass as conclusive evidence may be sad, but it happens. The adverse reaction which some diners (and all too many restaurateurs and sommeliers) have to sediment in wine is discussed on page 226, and is another common non-fault. But there are others, two of the more common being wine diamonds and wine sparkles respectively.

The non-faults

Wine diamonds is the name given by harassed German winemakers to the heavy deposits of potassium bitartrate crystals which frequently form at the bottom of bottles of their precious *Beerenauslesen* and *Trockenbeerenauslesen*. Commercial white wines made in significant quantities are almost invariably cold-stabilized to remove these harmless, tasteless and odourless deposits before the wine is bottled, and not a few red and fortified wines are similarly treated. The belief that the crystals are sand, glass or other lethal signs of incompetent winemaking is nonetheless widespread. Knowledge and education are the proper antidotes.

Wine diamonds

Wine sparkles, or spritz or *pétillance* is de rigueur for Muscadet and many Swiss wines, tolerated in most aromatic or light-bodied wines, frowned upon in full-bodied whites, and rejected in red wines. It may be carbon dioxide, but sometimes it is not, and here a little knowledge is a dangerous thing – particularly in the case of red wines. A sign of gas (in the form of a slight rim) may mean excess carbon dioxide from over-zealous protection (a minor fault which should correct itself with a few years' bottle-age). It may mean the presence of a mysterious substance which possibly comes from new oak and acts as a foam stabilizer, in the same way as products added to soap powder prevent the bubbles from immediately breaking. Minute quantities of gas in the wine (normally invisible) fill the bubbles caused by agitation; the difference between this type of foam and that caused by carbon dioxide is that there is no detectable prickle or sensation on the tongue when the wine is tasted. Finally, it may mean a secondary (probably malolactic) fermentation is underway, which is totally undesirable. A little knowledge is dangerous, because not a few New World 'experts' are prone instantaneously to diagnose the last cause without considering the other possibilities.

Wine sparkles

The Manipulation of Wine

Wine is arguably the most natural of all of the long-life food substances available. Compared to most packaged foods the number of added substances not naturally present in wines is tiny. What is more, the legislation of most wine-producing countries proceeds on an extraordinarily restrictive basis: a list of permitted additives exists, and everything not on that list is banned, however harmless (or indeed beneficial) it may be. This chapter looks at the principal additions legal in some or all of the major wine-producing countries, and at the controversial procedure of filtration, and endeavours to place them in the wider perspective of our concern about natural and unnatural foods.

Sulphur dioxide While the use of sulphur as a fumigant has been known since Roman times (chiefly by burning sulphur in wine casks), its deliberate use through all stages of vinification and conservation has been very much a creature of the 20th century. Whether this use is a transient abberation remains to be seen: certainly preoccupation with food additives of every kind is part of the nosophobia which is sweeping the Western world in the last decade of the 20th century, and in this context sulphur dioxide has been cast as public enemy number one.

The nature of sulphur dioxide Sulphur dioxide is widely used throughout the food and beverage industries because of its remarkable properties. It is both a germicide and an anti-oxidant at levels which are non-toxic to all but a tiny fraction of one percent of the population, and when used to excess it quickly betrays its presence by smell.

It is found in wine in both free (uncombined) and bound (combined) forms. The free sulphur dioxide (often simply referred to as sulphur) is by far the most important portion, both from the viewpoint of the wine and the wine drinker: it is the free sulphur which inhibits bacterial growth and prevents oxidation; it is the free sulphur which we smell and most readily taste; and it is the free sulphur which poses a threat to the acutely sensitive asthmatic or other allergy sufferer who must avoid sulphur dioxide. Free sulphur in turn exists in two forms, the most effective of which is molecular or un-ionized sulphur dioxide.

Levels of sulphur dioxide in wine and other substances Depending on a wine's pH, between 13 and 60 milligrams per litre of total free sulphur are required to control oxidation and microbial growth. In fact, relatively few premium quality dry table wines have total sulphur dioxide levels (free and bound) in excess of 100 milligrams per litre.

These levels are quite low by overall food standards. Fresh fruit salad or vegetable salad in health food bars frequently contains 200 milligrams per litre of free sulphur dioxide, while other semi-processed foods and beverages frequently contain significantly higher levels.

The need for sulphur dioxide The need for sulphur dioxide – and most particularly the level of use – is coming under increasing scrutiny. For the foreseeable future, mainstream winemaking around the world will continue to rely upon sulphur dioxide additions. However, increasing attention is being paid both to the quantity and the timing of additions, with the consequence that levels are steadily decreasing overall. It seems clear that white winemaking will continue to rely more heavily on sulphur dioxide than will red winemaking, although in both cases the technology exists to bypass the use of sulphur altogether. Finally, in the absence of those alternative technologies, grapes free from mould and of good chemical composition (in terms of pH, acid and sugar) require much lower levels of sulphur dioxide than do unsound grapes.

Skilfully and rationally used, the effect of sulphur dioxide is beneficial, particularly in the case of wines intended for medium- to long-term cellaring. It should not be detectable in the aroma, and certainly not in the taste. The fact that certain types of European wines (in particular) have in the past been heavily influenced by sulphur dioxide (and that a few continue to be influenced) is no more nor less than a reflection of ignorance, and cannot be seen as a legitimate part of regional tradition. (Sauternes, Chablis and white Bordeaux are examples of wines which were often heavily and adversely influenced by excessive additions.)

The effect of sulphur dioxide on colour, aroma and taste

American labelling law currently requires the words 'Contains sulfites' to appear on (effectively) all wine labels. In Australia the requirement is to specify either 'Preservative (220) added' or 'Sulphur dioxide added'. No such requirement exists in the EC. Indeed, such statements are actively discouraged.

Warning labels and health

One cannot help but wonder what these warnings achieve. The irony is that from the winemakers' viewpoint they may help in the defence of the hypothetical claim for damages by the consumer who alleges he or she has been harmed by the presence of sulphur dioxide in wine. The reality is that persons who are so sensitive to low levels of sulphur dioxide will surely be under strict medical supervision of their dietary intake, or will have long since encountered sulphur dioxide in far higher and presumably lethal levels in other foodstuffs. At the most mundane level, the introduction of the warnings brought forth letters of bitter complaint about the 'changes' being made to their wine, and demanding that winemakers continue to provide wines produced without newfangled additions. Anecdotal evidence abounds of consumers' claims of being able to taste the difference between the old and the new – when of course there was no difference at all in the wine, merely in the labelling.

Acidity adjustment

Ascorbic acid is frequently added to white wine in conjunction with sulphur dioxide as an anti-oxidant, but never to red wine. Its disclosure is required on Australian wine labels in similar terminology to that required for sulphur dioxide (either 'Antioxidant (300) added' or 'Ascorbic acid added'). The temptation has been to amend the warning to 'Vitamin C enriched', for that is what ascorbic acid essentially is, but the bureaucrats in Australia, like their American counterparts at the Bureau of Alcohol, Tobacco and Firearms, are not known for their sense of humour.

The health-conscious might be surprised, even alarmed, if grapes were labelled 'contains tartaric, malic and citric acid', but these are naturally present in the fruit.

The addition of tartaric acid is permitted by EC regulations only in certain zones, and only if chaptalisation has not been used. Those who have worked in Bordeaux and Burgundy will know the shrug that takes care of such regulations. The average French winemaker is nothing if not pragmatic, and by and large contemptuous of officialdom. (The same comment applies to the ritual of the 'official' and the supplementary (or unofficial) addition of sugar in poor years.)

In the New World the addition of acid is virtually standard winemaking practice; one point of agreement is that major additions are best made before or during fermentation, with only fine-tuning adjustments after the end of the malolactic fermentation and (perhaps) at bottling.

Because these acids are naturally present in grapes, the addition cannot sensibly be regarded as introducing something foreign, nor attacking the status of wine as an essentially natural product. What is more, they are added (if they are added at all) for one reason, and one reason alone: to make the wine a better product, both in terms of its taste and its chemical and bacterial stability. That does not prevent the average European winemaker from criticizing wines which have had acid added, and it does not help New World winemakers to know the criticism is essentially an unscientific one.

Chaptalisation   At this level of discussion New World winemakers can and do immediately turn the tables on Old World winemakers, and with about the same level of scientific justification, which is none at all. They also play tit-for-tat in claiming they can taste the after-effects. Chaptalisation has been discussed elsewhere (page 198); suffice to say it is used with the sole purpose of improving the quality of the wine, and in the vast majority of instances it does just that.

Additives in perspective   Wine-growers from the Old and New Worlds are in total agreement on one thing: the best grapes will require neither acidification nor chaptalisation; they will have a low pH and will produce a wine which will retain an acceptable pH after malolactic fermentation; and they will, of course, be free of mould, rot and other defects. The whole thrust of viticulture is directed to growing grapes with these characteristics. However, we do not live in a perfect world, and the perfect grape is a very rare commodity.

Moreover, even if it is produced, the perfect grape cannot produce perfect wine unaided. So additives of various kinds simply have to be used, however transient their presence. In almost all instances they do no more than bolster substances naturally present in fermenting grapes or wine (even sulphur dioxide technically falls into this category), and are simply intended to provide the balance which nature has temporarily or permanently neglected to provide.

The bottom line is that wine is a natural product which, given that the basic process of fermentation is a naturally occurring one, is subject to far less manipulation than any other long-life food substance, and that fewer unnatural additives are either used in its making or left in the wine when it is bottled (and thereby when it is drunk).

Filtration   The winemaker's and winelover's belief that wine is a natural substance can be a double-edged sword; for some, any interference with its natural state is anathema. An eloquent, indeed passionate, believer in natural wines is the San Francisco wine-importer Kermit Lynch, whose philosophy permeates every page of his book *Adventures on the Wine Route* (The Bodley Head, 1988). It is a wonderful book to read and there can be no doubting the sincerity of Mr Lynch's oft-repeated view that filtration absolutely destroys all wine. Speaking of a filtered version of a wine he normally liked he wrote:

> 'It tasted bland and innocuous. It smelled of cardboard because it had been filtered through sheets of cardboard. Wine is incredibly impressionable. It is influenced by the most subtle details, from the soil in which the vines grow to a neighbour's blackcurrant patch. Squeezed through the sterile pads, the poor wine expressed sterility and cardboard ... Three or four times I have seen an unfiltered wine go bad ... It may be unrealistic, but I believe customers who have such a wine should accept the loss and shut up about it. Complaining scares your wine merchant, who in turn scares the winemaker who then for reasons of security begins to sterilize his wines. And who gains from all that? If one loves natural wines, one accepts an occasional calamity. We would not castrate all men because some of them go haywire and commit rape. At least I wouldn't.'

Professor Peynaud takes the diametrically opposed view:

> 'The phrase "as clear as spring water" reflects the appeal of purity. Besides, a cloudy wine never tastes well, for several reasons. If there is a haze and a deposit in a wine that has been in bottle for only a few weeks, or even for two or three years, there is something wrong. Whatever has

caused the cloudiness will also have altered the wine's constitution and impaired its quality. Particles in suspension in a cloudy wine affect one's taste buds directly and adversely: the organoleptic qualities are masked by the screen of impurities in suspension and the flavour is distorted. A cloudy wine tastes rough and lacking in harmony. Conversely, the more a wine is clarified, the finer the filtration, the smoother and more supple the wine will taste. Filtration properly carried out does not strip or attenuate a wine; it clears it of internal impurities and improves it. To deny this is to say that a wine's quality is due above all to foreign substances in suspension.'

Kermit Lynch provides numerous real-life examples of what he perceives to be other filtration catastrophes, including the filtration of some 1983 burgundies which turned wines which were 'almost black' in the cask into 'pale orange' in bottle. He recounts his advice to the winemaker:

'I advised him to bottle his beautiful 1985s himself; why not ask one of the old-timers in the village how the bottling used to be done before the oenologist-entrepreneurs arrived, selling security from the back of a van.'

The qualified winemaker will notice the reference to cardboard in the first disaster, and the remarkable colour-change in the second example (coupled with the 1983 vintage). He will know that in the first instance the filtration was incorrectly carried out (removing the cardboard taste from filter pads requires a little care and patience, and a sensitive palate, but is an essential part of proper filtration procedure) and that in the second case laccase (the botrytis oxidase) was hard at work, perhaps aided by careless handling of the filtration equipment – oxidation is an ever-present risk.

Filtering tends to arouse great emotions among winemakers, Old World and New. Two glasses of Chardonnay, one before passing through the vacuum filter (in the background), one after. Filtered wine may look better, but is it stripped of flavour?

All intelligent winemakers think hard about both the cost and all the quality implications of anything they do with their wine. They are acutely aware how easily a great wine can be spoilt or diminished; and most are forever seeking ways to minimize pumping, bruising and, above all else, the risk of oxidizing fine wine. Large-scale commercial wine, however, is made with different aims in mind: it must be able to withstand all sorts of maltreatment (being left in the sun for a day or two, being left in the deep freeze, being served immediately after a 24 hour trip in the back of a car, or by a wine waiter trained in a fast food chain dispensary) and must never show a hair out of place.

The commercial winery has no effective option when it comes to filtration, maintenance of standard levels of sulphur dioxide and so forth: they are disciplines which logically have to be followed. But the criteria for the small producer may be different, and there is a tendency among some New World wineries to eliminate (or reduce as far as possible) filtration of red wines.

Ironically, one finds this in some of the most technically sophisticated wineries, such as Robert Mondavi in the Napa Valley, and Petaluma in Australia. They eliminate filtration by using extreme care in racking and fining their wines; by ensuring that the chemical balance between sulphur dioxide and pH is exactly correct; and by ensuring absolute sterility of the bottling equipment and bottling procedure. Through sophisticated microbiological plating procedures and the use of microscopes they will know precisely what is the bacterial and yeast status of the wine, and be in a position to determine with scientific certainty the likelihood of future problems.

Depending on the type of wine and the amount of fining or racking, the only 'problem' which such winemakers are likely to foresee and accept is the probability of a crust or deposit forming in the bottle. In educated wine-drinking circles on the American West Coast, this has become a badge of honour, and the whole process seems to be in danger of getting out of hand. Bottling and selling Pinot Noir which is distinctly cloudy right from the outset seems to some winemakers to be perfectly normal.

A straw poll of makers of fine burgundy would probably reveal that they are split down the middle on filtration; but those who oppose it tend to do so vocally, while those who practise it do so quietly and unostentatiously. Yet outside of the largest *négociant* houses (and ignoring the quaint habit of the house of Louis Latour in physically removing the sediment from its burgundies prior to shipment) the knowledge of the non-filtering producer about the bacterial status of his wine (and very possibly the pH and sulphur dioxide level) is non-existent. He does not filter his wine because he does not wish to, not because he does not need to.

In other words, the basis for eliminating filtration is carefully established by New World winemakers, and the obvious question is why – if filtration does not adversely effect wine – they go to so much trouble to do so. The answer is somewhat nebulous: but there are two things which can be said with certainty. First, filtration is an added expense; second, particularly for delicate red wines such as Pinot Noir, filtration adds to the shock of bottling. If one tastes any wine on its way through the bottling process (that is from the vat from which it is being drawn before it enters the bottling line and from a bottle taken off the line at the end of the process) there will be a marked difference. Even a wine as exalted as 1982 Château Pétrus showed the effect quite vividly at the time. If one adds an in-line membrane filter, and the wine is Pinot Noir, the effect is further magnified. But leave the wine for one, two or three months (one cannot tell how long the recovery process will take), and it is usually impossible to tell the filtered from the non-filtered wine, provided the filtration and bottling was skilfully carried out.

So in a sense the third reason is the most important, and is really without any scientific base. It seemingly puts the technocrat right into the Kermit Lynch camp:

Bottling straight from the cask here on the Loire means that the wines are unfiltered. They may have a certain 'spritz' – a slight prickle on the tongue – indicative of the minute yeast particles suspended in the wine, and taste very fresh and fruity.

the less a wine is (needlessly) tampered with, the better, and it may just be that an acceleration of the sedimentation and crusting process is a good thing.

There is, in fact, a difference between the Lynch and technocrat camps, which might simplistically be likened to the difference between the art and science of wine. Kermit Lynch likes to see wine made in old oak vats; he does not like sulphur dioxide; he does not like any of the soulless trappings, trimmings and equipment of the new winery. Great wine made this way is a truly magical thing, a spontaneous gift of nature in which the role of the winemaker is an ancient custodial one directed to preserving the traditions of the past. The technocrat arrives at the same destination having used an entirely different philosophy and entirely different tools of trade.

Nor does it stop there. Ask the non-filtering Burgundian why he does not filter his wine, and he will point to the old vintages in his cellar (which are absolute nectar) and to the fact that the numerous Michelin-starred restaurants of France who buy his wine have never once complained about any problems. The answer, of course, is that the wines have never been subjected to heat, and have only had one short journey in their lives. It is why Kermit Lynch found early on that refrigerated containers were essential if his artisan wines were to be guaranteed safe-passage to the United States.

The truth is that a good 50 percent of those artisan burgundies and Rhônes are bacterial time-bombs. In the best vintages and from the best winemakers, the pH levels may be sufficiently low and the sulphur dioxide levels sufficiently high to withstand the stress of transportation and heat (remembering that sooner or later the wines come out of refrigerated containers and that the United States is a very big country). In other years, even the greatest names may be no protection: it is one reason why domaine-bottled burgundies have such a chequered reputation outside of Europe.

The other problem lies with the sediment. Of course it is harmless; of course careful pouring and decanting will eliminate the problem; and of course any old wine, filtered or not, will throw a crust. The hard reality is that many restaurants and many consumers simply will not accept sediment in the relatively young wines they are used to handling and drinking, a problem of particular significance in emerging markets such as Japan.

In a world in which product-liability litigation is a grim reality, in which health concerns grow in direct proportion to our ever-increasing life span, and in which the bureaucratic imposition of unasked-for food standards has become an art form, the romantic ideals of people such as Kermit Lynch are becoming increasingly impractical. A high degree of technical knowledge and control is a prerequisite, even if it is directed to a hands-off rather than a hands-on approach to winemaking.

Glossary

Acetic acid Present in small amounts in all wines. In excess causes sharp vinegary aroma and taste.

Aguardiente Neutral grape spirit used to fortify port.

Amontillado Means 'in the style of Montilla'. Loosely, any medium sherry; specifically, a *fino* which has been further aged after the elimination of *flor* (qv) so that it develops a dry nutty flavour. Alcohol content of 16.5 to 18°.

Añada Term used in sherry production for young wine of a single year that has yet to be added to a *criadera* (qv).

Anthocyanins Coloured forms of tannins present in the skin of black grapes, responsible for colour of all red wines.

Anthracnose Fungal disease which stains grapes and shoots. esp. in warm, humid climates.

Assemblage French for blending. Putting together the components of, eg, champagne, Bordeaux.

Auslese German for selected, ie quality wine from selected grapes, hence extra ripe and usually sweet.

Autofermenter Vat in which natural pressure is used to mix juice and skins to extract colour. Esp. in Australia. Also called autovinifier.

Autolysis Progressive breakdown of walls of dead yeast cells in sparkling wine before disgorgement. Liberates nitrogenous compounds and amino acids which positively affect taste and structure of wine.

Back blending *Süssreserve* in German. Addition of blend component designed to give finished wine appropriate flavour and chemical balance; eg adding unfermented grape juice to sweeten finished wine. Also refers to back blending unoaked wine with an overoaked one.

Barrique 225-litre oak barrel, originally from Bordeaux. Holds 24 cases. Increasingly used outside France.

Baumé French system for gauging potential alcohol of a wine by measuring must weight. Determines timing of harvest. One degree Baumé corresponds to 17–18 grams of sugar in a litre of water. *See* comparative chart at end of glossary.

Beerenauslese Very sweet category of German quality wine made from nobly rotten (*see* Botrytis) grapes. Can only be made in certain years. Develops with long bottle age (qv).

Black rot Fungal disease causing black staining of leaves and shrivelling of the fruit esp. in hot humid conditions.

Bodega Spanish for wine cellar. May also apply to the winery, the company producing the wine, or a shop selling wine.

Bordeaux mixture *Bouillie Bordelaise* in French. Bright blue mixture of copper sulphate, lime and water. Treatment for fungal diseases. Approved by organic growers.

Botrytis cinerea Latin name of the fungus which causes noble rot (*pourriture noble*). Attacks ripening grapes in autumn when morning mist and warmth provide humid conditions for its development.

Bottle age Characteristic of maturity which develops in bottle. Mark of quality.

Brine A liquid used in refrigeration systems.

Brix American/Australian system for gauging potential alcohol of a wine by measuring must weight (qv). *See* comparative chart at end of glossary. One degree Baumé (qv) equals 1.8 Brix.

Bunch thinning Selective removal of a portion of the crop, usually at or around *véraison* (qv). Designed to concentrate flavour and colour of remaining crop.

Cap The mass of grape skins which accumulates on the fermenting must in the vat.

Carbonic maceration French: *macération carbonique*. Fermentation method using whole bunches of grapes which begin to ferment inside their skins in a CO_2-saturated atmosphere. Juice at the bottom of the vat, squeezed out under weight of the fruit, takes colour and fruit, but not tannin, from the grapes. Results in fresh fruity red wines, not for ageing.

Chaptalisation Addition of sugar to fermenting must to increase alcoholic content. All sugar converts to alcohol: it is not to sweeten. Not necessary (indeed, not allowed) in the New World. Important in the northern hemisphere where grapes are naturally more acid. Permitted in France (Monsieur Chaptal was Napoleon's Minister of Agriculture) and most of Germany; not in Italy where concentrated must is used instead.

Charmat process Also called *cuve close*. Process for making sparkling wine in bulk. The second fermentation takes place in the vat, not the bottle. Consistent, cheap, labour-saving method of making sparkling wine. No substitute for the *méthode champenoise*.

Classed growth *Cru classé* in French. Usually refers to the 1855 Bordeaux classification of top 60 or so châteaux in Haut-Médoc, Sauternes and one in Graves. Also used of similar rankings in St Emilion.

Cold settle Natural clarification of white grape juice after pressing and before the commencement of fermentation.

Cold stabilization Chilling wine to about -5°C to precipitate out tartrate crystals which may otherwise be deposited in bottle.

Crémant French term for fully sparkling wine from Alsace, Burgundy and the Loire, but a softer sparkle than champagne. For distinction, the term is being phased out in Champagne.

Criadera First stage in a sherry *solera* (qv) where the youngest wine is beginning to age. Translates as 'nursery'.

Crusher-destemmer English term for *fouloir égrappoir*. Device which first crushes grapes between rollers, then removes stems by beaters revolving in a cage.

Cultured yeasts Laboratory-bred strains of natural yeast. Usually subtle in flavour and resistant to higher levels of alcohol or sulphur dioxide in wine. *See also* Wild yeasts.

Destemmer-crusher Destems the grapes before crushing cycle begins.

DOC, DOCG Denominazione de Origine Controllata e Garantita. Highest categories of Italian wine. New laws from 1992 will modify their status.

Downy mildew Fungus esp. prevalent in warm humid conditions which attacks the leaves. Selective chemicals now used in conjunction with dosing with copper sulphate or Bordeaux mixture (qv).

Esters Formed by reaction between acids in a wine and its alcohol. Flavourful and usually volatile. Over 100 different esters occur in most wines. Can contribute sweet fruity aromas.

Esterification The chemical process by which esters are formed, involving interaction of oxygen with acids and alcohol.

Estufagem Portuguese term describing the process of heating Madeira in an *estufa* or stove, a specially heated tank, in which the wine is 'cooked'.

Ethyl acetate Formed by acetic acid bacteria. Present in conjunction with acetic acid. Difficult to measure scientifically; easy to detect with your nose. Causes acetic or vinegary smells or tastes.

Fan leaf *Court noué* in French. A virus spread in the soil. Causes degeneration in the vine, seen in yellowed leaves, dramatic reduction of yield and shortening the life of the vine.

Filtration Sieving process to remove suspended particles. Less gentle clarification than fining (qv). Arouses strong feelings among those who believe filtering strips character, as well as less desirable elements. Very fine filters to remove yeasts and bacteria make the wine 'star bright'.

Fining Removal of particles by adding a substance which coalesces fine particles, such as bentonite clay or egg white.

Flash pasteurization Rapid sterilization of sweet or semi-sweet table wine by heating to about 90°C for one minute, then quickly cooling. Prevents undesirable bacterial activity or further fermentation.

Flor Surface yeast developing on *fino* and *manzanilla* sherry during its ageing period in barrel. Gives a distinctive taste and prevents wine from oxidizing. Occurs naturally in the Jerez region.

Free-run Juice which runs out of the vat under the natural weight of the fruit. Widely considered to be of better quality than press wine (qv).

Governo Sometimes used in making Chianti. Concentrated must from a small percentage of semi-dried grapes is added to vats of normally fermented wine. Induces slight refermentation and softens the wine.

Goût de terroir Describes a smell or flavour in wine, believed by the French to derive from the soil of the particular vineyard from which the wine came.

Grey rot Unwelcome form of noble rot (*See* Botrytis cinerea) esp. in humid conditions without sufficient warmth to dry and concentrate the grapes. Spoils the taste of the wine as well as leaves of the vine.

Header-boards Also known as heading-down boards. Means of keeping the cap of grape skins submerged in the vat.

Heat exchanger Device for rapidly cooling or warming wine, grape juice or must, often employing a tube-within-a-tube configuration.

Hyperoxidation Forced oxidation of juice by blowing oxygen through it.

Juice run-off Known as *saignée* in Burgundy; typically involves removal of 100 litres of juice from each 1000 litres of must to concentrate the remaining wine.

Laccase Enzyme which can occur in grapes (esp. in wet conditions). Causes rapid and damaging oxidation of juice and wine.

Lagar Old fashioned wine press in form of stone trough used for treading grapes.

Late harvest *See* Vendange Tardive.

Leafroll Airborne virus causing curling of leaves and reduction in yield and vigour.

Lees Sediment comprising dead yeast cells and other particles remaining in wine after fermentation. Red wine is racked off this sediment. Some whites (eg Muscadet, champagne and some Chardonnay) are left on their lees (*sur lie*) to add flavour and complexity.

Liqueur d'expédition Blend of wine, sugar and (perhaps) grape spirit added to champagne after disgorgement to balance sweetness.

Liqueur de tirage Solution of wine, yeast and sugar added to champagne to induce second fermentation.

Maceration Refers to period during which the must or wine remains in contact with the grape skins. Alcohol acts as a solvent, extracting colour, tannin and aroma from the skins.

Macération carbonique *See* carbonic maceration.

Maderized Critical term for overmature white wine that has darkened in colour and become flat. *Maderisé* in French.

Malic acid Component of wine. Accounts for green and sour taste of wine made from unripe grapes. *See* Malolactic fermentation.

Malolactic fermentation Conversion by bacteria (not yeast) of malic acid into lactic acid. Softens wine and reduces overall acidity. A process now applied to all red, but not all white wines.

Marc French word for residue of stalks, skins and pips left after pressing. Pomace in English. Also term for spirit made from distilled pomace.

Mercaptan Derives from hydrogen sulphide and manifests itself in range of unpleasant odours (rotten eggs, burnt rubber, gamey meat, garlic, stale cabbage).

Méthode rurale Similar to *méthode champenoise* but without benefit of *remuage* (qv) which produces more sophisticated sparkling wine.

Mousseux French for fully sparkling. Usually implies the *cuve close* method of production.

Must Freshly crushed grape juice (with or without skins), pre-fermentation. *Moût* in French.

Must weight A measure of the amount of sugar the grapes contain, itself an indication of ripeness. Regularly measured to determine optimum picking date.

Noble rot *See* Botrytis cinerea.

Nouveau French term for new wine, esp. Beaujolais, which by tradition is released on the third Thursday in November – just weeks after the harvest. *Primeur* means the same – to be drunk very young.

Oechsle German system for gauging potential alcohol of a wine by measuring must weight. *See* comparative chart at end of glossary.

Oidium *See* Powdery mildew.

Oloroso The opposite of *fino*: sherry which is naturally full-bodied and pungent. Completely dry unblended, but often the base for cream sherry, blended with sweet wines.

Osmosis Concentration of wine or grape juice by removal of water molecules through a special filter. With **Reverse osmosis** the wine or juice to be concentrated passes through the filter, leaving the water behind.

Oxidation Chemical reaction of wine to oxygen in the air. Indispensable in ageing of wines. Occurring involuntarily it can damage colour, aroma and taste.

Oxidases Naturally occurring enzymes causing oxidative changes including browning, astringency and coarseness.

Oxidized Of wine that has gone stale and flat from excessive contact with the air.

Passito Italian wine made from semi-dried grapes, traditionally on straw mats, before pressing. Concentrated juice makes strong sweet wine.

Pasteurization Heating wine to 65–70°C for a few minutes to kill any bacteria, prevent further fermentation and stabilize the wine.

Pétillant French for slightly sparkling. German: *spritzig*. Describes wines which undergo secondary fermentation in bottle and produce a small amount of carbon dioxide which dissolves in the wine. *See also* Crémant, Mousseux.

pH Measure of hydrogen ions or acidity in a wine. The lower the pH the higher the acidity.

Phenols Group of closely related substances called anthocyanins (qv), flavones and leucoanthocyanins which congregrate in the skins and pips of the grape. **Phenolic** is used mainly to describe coarse or heavy white wines which, while having much lower levels of phenols than do red wines, are more susceptible to being flawed by excessive phenolic content.

Pierce's Disease Spread by insects ('sharpshooters'), esp. in California. Causes leaves to yellow, fruit to wilt. Ultimately the vine may die.

Pigeage French term for treading grapes and mixing the skins with the fermenting must. Traditionally done with bare feet.

Pipes A large cask with tapered ends – the traditional measure for buying, storing and selling port. Contains about 56 dozen bottles.

Polymerization Aggregation of anthocyanins and tannins into larger particles, leading to colour changes of red wine as it ages and ultimately to deposit of crust or sediment in bottle.

Pomace *See* Marc.

Powdery mildew Also known as oidium. Vine disease which attacks leaves and berries, eventually killing the vine. Detectable in the taste of wine if made with affected grapes.

Press Equipment used to separate juice or wine from skins and pips. The most traditional is the basket press, used for five centuries or more. The most common modern alternative is the membrane or airbag press (also known as bladder or pneumatic press). Other innovations are the continuuous press (highly efficient but rough) and the impulse press.

Press wine Red wine pressed from the grapes after the free-run (qv) has been drained off. Often extremely tannic.

Prise de mousse Champagne-making term for the second fermentation when the *liqueur de tirage* (qv) is converted to alcohol and release of carbon dioxide creates the sparkle in the wine.

Protective winemaking New World approach designed to rigorously exclude effects of oxidation on both juice and wine by use of inert gases, chemicals (sulpher dioxide and, with white wines, ascorbic acid) and extensive refrigeration.

Pumping over Refers to fermenting must being drawn over the cap of skins in vat. Known in France as *remontage*. Essential in red winemaking.

Quinta Wine or port (or agricultural) estate in Portugal, large or small.

Racking Transfer of wine off its lees (qv) from one barrel to another.

Rancio Taste of old often fortified wine, maderized (qv) on purpose.

Reduction Indicates smells in wine resulting from sulphur combined with hydrogen, not oxygen.

Reductive environment One in which there are decreasing amounts of oxygen available for chemical changes of maturation (eg in a bottle).

Refermentation Fermentation initiated by addition of yeast and nutrients (probably sugar) to a wine which has previously completed its fermentation.

Remontage *See* pumping over.

Remuage Ridding champagne of sediment in the bottle after second fermentation. Turning and gradually tilting bottles, from horizontal to perpendicular, coaxes the sediment down the neck for removal.

Residual sugar Natural grape sugar left after fermentation which is usually stopped artificially to retain sweetness in a wine.

Reverse osmosis *See* Osmosis.

Rotary drum vacuum filter Equipment which recovers grape juice from the creamy mud gathered after cold settling (qv); also used for filtration of wines, esp. sweet wines.

Saignée *See* Juice run-off. Used particularly of rosés so made.

Seasoning Ageing of oak in air after it has been cut but before it is made into barrels.

Sélection des grains nobles Alsace term for wines made from grapes esp. rich in sugar, perhaps nobly rotted. Chaptalisation is not permitted. Wines may be sweet or fermented completely dry.

Solera Fractional blending system used particularly in Jerez. Old wine drawn off a barrel is replaced by younger wine.

Sterile filtration Filtration through an ultra-fine medium (often a membrane) which removes all bacteria.

Sur lie 'On the lees'. The best Muscadet is bottled straight from the vat to maintain contact with some of the sediment (lees) from fermentation. Usually detectable as a slight *spritz* and gives flavour and freshness.

Süssreserve Sweet reserve. Unfermented grape juice added to wine to bring it to the required level of sweetness. Used in German winemaking up to and including Auslese level. *See also* back blending.

Tartaric acid The most important grape (and wine) acid. Cold stabilization (qv) causes the acid to be precipitated out in crystal form. May be added to wine lacking in acidity.

Teinturiers Black grapes that have red, not white, pulp and juice, eg Alicante Bouschet. Used to supplement colour of varieties with fewer pigments.

Titratable acidity Usually abbreviated to TA. Expression of level of acid present in a wine. In Europe expressed as sulphuric acid; in New World as tartaric acid.

Tries French term for passes made through vineyards to pick (eg) individual grapes wines affected by botrytis for making sweet wines.

Trockenbeerenauslese Selected very sweet grapes, often infected with noble rot. Make the sweetest and most expensive German wine.

Ullage Space between cork and level of wine in the bottle. In young wine indicates a faulty cork.

Vendange Tardive Late harvest. Term used in Alsace for wines from late-picked grapes. Must be from a single vintage. Same as *Spätlese* but a bigger, richer style of wine.

Véraison Point at which grapes change colour from green to yellow green or reddish purple. Marks commencement of final ripening stage.

Vino da tavola Italian for table wine. No precise provenance, nor grape varieties, may be stated on label.

Vin de garde Wine for ageing in bottle.

Volatile acidity Derives from acetic acid, caused by bacteria spoiling a wine exposed to air. A small amount enhances bouquet and flavour.

Wild yeasts Naturally occurring yeast which can be seen as the 'bloom' on skins of ripe grapes; commonly relied on to initiate fermentation in the Old World, rarely in the New World. *See also* Cultured yeasts.

Sugar to alcohol: potential strength

Specific Gravity	°0 °Oechsle	Baumé	Brix	% Potential Alcohol v/v
1.065	65	8.8	15.8	8.1
1.070	70	9.4	17.0	8.8
1.075	75	10.1	18.1	9.4
1.080	80	10.7	19.3	10.0
1.085	85	11.3	20.4	10.6
1.090	90	11.9	21.5	11.3
1.095	95	12.5	22.5	11.9
1.100	100	13.1	23.7	12.5
1.105	105	13.7	24.8	13.1
1.110	110	14.3	25.8	13.8
1.115	115	14.9	26.9	14.4
1.120	120	15.5	28.0	15.0

*Each country has its own system for measuring the sugar content or ripeness of grapes, known in English as the **must weight**. The chart relates the three principal ones (German, French and American/Australian) to each other, to specific gravity, and to the potential alcohol of the wine if all the sugar is fermented.*

Index

acetic acid 213
acidity 91, 199-201, 221
ageing 202-11; *see also* maturation
aguardiente 179-80, 183
alcohol 197-8
aldehyde 216
Aligoté 87
almacenistas 189
Alsace 91-2, 95, 96-7
amontillado 176-7, 188-91
añada 189
Anaheim Disease *see* Pierce's Disease
anthocyanins 202, 205
anthracnose 58
Antinori, Piero 25, 157
Apfelsaüre 91
apoplexy 65; *see also* irrigation
appellation control 77; *see also* classification
Argentina 23, 64, 98
aroma 94-3, 203-4, 206, 216; *see also* bouquet
ascorbic acid 221
assemblage 113, 115, 130; *see also* blending
Asti Spumante 121
Aszú 132-3
Auslese 87, 90, 92, 130-2
Australia:
 appellations 24
 Cabernet Sauvignon 166-7
 Chardonnay 69, 84, 110-11, 122
 Chenin Blanc 98
 fortified wines 181, 191
 irrigation 63-5
 Pinot Noir 33, 122, 153
 Riesling 34, 84, 92-3, 135
 rosé wines 139
 Shiraz (Syrah) 34, 61, 84, 160-1
 sparkling wines 121-3
 sweet table wines 135-6
 terroir 19-20
 vine varieties 33-5, 37, 153
 winemaking 13, 84, 101, 110-11, 160-1, 166-7, 198
 yields and quality 55
Austria 92, 134
AVAs (Approved Viticultural Areas) 12, 24

back-blending 90; *see also* blending
Barbaresco 170-3
Barolo 170-3
Barossa Valley 24, 161
barrels, oak 79-80, 107, 148, 152, 154, 167-8, 192-5; *see also* barriques
barriques 156-7, 162, 165, 195
Barsac 101, 128

battonage 107
Beaucastel, Château de 160
Beaujolais 71, 142-4
Beerenauslese 58, 93, 130-2, 134-5, 219
black rot 58
Blanquette de Limoux 121
blending 38, 84, 148, 164-5, 168, 173, 177, 180-1, 183, 185, 189-90; *see also* *assemblage*, back-blending
Bordeaux 35, 38, 50, 54, 58-9, 101, 164-5, 206
Bordeaux mixture 45, 58, 60, 218
Botrytis cinerea 58, 124-6, 130
bottle-shock 204
bottle-stink 207
bottling 95, 173, 183, 204
bouquet 204, 206-7; *see also* aroma
breeding, of vines 17-18, 41-2
Brett (*brettanomyces*) 219
Bual 184, 186, 187
Burgundy:
 climate 28
 wines 9-10, 26, 33, 58, 103, 107-8, 149-55

Cabernet Sauvignon 37, 49, 84, 156-7, 164-9
 aroma 206
 blending 38, 84, 164, 168
 and climate 33
 colour 205
 yields 53
California:
 Chardonnay 33, 103, 108-10
 Chenin Blanc 35, 98
 fortified wines 81, 181
 Pinot Blanc 103
 Pinot Noir 33, 121-2, 153
 Riesling 34, 98, 135
 rosé wines 139
 Sauvignon Blanc 34-5, 101
 sparkling wines 121-3
 sweet table wines 135
 and *terroir* 135
 vines 33-5, 37, 110, 153
 winemaking 81-4, 101, 108-10, 165-6
California Sprawl 49, 110
carbonic maceration 140, 143-4, 162
catechin 203
Caucasus 11, 15
cava 120-1
Chablis 33, 76-7
Champagne 23, 69, 71, 112-20, 201
chaptalisation 151, 155, 169, 198, 222
Chardonnay 33, 69, 81, 84, 103-11
 alcohol levels 197
 aroma 203-4
 bouquet 204
 and climate 33

colour 203, 215
 sparkling wines 122
Chasselas 86-7, 99
Châteauneuf-du-Pape 38, 159-60
Chenin Blanc 35, 87, 98, 205
Chianti 38, 144-7
Chile 35, 61, 64, 85, 98
citric acid 199-200
clarete 148
clarification 95, 105, 115-16, 182
classification 12, 22-5, 77, 81
climate 12, 27-35, 63, 76; *see also* weather
Clodosporium cellare 133
clonal selection 18, 38-9, 41, 54; *see also* breeding
cold stabilization 95, 183, 201
Colombard 87
colour 150-1, 201-3, 205-6, 215-16
Commandaria 136
Constantia 136, 181
Coonawarra 20, 24, 46, 122
copper 218
Cordoníu 120
Côte Rôtie 34, 66, 158, 174
crémant 121
criadera 176-7, 189
Croser, Brian 22, 79, 101
crossing 40, 99
crushing 71, 88, 94-5, 104-6, 140, 154-5, 162-3, 168-9, 176, 182-3, 186-7
Cyprus 61, 136
Czechoslovakia 92

débourbage 114
demi-muids see oak barrels and vats
destemmer 71
diseases 57-62; *see also* phylloxera
Dom Pérignon 38, 112-13, 118
Domaine Chandon 122, 123
doughnut effect 38
downy mildew 60
Drouhin, Robert 72, 74, 153
Durup, Jean 76-7

Edelfäule 58, 130-2
Eiswein 126, 131-2, 134, 198
Essencia 132
esterification 202
esters 207
estufa 185, 187
estufagem 186
ethyl acetate 213
Evans, Len 13, 128

fan leaf 60
faults, in wine 212-19
Fendant 99
fermentation 12, 73-4, 78, 88-9, 90, 92-3, 95, 105-7, 115-16, 129-30, 131, 140, 143-4, 146-7, 154-5, 160-3, 168-9,

172-3, 176-9, 186-7
fertilizers 18, 45
Fèvre, William 76-7
filtration 74, 89, 95, 141, 153, 155, 169, 187, 222-6
fining 89, 115-17, 141, 155, 169, 187
fino 176-7, 189-90
flavones 203
flor 176-7, 188-9
fortified wines 175-91, 201
 Australia 181, 191
 Portugal 178-87
 South Africa 136, 181
 Spain 176-7, 188-91
 USA 81, 181
foudres see oak barrels and vats
France; *see also* names of main wine regions
 Chardonnay 103-8
 Chenin Blanc 35, 98
 irrigation 63
 Pinot Blanc 102
 Pinot Noir 33, 149-53
 Riesling 91-2, 94-5
 rosé wines 138-9
 Sauvignon Blanc 100-1
 Sémillon 35
 sparkling wines 112-21
 sweet table wines 134
 Syrah 34
 Viognier 97, 102
 winemaking 9-10, 76-80, 101, 112, 114-20, 134, 149-55, 162-5
 yields 54, 128, 159
freezing *see* Eiswein
Freixenet 120
Fromenteau 97; *see also* Pinot Gris
Füders see oak barrels and vats
fungicides 18, 44, 60, 216-17

Gaja, Angelo 81, 170-1
genetic engineering 40-1
Germany:
 climate 30
 Gewürztraminer 96
 quality 54-5
 red wines 33, 153
 Riesling 34, 54, 87, 90-1, 95, 121, 131-2, 203, 205
 sparkling wines 121
 Spätburgunder 153
 sweet table wines 126, 130-2, 198
 Weissburgunder 102-3
 winemaking 87, 90-1, 130-2, 198
 yields 54-5, 87, 90
Gevrey-Chambertin 20
Gewürztraminer 86, 96, 203
Gigondas 160
gönci 132-3
Goria Law 157
governo 147
Grains Nobles 91
grains rôtis 128

grapes; see also vines
    choice of 94
    growing methods 124, 126, 135-6
    transportation of 68-9
    varieties 28, 36-42, 53, 146, 162-3
Grivot, Etienne 50
Grüner Veltliner 86
Guigal, Marcel 34, 158, 174
gypsum 188
gyropalettes 120

harvesting 28, 44, 67-9, 88, 104-6, 173; see also picking
Haut-Brion, Château 80, 164
heat exchangers 72
Hermitage 174; see also Grange Hermitage
Hugel, Jean and Marc 92
humidity, in cellars 209
Hungary 61, 97, 132-4
Hunter Valley 35, 161, 212
hybrids 40
hydrogen sulphide 212, 217-18

ion exchange 201
irrigation 44, 63-5
Italy; see also Chianti, Piedmont
    Pinot Bianco 102
    Pinot Grigio 97
    sparkling wines 121
    winemaking 80-1, 146-7, 156-7, 172-3

Jaboulet, Gérard 34
Jordan, Tony 79
Jerez 188, 190, 192

labelling 24-5, 37, 221; see also classification
labour 66-7, 78
laccase 214-15
lactic acid 199-200
Lafite, Château 38, 211
lagares 176, 178
Latour, Château 80, 164
layering 58-9
leafroll 60
lees 98-9, 105, 107, 116, 154
legislation 12, 23-4, 63, 77, 118, 148
Loire Valley 134, 142
Long, Zelma 68, 108, 109, 110, 166
Lynch, Kermit 222-3, 225-6

macération carbonique see carbonic maceration
Madeira 184-7
maderization 204
malic acid 199-200
Malmsey 184, 186
malolactic fermentation 89, 105, 107, 140, 147, 169, 173, 199-200
Malvasia see Malmsey
Malvoisie 97; see also Pinot Gris

marcottage see layering
Margaux, Château 38, 78
Marsanne 87, 99
maturation 89, 105, 141, 147, 148, 154-5, 162-3, 168-9, 172-3; see also ageing
mechanization 17, 46-8, 66-9
Médoc 18, 28, 63
Melon de Bourgogne (Muscadet) 87, 98-9
Mentzelopoulos, André 78
mercaptans 212, 218
Merlot 164
méthode ancienne 72
méthode champenoise 120
méthode rurale 121
Moët & Chandon 23, 113, 120, 123
MOG 67
Mondavi, Robert 80, 101, 153, 165, 234
Mondavi, Tim 108, 110, 166
mousiness 219
mousseux 121
Muligny 9-10
Müller-Thurgau 40, 86
Muscadet 87, 98-9, 204
Muscat 86, 191, 203

Napa Valley 19, 28, 61, 93, 110; see also California
Nebbiolo 170-2, 205-6
nematodes 42
New Zealand
    Chenin Blanc 35, 98
    Pinot Gris 97
    Pinot Noir 33, 153
    Riesling 34, 92-3
    Sauvignon Blanc 24, 35, 84, 102
    Sémillon 35
    winemaking 69, 84-5

oak barrels and vats 73, 79-80, 107, 148, 152, 154, 167-8, 192-5; see also barriques
oidium (powdery mildew) 59, 218
oloroso 176-7, 189, 191
Oregon 33, 93, 110, 153
osmosis 198
osmotic concentration 126
oxidases 214-15
oxidation 68, 104, 109, 214-16

Padouen, Château 128-9
Paradis 203
Penedès 28, 33, 120-1, 153
Penfolds 26, 34, 161, 213
pest control 45
pétillance 99, 121, 219
Peynaud, Professor Emile 79, 81, 202, 213, 222
pH levels 200-1, 205
phylloxera (Phylloxera vastatrix) 41-2, 59, 61
picking 95, 126, 128-9, 131, 154-5, 168-9, 183; see also

harvesting
Piedmont 81, 170-3
Pierce's Disease 61
pigeage 71, 162
Pinotage 85
Pinot Beurot 97; see also Pinot Gris
Pinot Bianco 102; see also Pinot Blanc
Pinot Blanc 39, 102-3
Pinot Droit 39
Pinot Fin 39
Pinot Grigio 97; see also Pinot Gris
Pinot Gris 39, 97-8
Pinot Meunier 39, 122
Pinot Noir 36, 39, 149-55
    aroma 206
    and climate 33
    clones 39, 41
    colour 150-1, 205
    harvesting 69
    and sparkling wines 122
    and yields 53
planting 44
planting densities 17, 49
polyphenoloxidase 214
port 178-83
Portugal 61-2
    fortified wines 178-81, 182-3
    making port 178-81, 182-3
    rosé wines 139
pourriture grise 58
pourriture noble 58
powdery mildew see oidium
Prats, Bruno 19, 50, 54, 56
pressing 72-3, 88, 95, 105-6, 114, 129, 114, 140, 176, 183, 186-7
Prosecco 121
pruning 16, 43-4, 46-9, 67
pumps 74
puttonyos 132-3

quality 17, 50-6, 64-5, 76-8, 112

Rahoul, Château 101
rainfall 30; see also irrigation
Rainwater (Madeira) 186
raising 126, 135-6
RD (récemment dégorgé) 120
recorking 209, 211
red wines 71, 137-74
    ageing 202
    aroma 206, 216
    bouquet 206-7
    colour 205, 216
    oxidation 216
    pH levels 201
    quality 56
    yield 56
remuage, remueurs 116, 120
reserve wines 115, 118
reverse osmosis 197, 198
Rhône 138-9, 158-60, 162-3, 174
Ricard, Claude 101

Riesling 36, 54-5, 84, 86-93, 135
    ageing 205
    aroma 203
    bouquet 204
    and climate 34
    colour 203
    fermentation 90, 92-3
Rioja 38, 81, 148
Rkatsiteli 87
rootstocks 41-2, 60-1
rosé wines 138-9
Rothschild, Baron Philippe de 165
Roussanne 87, 99
Ruländer 97; see also Pinot Gris

Sangiovese 144-5, 156-7
Sangiovete 145
Sauternes 35, 126, 128-30
Sauvignon Blanc 34-5, 49, 69, 84, 98, 100-2, 203
Scheurebe 99
Schubert, Max 213
Sekt 121
Sémillon 35, 49, 84, 102, 136, 204-5
Sercial 184-6
shade 49
sherry 176-7, 188-91
Shiraz 34, 61, 84, 160-1; see also Syrah
Sichel, Peter 20-2, 26, 54
Sieggerebe 99
Smart, Richard 49, 55, 110
soil 20, 24, 45-7
solera system 176-7, 186, 189-90
South Africa 12, 62
    Chenin Blanc 35, 98
    fortified wines 136, 181
    Sauvignon Blanc 35, 98
    white wines 34, 85, 98
    winemaking 85
Spain:
    fortified wines 188-91
    red wines 33, 148, 153
    Rioja 38, 81, 148
    sherry 176-7, 188-91
    sparkling wines 120-1
    winemaking 81, 176-7, 188-91
sparkling wines 71, 112-23, 201
Spätlese 33, 87, 90, 92, 130-2
sprays 18, 45, 216-17
Steen 98; see also Chenin Blanc
Stücks see oak barrels and vats
sulphur 216-18, 220
sulphur dioxide 77, 204, 212, 216, 220-1
sulphuric acid 201
süssreserve 90, 198
sweet table wines see table wines
Switzerland 87, 99
Syrah 49, 158, 162-3; see also Shiraz
    aroma 206
    and climate 34

yields 53
Sylvaner 86
Szürkebarát 97; *see also* Pinot Gris

table wines, sweet 124-36
Chateau Tahbilk 61
tanks *see* vats
tannins 202
tartaric acid 199-201, 221
tasting 51, 55-6, 112, 204, 207-8
Tavel 138-9
TCA *see* Trichloroanisole
temperature (climatic) 28-30
temperature (fermentation) 12, 90, 92-3, 95, 105, 107, 186-7, 209
terroir 19-26, 76, 78, 108, 118
tinto 148
toasting 193
Tokay 132-4, 191
Tokay d'Alsace 97
Torres, Miguel 25
training of vines 45
Trebbiano 81, 87, 99
Trichloroanisole (TCA) 218-19
tries 128-9; *see also* picking
trimming 43, 45-6; *see also* pruning
Trockenbeerenauslese 58, 128, 129, 130-2, 134-5, 219
tyrosinase 214

ullage 204, 211
USA *see* California, Oregon, Washington State

vats 73-4, 164-5, 173, 192
Verdelho 97, 184, 186
Vinding-Diers, Peter 101, 128
vines 15-18, 110; *see also* grapes
    American 57-8
    breeding of 17-18, 38-9, 41-2, 54
    growth of 28-35, 37, 43-5, 49, 63-5, 110
vinho surdo 184
vini passiti 126, 136
vins de paille 126, 136
vintages 118, 186
Viognier 97, 102
viruses 60-2; *see also* diseases
volatile acidity 201, 212-14;
volatility *see* volatile acidity

Washington State 35, 93
weather 22, 27-35; *see also* climate
weed control 47
Weinsäure 91
Weissburgunder 102-3; *see also* Pinot Blanc
Welschriesling 86
white wines 86-111
    ageing 203-5
    aroma 94-5

and oxidation 215-16
pH levels 201
quality 56
yield 56
wind, effect of 31
wine diamonds 219
wine sparkles 219
winemaking 9-13, 15, 20, 22, 71-5
    aromatic white wines 94-5
    Australia 13, 84, 101, 110-11, 160-1, 166-7, 198
    Bordeaux 164-5
    Burgundy 9-10, 149-55
    Cabernet Sauvignon 167-9
    California 81-4, 101, 108-10, 165-6
    champagne 112, 114-20; process chart 114-17
    Chardonnay 104-5
    Chianti 146-7
    Chile 85
    fortified wines 175, 178-80, 182-3, 188-91
    France 9-10, 76-80, 101, 112, 114-20, 134, 149-55, 162-5
    Germany 87, 90-1, 130-2, 198
    Italy 80-1, 146-7, 156-7, 172-3
    Madeira 184-7
    New Zealand 69, 84-5

Oregon 33, 93, 110, 153
Piedmont 172-3
port 178-80, 182-3
Portugal 178-87
red wine, process chart 140-1
Rhône 158-160, 162-3
Rioja 148
sherry 188-91; process chart 176-7
South Africa 85
Spain 81, 188-91
sweet wines 124-8
Syrah 162-3
white wine, process chart 88-9
wines; *see also* fortified wines, red wines, rosé wines, sparkling wines, table wines, white wines
    history 11, 15-16, 19, 124-5, 128
    naming of 24-6, 37

Yarra Valley 13, 24, 28, 153
yeasts 78, 95, 119-20, 188-9, 214, 218; *see also* lees
yeso 188
yields 17-18, 49-56
    Australia 55
    France 54, 128, 159
    Germany 54-5, 87, 90
    and irrigation 63-5
Yquem, Château d' 125, 128-30

Acknowledgments

The publishers wish to thank the following organizations and individuals for their kind permission to reproduce the photographs in this book:

Bridgeman Art Library/Eaton Gallery, Prince's Arcade, London: 8
Michael Busselle: 44, 66 left, 91, 100, 119 left and top right, 155 centre, 163 top
Cephas: Nigel Blythe 27, 217 right/ Andy Christodolo 60 left, 86, 153/ R & K Muschenetz 122/ Mick Rock 25 left and right, 29, 31, 37 right, 40, 45 left, 48, 51 left, 52-3, 57, 60 right, 62, 63, 64 left, 68, 70, 72 right, 74 right, 79, 92, 93 left and right, 96-7, 103, 105 right, 108 left and right, 111, 119 bottom, 120, 123, 125, 143, 146 bottom, 147, 148 top and bottom, 155 bottom, 162 top, 167, 169, 170-1, 171, 172, 173, 178, 183 top, 189, 190, 191, 193, 194 left and right, 196, 199, 213, 215, 217 left, 221, 223, 225/ Ted Stefan 36, 47, 65/ Mike Taylor 16 left/ WINE Magazine 135
Sally Cushing: 64 right
Patrick Eager: 16 right, 46, 72 left, 85, 95 top, 106, 129 right, 208
Luzio Grossi: 2
Claus Hansmann: 43
Image Bank: 105 left
Kevin Phillips: 184, 185, 187

Kim Sayer: 205 top and bottom
Scala: 124
Scope: Jean Luc Barde 39 right, 42 right, 137, 145, 146 top, 149, 152, 155 top, 157, 162 bottom, 163 bottom/ Jacques Guillard 20, 23, 30, 37 left, 39 left, 42 left, 45 right, 52, 76, 77, 94 left, 113, 139, 158, 159, 160, 174, 179, 180, 182, 183 bottom/ Michel Guillard 17, 19, 28, 51 right, 58, 73 right, 78, 127 top left and top right, 129 left, 130, 132, 133 left and right, 165, 195, 210, 211, 224/ Jacques Sierpinski 32/ Jean Daniel Sudres 69, 104 left, 142 left and right, 150-1, 158-9, 168 bottom, 192, 207
Alan Williams: 14, 74 left, 82-3, 104 right
Jon Wyand: 94 right, 95 bottom, 109, 168 top
Zefa Picture Library: 66 right, 127 bottom, 200

Picture Researcher: Christine Rista

Illustrators:
Jane Cradock-Watson: 88-9, 114-17, 140-1, 176-7
Eugene Fleury: 21
Mick Saunders: 59